FATHERHOOD

FATHER

HOOD

AN ANTHOLOGY

Edited and introduced by
JOHN LEWIS-STEMPEL

THE OVERLOOK PRESS
Woodstock & New York

For my wife and children, without whom I would
never have had the honour of being a father.
And for my father, too.
Thank you.

First published in the United States in 2003 by
The Overlook Press, Peter Mayer Publishers, Inc.
Woodstock & New York

WOODSTOCK:
One Overlook Drive
Woodstock, NY 12498
www.overlookpress.com
[for individual orders, bulk and special sales, contact our Woodstock office]

NEW YORK:
141 Wooster Street
New York, NY 10012

Library of Congress Cataloging-in-Publication Data

Fatherhood : an anthology / edited and introduced by John Lewis-Stempel.
p. cm.
Includes bibliographical references
1. Father—Literary collections. 2. Fatherhood—Literary collections.
I. Lewis-Stempel, Joh.
PN6071.F3F35 2003   808.8'9920431—dc21   2003042890

Printed in the United States of America
ISBN 1-58567-419-2
FIRST EDITION
1 3 5 7 9 8 6 4 2

Contents

PART 2

Fathers and Sons

PART 3
Daddy's Girl

PART 4

The Sins of the Father

PART 6

Patrimony

Introduction

Fatherhood: ME . . . 1. The relation of a father to a child;
paternity. Also *fig*. +2.
Authority of or as of a father – 1690
The Oxford English Dictionary

I should declare an interest. Seven years ago I watched my son
being born. He was, to borrow a phrase of Laurie Lee's, 'an ordinary miracle', but as I gazed in near-religious wonder at that
blue-eyed boy I realised many brilliant things, not least that he
wasn't the only thing born in that moment. I had become a Father.
Out of the old me, fallen like a husk on the floor of the oper-
ating theatre, stepped a new me, a pater, a daddy, a Father, a
man with awesome responsibility, the care – with my partner,
soon to become my wife (we got married in church, very grown-
uply) – of this tiny, precious parcel of humanity. For ever.

My head also filled with a grateful image of my own father,
whose discarded Christmas-present underpants I was wearing as
a lucky charm (no, really), for I had suddenly, in the pitiful music
of an infant's cry, become what he had always been to me. Dad.

And so is the mantle of fatherhood passed down the ages.

The problems began when we got home from the hospital. For
I hadn't the faintest idea of what being a father actually meant.
Or, what a father was actually required to do. There was a vague
thirtysomething notion of being emotionally more hands-on than
my own father (though, in truth he was a good dad, and even
raised me alone for a period of my early childhood) but not much
else. It took me some time to realise that my personal bafflement
was not really personal at all.

This was 1994 and society had long before lost the plot on
fathers. Newspapers and government castigated 'deadbeats dads',
'new dads' were the advertisers' darlings, some dads had given
up the rat race to become SAHDs (stay-at-home-dads, with their
spouses earning the family mortgage), certain influential

psychologists promoted androgynous parenting, while numerous radical feminists suggested that fathers were not only unnecessary but a total, utter hindrance to a child's development. And lurking under the mixed messages was a devastating social development: the nuclear family had fallen apart and fathers were lost in the wreckage. By 1994, divorce, and birth outside marriage, meant that nearly one in five British children was going to sleep at night without their biological father in the home.

Four years on, my own experience of fatherhood was only confirmed by the arrival of an unfeasibly lovely daughter (the wonder of it all never diminishes), while the whatistobedonewithdad? din outside only loudened. To someone who is a writer and anthologist by trade, an anthology of paternity in all its diversity seemed timely. But to be honest my motives were private. I believed that, if I could trawl through as many sources on fatherhood as I could find, from ancient Greek plays to Freudian psychology, from Russian literature to Bob Dylan, from poetry to *The Simpsons*, from newspaper reports to Groucho Marx, I myself might glean some clues as to my job as father. And then pass the clues on. Because I'm a believer in fatherhood. You might as well know that now.

So, what follows is a celebration of fatherhood, but also a revelation. It shows, I hope, what fatherhood is like and why it is like it is. It's a sort of literary toolkit for fathers and anybody who wants to understand the mystery of his or her own father (because everybody has a father, be he good or bad, close or never known). There's nothing new under the paternal sun; every fatherly deed, thought or doubt has been expressed by someone somewhere. It helps to know it and to read it, so as to understand it, even fix it. Dad – unwarrantedly chastised your so-small son? Then read Coventry Patmore's Victorian poem 'The Toys'. Feel like announcing the joyous news of your child's birth from the rooftops? Of course you do, just like Hector in Homer's *Iliad*. Realised that in becoming a father your ambition has dipped? Francis Bacon was writing about just that in 1601.

1601. Homer's Ancient Greece. The Victorian era. The past speaks clearly about fatherhood for anyone wishing to hear it. Paternal affection and care is not a modern invention; it's as old as man himself. One reason why is reported in *The Times* of 6 January 2000 (see page 11); on becoming fathers, men undergo a hormonal change (testosterone levels crash) which makes them protective and caring of their offspring. So do nearly all animals. If paternal affection is a transcendent natural truth, fatherhood is nonetheless largely socially conditioned. And until the 1800s, no one doubted that a man's place was in the family (childcare manuals of the 1700s – yes, they had them even then – were invariably addressed to the father), but then came the Industrial Revolution and its ravening factories. Work went out of the home, and with it went father. He couldn't be in two places at once. Separated from the family hearth, Dad became a more distant figure, and probably more disciplinarian. Unable to guide children by the example of living and working alongside them, he relied on coercion to assert his authority. The Victorian Sunday pater was born, depicted in all his spanking infamy in Samuel Butler's *The Way of All Flesh*. And yet it is clear from Patmore and a thousand Victorian fathers' letters that many Victorian men cherished their children and wished a more companionate relationship with them. The ebb of 'progress' was against them.

Father's lot has improved little since. He has, valiant individual efforts aside, been pushed to the margin of the magic family circle, assigned to the sole role of breadwinner. By the 1980s even that role had been denied him, lost to unemployment and the expansion of the female labour force. With no clear role in view, it is small wonder that many men, after kindly donating their sperm, fail to pick up the gauntlet of fatherhood. As the poet Les Murray puts it, 'Becoming a father, that is no/Achievement. Being one is, though.'

Because, let's face it, fatherhood is a challenge. It's the worst job in the world. There's no pay, no job description, no training, no medals, the hours are endless and you never, ever, retire. I still phone *my* father (75) for advice and worry him silly ('Drive carefully . . . ring us when you get home'). It is also, alongside motherhood, the best job in the world; the raising and care of another human being. And the most important. Here's why. Children with a father on hand are more likely to do well at school, be caring as an adult, be happier; they are less likely than the fatherless to be delinquent, to rape (if male), become pregnant as a teenager, be poor, go to prison, murder, have emotional problems, commit suicide. They are even less likely to smoke.

No, not all fathers are perfect. There are plenty of ogres in

'The Sins of the Father'. But in general the world is better for
having fatherhood in it. (Those who wish to serve as fathers,
incidentally, will find advice in this book from Jean-Jacques
Rousseau, *Esquire* magazine, Bill Cosby, Shakespeare, the
National Fatherhood Initiative, and scores more.)

And for those who do serve as fathers the pleasures are great.
The smiling upturned face of your child . . . well, there's nothing
to compare to that.

It's as good as it gets.

1

A Father is Born

Letter to Daniel

Fergal Keane, 1996

My dear son, it is six o'clock in the morning on the island of
Hong Kong. You are asleep cradled in my left arm and I am
learning the art of one-handed typing. Your mother, more tired
yet more happy than I've ever known her, is sound asleep in the
room next door and there is soft quiet in our apartment.

Since you arrived, days have melted into night and back again
and we are learning a new grammar, a long sentence whose punc-
tuation marks are feeding and winding and nappy changing and
these occasional moments of quiet.

When you're older we'll tell you that you were born in Britain's
last Asian colony in the lunar year of the pig and that when we
brought you home, the staff of our apartment block gathered to
wish you well. 'It's a boy, so lucky, so lucky. We Chinese love
boys,' they told us. One man said you were the first baby to be
born in the block in the year of the pig. This, he told us, was
good Feng Shui, in other words a positive sign for the building
and everyone who lived there.

Naturally your mother and I were only too happy to believe
that. We had wanted you and waited for you, imagined you and
dreamed about you and now that you are here no dream can do
justice to you. Outside the window, below us on the harbour, the
ferries are ploughing back and forth to Kowloon. Millions are
already up and moving about and the sun is slanting through the
tower blocks and out on to the flat silver waters of the South
China Sea. I can see the contrail of a jet over Lamma Island and,
somewhere out there, the last stars flickering towards the other
side of the world.

We have called you Daniel Patrick but I've been told by
my Chinese friends that you should have a Chinese name as
well and this glorious dawn sky makes me think we'll call
you Son of the Eastern Star. So that later, when you and I
are far from Asia, perhaps standing on a beach some evening,

I can point at the sky and tell you of the Orient and the times and the people we knew there in the last years of the twentieth century.

Your coming has turned me upside down and inside out. So much that seemed essential to me has, in the past few days, taken on a different colour. Like many foreign correspondents I know, I have lived a life that, on occasion, has veered close to the edge: war zones, natural disasters, darkness in all its shapes and forms.

In a world of insecurity and ambition and ego, it's easy to be drawn in, to take chances with our lives, to believe that what we do and what people say about us is reason enough to gamble with death. Now, looking at your sleeping face, inches away from me, listening to your occasional sigh and gurgle. I wonder how I could have ever thought glory and prizes and praise were sweeter than life.

And it's also true that I am pained, perhaps haunted is a better word, by the memory, suddenly so vivid now, of each suffering child I have come across on my journeys. To tell you the truth, it's nearly too much to bear at this moment to even think of children being hurt and abused and killed. And yet looking at you, the images come flooding back. Ten-year-old Andi Mikail dying from napalm burns on a hillside in Eritrea, how his voice cried out, growing ever more faint when the wind blew dust on to his wounds. The two brothers, Domingo and Juste, in Menongue, southern Angola. Juste, two years old and blind, dying from malnutrition, being carried on seven-year-old Domingo's back. And Domingo's words to me. 'He was nice before, but now he has the hunger.'

Last October, in Afghanistan, when you were growing inside your mother, I met Sharja, aged twelve. Motherless, fatherless, guiding me through the grey ruins of her home; everything was gone, she told me. And I knew that, for all her tender years, she had learned more about loss than I would likely understand in a lifetime.

There is one last memory. Of Rwanda, and the churchyard of the parish of Nyarabuye where, in a ransacked classroom, I found a mother and her three young children huddled together where they'd been beaten to death. The children had died holding on to their mother, that instinct we all learn from birth and in one way or another cling to until we die.

Daniel, these memories explain some of the fierce protectiveness I feel for you, the tenderness and the occasional moments of blind terror when I imagine anything happening to you. But there is something more, a story from long ago that I will tell you face to face, father to son, when you are older. It's a very personal story but it's part of the picture. It has to do with the long lines of blood and family, about our lives and how we can get lost in them and, if we're lucky, find our way out again into the sunlight.

It begins thirty-five years ago in a big city on a January morning with snow on the ground and a woman walking to hospital to have her first baby. She is in her early twenties and the city is still strange to her, bigger and noisier than the easy streets and gentle hills of her distant home. She's walking because there is no money and everything of value has been pawned to pay for the alcohol to which her husband has become addicted.

On the way, a taxi driver notices her sitting, exhausted and cold, in the doorway of a shop and he takes her to hospital for free. Later that day, she gives birth to a baby boy and, just as you are to me, he is the best thing she has ever seen. Her husband comes that night and weeps with joy when he sees his son. He is truly happy. Hungover, broke, but in his own way happy, for they were both young and in love with each other and their son.

But, Daniel, time had some bad surprises in store for them. The cancer of alcoholism ate away at the man and he lost his family. This was not something he meant to do or wanted to do, it just was. When you are older, my son, you will learn about how complicated life becomes, how we can lose our way and how people get hurt inside and out. By the time his son had grown up, the man lived away from the family, on his own in a one-roomed flat, living and dying for the bottle.

He died on the fifth of January, one day before the anniversary of his son's birth, all those years before in that snowbound city. But his son was too far away to hear his last words, his final breath, and all the things they might have wished to say to one another were left unspoken.

Yet now, Daniel, I must tell you that when you let out your first powerful cry in the delivery room of the Adventist Hospital and I became a father, I thought of your grandfather and, foolish though it may seem, hoped that in some way he could hear, across the infinity between the living and the dead, your proud statement of arrival. For if he could hear, he would recognise the distinct voice of family, the sound of hope and new beginnings that you and all your innocence and freshness have brought to the world.

To Ianthe

Percy Bysshe Shelley, 1792–1822

I love thee, Baby! For thine own sweet sake;
Those azure eyes, that faintly dimpled cheek,
Thy tender frame, so eloquently weak,
Love in the sternest heart of hate might wake;
But more when o'er thy fitful slumber bending
Thy mother folds thee to her wakeful heart,
Whilst love and pity, in her glances bending,
All that thy passive eyes can feel impart:
More, when some feeble lineaments of her,
Who bore thy weight beneath her spotless bosom,
As with deep love I read thy face, recur! –
More dear art thou, O fair and fragile blossom;
Dearest when most thy tender traits express
The image of thy mother's loveliness.

'I think I was reasonably shaken'

From Laurie Lee, *The Firstborn*, 1964

She was born in the autumn and was a late fall in my life, and lay purple and dented like a little bruised plum, as though she'd been lightly trodden in the grass and forgotten.

Then the nurse lifted her up and she came suddenly alive, her bent legs kicking crabwise, and her first living gesture was a thin wringing of the hands accompanied by a far-out Hebridean lament.

This moment of meeting seemed to be a birthtime for both of us; her first and my second life. Nothing, I knew, would be the same again, and I think I was reasonably shaken. I peered intently at her, looking for familiar signs, but she was convulsed as an Aztec idol. Was this really my daughter, this purple concentration of anguish, this blind and protesting dwarf?

Then they handed her to me, stiff and howling, and I held her for the first time and kissed her, and she went still and quiet as though by instinctive guile, and I was instantly enslaved by her flattery of my powers.

The biological programming of fatherhood

News article in *The Times*, 6 January 2000

Men are biologically programmed to become soppy after their children are born. A study shows that hormone changes put fathers through a similar emotional rollercoaster to that experienced by mothers.

Levels of testosterone, the male sex hormone, crash by an average of a third just after a baby is born. The lower it goes, the more a father dotes on the newborn. The effects, reported in *New Scientist*, are thought to be an evolutionary device to create an emotional bond with mother and child and make men less likely to stray.

Recent studies show that most male birds, rats and some primates are primed for their young in this way, but Anne Storey, a researcher at Memorial Hospital, in St John's, Newfoundland, is the first to find the effect in human beings. Dr Storey analysed blood samples from 34 couples. Hormone changes in fathers were triggered even by watching videos of newborn babies.

Being there

From figures presented to the Fatherhood Research
Group by Anne Wollett, 1985, and the records of the
Royal College of Midwives, 2000

Fathers at Birth	1940s	1950s	1960s	1970s	1980s	1990s
Mother wanted father to be present:	14.3%	38.9%	50.0%	73.1%	–	–
Father was present	none	8.5%	32.2%	64.0%	76.0%	92.1%

Soul man

From *The Rainbow* by D. H. Lawrence, 1915

FROM the first, the baby stirred in the young father a deep, strong emotion he dared scarcely acknowledge, it was so strong and came out of the dark of him. When he heard the child cry, a terror possessed him, because of the answering echo from the unfathomed distances in himself. Must he know in himself such distances, perilous and imminent?

He had the infant in his arms, he walked backwards and forwards troubled by the crying of his own flesh and blood. This was his own fiesh and blood crying! His soul rose against the voice suddenly breaking out from him, from the distances in him.

Sometimes in the night, the child cried and cried, when the night was heavy and sleep oppressed him. And half asleep, he stretched out his hand to put it over the baby's face to stop the crying. But something arrested his hand: the very inhumanness of the intolerable, continuous crying arrested him. It was so impersonal, without cause or object. Yet he echoed to it directly, his soul answered its madness. It filled him with terror, almost with frenzy.

He learned to acquiesce to this, to submit to the awful, obliterated sources which were the origin of his living tissue. He was not what he conceived himself to be! Then he was what he was, unknown, potent, dark.

He became accustomed to the child, he knew how to lift and

balance the little body. The baby had a beautiful, rounded head that moved him passionately. He would have fought to the last drop to defend that exquisite, perfect round head.

He learned to know the little hands and feet, the strange, unseeing, golden-brown eyes, the mouth that opened only to cry, or to suck, or to show a queer, toothless laugh. He could almost understand even the dangling legs, which at first had created in him a feeling of aversion. They could kick in their queer little way, they had their own softness.

One evening, suddenly, he saw the tiny, living thing rolling naked in the mother's lap, and he was sick, it was so utterly helpless and vulnerable and extraneous; in a world of hard surfaces and varying altitudes, it lay vulnerable and naked at every point. Yet it was quite blithe. And yet, in its blind, awful crying, was there not the blind, far-off terror of its own vulnerable nakedness, the terror of being so utterly delivered over, helpless at every point. He could not bear to hear it crying. His heart strained and stood on guard against the whole universe.

~~

High anxiety

James Boswell, 1740–95

Diary: Monday, 9 October 1775

My wife having been seized with her pains in the night, I got up about three o'clock, and between four and five Dr Young came. He and I sat upstairs mostly till between three and four, when, after we had dined, her labour became violent. I was full of expectation, and meditated curiously on the thought that it was already certain of what sex the child was, but that I could not have the least guess on which side the probability was. Miss Preston attended my wife close. Lady Preston came several times to inquire, but did not go into the room. I did not feel so much anxiety about my wife now as on former occasions, being better used to an inlying. Yet the danger was as great now as ever. I was easier from the same deception which affects a soldier who has escaped in several battles. She was very ill. Between seven and eight I went into the room. She was just delivered. I heard her say, 'God be thanked for whatever he sends.' I supposed then the child was a daughter. But she herself had not then seen it. Miss Preston said, 'Is it a daughter?' 'No,' said Mrs Forrest, the nurse-keeper, 'it's a son.' When I had seen the little man I said that I should now be so anxious that probably I should never again have an easy hour. I said to Dr Young with great seriousness, 'Doctor, Doctor, let no man set his heart upon anything in this world but land or heritable bonds; for he has no security that anything else will last as long as himself.' My anxiety subdued a flutter of joy which was in my breast.

Serenade

Thomas Hood, 1799–1845

'Lullaby, oh lullaby!'
Thus I heard a father cry,
'Lullaby, oh, lullaby!
The brat will never shut an eye;
Hither come, some power divine!
Close his lids, or open mine!' . . .
'Lullaby, oh, lullaby!
Two such nights, and I shall die!
Lullaby, oh, lullaby!
He'll be bruised, and so shall I.
How can I from bedpost keep,
When I'm walking in my sleep?'

From IVF to paternity

From 'Trying Times' by Charles Spencer, 1997

IVF is hellishly expensive, about £2000 a time, and several hundred quid more if a cost-conscious GP refuses to prescribe fertility drugs on the NHS as they sometimes, cruelly, do. A few months ago there was a news story about a woman who stole £20,000 from her employer but was spared a prison sentence when the judge, an unusually enlightened one, heard she had used the money to pay for test-tube baby treatment (it worked, I'm delighted to report). We could afford our treatments, just about, but I can't put my hand on my heart and say Nicki and I wouldn't have resorted to dishonesty if we'd been broke and had found an illegal opportunity of getting our hands on the cash.

The desperation of infertility is, I think, truly appreciated only by those who have been through the whole heartbreaking business. What's more, I feel like something of an impostor writing all this, because there is little doubt that women suffer far more than their men when they try and repeatedly fail to have a baby.

As someone who enjoys a gamble, I found the best way of handling the whole bizarre and ruinously expensive business was to imagine that IVF treatment was a form of roulette: a minimum stake of £2000 with the big pay-off of a child if your number came up. Even now, nineteen years after the birth of the first test-tube baby, Louise Brown, the odds are lousy. The average live-birth rate for IVF treatments in Britain in 1994–95 was 14.5 per cent. Some clinics managed almost 25 per cent: the worst managed less than 5 per cent. During our treatment we always thought our hospital had one of the highest rates of success, but I see from recently published data that last year it actually achieved only 9 per cent. IVF is big business and it was apparently not unknown in the past for clinics to massage their figures to attract punters to their high-stakes game.

For my wife, it was far harder to regard IVF dispassionately as a gamble against the odds. The fertility drugs, which I have a horrible suspicion come from human corpses, play merry havoc with the emotions as well as the hormones, and Nicki had to go to the doctor's each day for an injection like some helpless junkie. There were also regular, invasive ultrasound scans.

On the big day itself, however, when the woman's eggs are removed under anaesthetic, the onus is all on the chap. You have to produce your sperm on the hospital premises and the thought of humiliating failure in such desperate circumstances doesn't exactly set the libido racing. After producing endless samples over the years of treatment, I felt I could masturbate for England by now, but there were nevertheless some exceptionally dodgy moments.

On arrival at the hospital, while the woman gets enjoyably spaced-out on the pre-med, the man is dispatched to what I came to know as the wanking room. At our swanky hospital, it was got up to look like an anonymous four-star hotel room, complete with sofa, inoffensive modern art prints and expensive table lamps. I half expected to find a courtesy bowl of fruit and a mini-bar, and the latter would certainly have been most welcome. On one of the occasional tables a pile of well-thumbed soft-porn magazines is coyly placed. In one hand you clutch your little plastic pot, in the other . . . well, you can guess the rest. Ridiculously, for a room entirely devoted to masturbation, there was no lock on the door. The memory of a nurse bursting in, without knocking, while I was in mid-wank, still brings me out in a hot flush of embarrassment.

Two days later, if the eggs have been satisfactorily fertilised by the sperm after being mixed together by white-coated technicians in the lab, the tiny four-cell embryos are placed in the womb. On the fourth treatment we saw them, three in number, projected on to a wall with a magnifying epidiascope. Our doctor thought one of them looked suspect, so only two were actually used: the thought that those two amoeba-like blobs might one day become babies was almost unbearably moving.

After the embryos have been put into the womb, the agonising wait begins. Feverish hope alternates with a morbid conviction of failure, hour by hour, sometimes minute by minute. When it becomes clear that a treatment has failed – either because the woman's period starts, or following a pregnancy test at the hospital – the sense of desolation is indescribable. The emotional roller-coaster is so gruelling that both Nicki and I decided that we would make the fourth attempt our last – whatever the result. We simply couldn't take the pressure any more.

Nicki became increasingly convinced that it would be yet another failure. Oddly enough, seeing those strange, alien creatures on the wall of the hospital made her feel even more

despairing. So near and yet so far. She decided that she wanted
to be alone when the result came through to give her a chance
to howl in peace, so I was packed off to France for a few days
with a friend. I too was convinced of failure and got blind and
maudlin drunk on the ferry and continued drinking deep into
the night. The following day, horribly hungover, fearful and
trembling, I phoned her from a Normandy seaside resort. She
was officially pregnant, though the pregnancy would be precarious for the first three months. The hangover disappeared,
just like that, and I tucked into a giant celebratory plate of
fruits de mer.

In the early hours of 16 April 1993, Edward was born by
caesarean section and I held him in my arms for the first time.
What had once seemed like sinister science fiction now felt like
nothing less than a miracle.

～

Echo, homo

From a letter by Lafcadio Hearn, 1850–1904

Last night my child was born – a very strong boy, with large
black eyes. If you ever become a father, I think the strangest and
strongest sensation of your life will be hearing for the first time
the thin cry of your own child. For a moment you have the
strange feeling of being double; but there is something more,
quite impossible to analyse – perhaps the echo in a man's heart
of all the sensations felt by all the fathers and mothers of his
race at a similar instant in the past. It is a very tender, but also
a very ghostly feeling.

～

To father is to be human

From Margaret Mead, *Male and Female*, 1949

Somewhere at the dawn of human history, some social invention was made under which males started nurturing females and their young. We have no reason to believe that the nurturing males had any knowledge of physical paternity, although it is quite possible that being fed was a reward meted out to the female who was not too fickle with her sexual favours. In every known human society, everywhere in the world, the young male learns that when he grows up, one of the things which he must do in order to be a full member of society is to provide food for some female and her young. Even in very simple societies, a few men may shy away from the responsibility, become tramps or ne'er-do-wells or misanthropists who live in the woods by themselves. In complex societies, a large number of men may escape the burden of feeding females and young by entering monasteries – and feeding each other – or by entering some profession that their society will classify as giving them a right to be fed, like the Army and the Navy, or the Buddhist orders of Burma. But in spite of such exceptions, every known human society rests firmly on the learned nurturing behaviour of men.

⌒

Frost at Midnight

Samuel Taylor Coleridge, 1798

The Frost performs its secret ministry,
Unhelped by any wind. The owlet's cry
Came loud – and hark, again! loud as before.
The inmates of my cottage, all at rest,
Have left me to that solitude, which suits
Abstruser musings: save that at my side
My cradled infant slumbers peacefully.
'Tis calm indeed! so calm, that it disturbs
And vexes meditation with its strange
And extreme silentness. Sea, hill, and wood,
This populous village! Sea, and hill, and wood,

With all the numberless goings on of life,
Inaudible as dreams! the thin blue flame
Lies on my low burnt fire, and quivers not;
Only that film, which fluttered on the grate,
Still flutters there, the sole unquiet thing.
Methinks, its motion in this hush of nature
Gives it dim sympathies with me who live,
Making it a companionable form,
Whose puny flaps and freaks the idling Spirit
By its own moods interprets, every where
Echo or mirror seeking of itself,
And makes a toy of Thought.

                But O! how oft,
How oft, at school, with most believing mind,
Presageful, have I gazed upon the bars,
To watch that fluttering *stranger*! and as oft
With unclosed lids, already had I dreamt
Of my sweet birth-place, and the old church tower,
Whose bells, the poor man's only music, rang
From morn to evening, all the hot Fair-day,
So sweetly, that they stirred and haunted me
With a wild pleasure, falling on mine ear
Most like articulate sounds of things to come!
So gazed I, till the soothing things I dreamt
Lulled me to sleep, and sleep prolonged my dreams!
And so I brooded all the following morn,
Awed by the stern preceptor's face, mine eye
Fixed with mock study on my swimming book:
Save if the door half opened, and I snatched
A hasty glance, and still my heart leaped up,
For still I hoped to see the *stranger's* face,
Townsman, or aunt, or sister more beloved,
My play-mate when we both were clothed alike!

Dear Babe, that sleepest cradled by my side,
Whose gentle breathings, heard in this deep calm,
Fill up the interspersed vacancies
And momentary pauses of the thought!
My babe so beautiful! it thrills my heart
With tender gladness, thus to look at thee,
And think that thou shalt learn far other lore,
And in far other scenes! For I was reared

In the great city, pent 'mid cloisters dim,
And saw nought lovely but the sky and stars.
But *thou*, my babe! shalt wander like a breeze
By lakes and sandy shores, beneath the crags
Of ancient mountain, and beneath the clouds,
Which image in their bulk both lakes and shores
And mountain crags: so shalt thou see and hear
The lovely shapes and sounds intelligible
Of that eternal language, which thy God
Utters, who from eternity doth teach
Himself in all, and all things in himself.
Great universal Teacher! he shall mould
Thy spirit, and by giving make it ask.

Therefore all seasons shall be sweet to thee,
Whether the summer clothe the general earth
With greenness, or the redbreast sit and sing
Betwixt the tufts of snow on the bare branch
Of mossy apple-tree, while the nigh thatch
Smokes in the sun-thaw; whether the eave-drops fall
Heard only in the trances of the blast,
Or if the secret ministry of frost
Shall hang them up in silent icicles,
Quietly shining to the quiet Moon.

⌒

The Birthnight: To F.

Walter de la Mare, 1873–1956, written for
his daughter Florence

Dearest, it was a night
That in its darkness rocked Orion's stars;
A sighing wind ran faintly white
Along the willows, and the cedar boughs
Laid their wide hands in stealthy peace across
The starry silence of their antique moss:
No sound save rushing air
Cold, yet all sweet with Spring,
And in thy mother's arms, crouched weeping there,
Thou, lovely thing.

⌒

Lie still with thy daddy

Anonymous lullaby, from *Songs from the Nursery*,
1805

Hush thee, my babby,
Lie still with thy daddy,
Thy mammy has gone to the mill,
To grind thee some wheat
To make thee some meat,
Oh, my dear babby, lie still.

An affair of the heart

From Honoré de Balzac, *Old Goriot*, 1834

Some day you will know that a father is much happier in his children's happiness than in his own. I cannot explain it to you: it is a feeling in your body that spreads gladness through you. In short, I live three times over. Shall I tell you something strange? Well, when I became a father I understood God. He is there complete in everything because creation sprang from Him. It is just like that with me and my daughters. Only I love my daughters more than God loves the world, for the world is not as beautiful as God is, and my daughters are more beautiful than I.

Clenched in it was my heart

Hugo Williams, from 'What Shall We Do Now That
We Have Done Everything?', 1992

It wasn't so long ago really, 1966, and yet I was given the impression by St Mary's, Paddington, that I was the first father ever to attend the birth of his child. I had a letter from our GP saying I could be present if I wanted to and I put on my tweediest suit and daddyest tie to combat the hospital bureaucracy. I was a knight errant on some ill-defined mission to save his lady, though from what I had only the vaguest idea.

As a father barely out of my teens, I was intoxicated by self-importance. I might not be the star, but I was aware of having a plum part in this traditional drama: prestige without pain. I thought it would be easy for me to turn in a convincing performance without getting too involved. Mine would be a cameo role with a certain amount of glory attached to it by association. I would drink a lot, go unshaved for a day or two, become 'stubbly with goodness'.

For my wife there were no such options available. When a nurse came to shave her there was nothing I could do to save her from defilement. The razor-blade packet had a little blue bird printed on it and we seized on this with relief. Did the NHS have a contract, we asked, with this obscure brand of blunt razor blade? The nurse didn't answer. The blue bird was put away for the scrapbook.

A little while later, when the agony began, Hermine asked me to find one of these inadequate weapons so she could commit suicide. My eyes must have been popping out of my head as I caught my first glimpse of what was really going on here.

'The worst thing was if a nurse came in during a contraction', she wrote afterwards. 'They didn't seem to understand the mental effort one was making. They would start talking inanely, asking me questions, so that I had to blurt out, *"I am having a contraction!"* I didn't want to alienate them, but if I didn't get them to stop they would go on shouting at me and touching my stomach, which became intolerable.'

She had already had one injection, which was supposed to be enough. The Natural Childbirth was supposed to take care of the rest, but it wasn't working. I should have sat tight, but I was still doing everything I was told by Hermine in those days. I ran all over the hospital, looking for a sister who would sign a chit authorising a nurse to open a cabinet and give my wife another jab.

I think of all those wasted evenings practising natural childbirth, my wife and I breathing heavily in and out while raising our right arm and left leg. The idea was to learn to relax your muscles independently so they didn't get tangled up in the 'natural' birth process. The exercises were so excruciatingly boring we invariably ended up asleep.

'The injection came and I remember no more, till half waking in a new room with a new, lesser pain, I thought vaguely that I was on the lavatory and I began crying because I had given birth unknowingly.'

After all the trouble she'd been to, this is what it came to: I was there and she wasn't; I had seen someone coming out of someone and she hadn't. Whether she blames me for this I don't know. I blame myself.

Our daughter, meanwhile, was fast asleep herself, one little hand showing above the bedclothes. Clenched in it was my heart.

To My Son

George Gordon, Lord Byron, written in 1807

Those flaxen locks, those eyes of blue,
Bright as thy mother's in their hue;
Those rosy lips, whose dimples play
And smile to steal the heart away,
Recall a scene of former joy,
And touch thy father's heart, my Boy!

And thou canst lisp a father's name –
Ah, William, were thine own the same, –
No self-reproach – but, let me cease –
My care for thee shall purchase peace;
Thy mother's shade shall smile in joy,
And pardon all the past, my Boy!

Her lowly grave the turf has prest,
And thou hast known a stranger's breast;
Derision sneers upon thy birth,
And yields thee scarce a name on earth:
Yet shall not these one hope destroy, –
A Father's heart is thine, my Boy!

Why, let the world unfeeling frown,
Must I fond Nature's claims disown?

Ah, no – though moralists reprove,
I hail thee, dearest child of love,
Fair cherub, pledge of youth and joy –
A Father guards thy birth, my Boy!

Oh, 'twill be sweet in thee to trace,
Ere age has wrinkled o'er my face,
Ere half my glass of life is run,
At once a brother and a son;
And all my want of years employ
In justice done to thee, my Boy!

Although so young thy heedless sire,
Youth will not damp parental fire;
And, wert thou still less dear to me,
While Helen's form revives in thee,
The breast which beat to former joy,
Will ne'er desert its pledge, my Boy!

Little Brown Baby

Paul Laurence Dunbar, African-American poet,
1872–1906

Little brown baby wif spa'klin' eyes,
Come to yo' pappy an' set on his knee.
What you been doin', suh – makin' san' pies?
Look at dat bib – you's ez du'ty ez me.
Look at dat mouf – dat's merlasses, I bet;
Come hyeah, Maria, an' wipe off his han's.
Bees gwine to ketch you an' eat you up yit,
Bein' so sticky an sweet – goodness lan's!

Little brown baby wif spaklin' eyes,
Who's pappy's darlin' an' who's pappy's chile?
Who is it all de day nevah once tries
Fu' to be cross, er once loses dat smile?
Whah did you git dem teef? My, you's a scamp!
Whah did dat dimple come f'om in yo' chin?
Pappy do' know you – I b'lieves you's a tramp;
Mammy, dis hyeah's some ol' straggler got in!

Let's th'ow him outen de do' in de san',
We do' want stragglers a-layin' roun' hyeah;
Let's gin him 'way to de big buggah-man;
I know he's hidin' erroun' hyeah right neah.
Buggah-man, buggah-man, come in de do',
Hyeah's a bad boy you kin have fu' to cat.
Mammy an' pappy do' want him no mo',
Swaller him down f'om his haid to his feet!

Dah, now, I t'ought dat you'd hug me up close.
Go back, ol' buggah, you sha'n't have dis boy.
He ain't no tramp, ner nor straggler, of co'se;
He's pappy's pa'dner an' playmate an' joy.
Come to you' pallet now – go to yo' res';
Wisht you could allus know ease an' cleah skies;
Wisht you could stay jes' a chile on my breas'—
Little brown baby wif spaklin' eyes!

Small men, big fathers

From Barry Hewlett's study *Intimate Fathers*, 1991

The Aka Pygmies of the African Congo perform more infant
care than any other fathers in known society.

The Aka data point to the importance of quantity time rather
than quality time. Aka fathers do provide some quality time,
but most (about 75 per cent) of their time with infants is spent
in basic caregiving (holding, watching, feeding). The Aka
father–child relationship is intimate not because of quality time
but because the father knows his child exceptionally well
through regular interaction. Aka fathers do not often play with
their infants because they can communicate their love and
concern in other ways. They know subtle means of interacting
with their children. They sleep with their infants and have
physical contact throughout the day. The Aka data suggest
that intimate parent–child relations contribute to emotional
security. I would suggest that the intimate parent–child relations

contribute substantially to the development of autonomy and self-assuredness. Aka children develop these characteristics at a very early age (five to six years old), while it may take a lifetime for many Americans. It is impossible for American parents today to spend as much time with their children as Aka parents do, but the Aka data do suggest that whenever possible it is important for American parents to hold or be near their children. This may mean sleeping with young children, taking children to adult activities, holding infants more often rather than letting them sit in infant carrying devices, or allowing children to play around grown-ups engaged in adult activities.

Exponential fatigue

Ogden Nash, 1902–71

As a father of two there is a respectful question which I wish to
    ask of fathers of five:
How do you happen to be still alive?

Birth wrong

From Sophocles, *Oedipus Rex*, *c.* 430 BC, translated
by Sir George Young, 1887

OEDIPUS: I am the son of Polybus of Corinth,
And of a Dorian mother, Merope.
And I was counted most preëminent
Among the townsmen there; up to the time
A circumstance befell me, of this fashion –
Worthy of wonder, though of my concern
Unworthy. At the board a drunken fellow
Over his cups called me a changeling;
And I, being indignant – all that day
Hardly refrained – but on the morrow went
And taxed my parents with it to their face;

Who took the scandal grievously, of him
Who launched the story. Well, with what they said
I was content; and yet the thing still galled me;
For it spread far. So without cognisance
Of sire or mother I set out to go
To Pytho. Phoebus sent me of my quest
Bootless away; but other terrible
And strange and lamentable things revealed,
Saying I should wed my mother, and produce
A race intolerable for men to see,
And be my natural father's murderer.
When I heard that, measuring where Corinth stands
Even thereafter by the stars alone,
Where I might never think to see fulfilled
The scandals of ill prophecies of me,
I fled, an exile. As I journeyed on,
I found myself upon the self-same spot
Where, you say, this king perished. In your ears,
Wife, I will tell the whole. When in my travels
I was come near this place where three roads meet,
There met me a herald, and a man that rode
In a colt-carriage, as you tell of him,
And from the track the leader, by main force,
And the old man himself, would thrust me. I,
Being enraged, strike him who jostled me –
The driver – and the old man, when he saw it,
Watching as I was passing, from the car
With his goad's fork smote me upon the head.
He paid, though! duly I say not; but in brief,
Smitten by the staff in this right hand of mine,
Out of the middle of the carriage straight
He rolls down headlong; and I slay them all!
But if there be a semblance to connect
This nameless man with Laius, who is now
More miserable than I am? Who on earth
Could have been born with more of hate from heaven?
Whom never citizen or stranger may
Receive into their dwellings, or accost,
But must thrust out of doors; and 'tis no other
Laid all these curses on myself, than I!

Yea, with embraces of the arms whereby
He perished, I pollute my victim's bed!
Am I not vile? Am I not all unclean?
If I must fly, and flying, never can
See my own folk, or on my native land
Set foot, or else must with my mother wed,
And slay my father Polybus, who begat
And bred me? Would he not speak truly of me
Who judged these things sent by some barbarous
    Power?
Never, you sacred majesties of Heaven,
Never may I behold that day; but pass
Out of men's sight, ere I shall see myself
Touched by the stain of such a destiny!

⌒

Artistic representations of Joseph the Father

From Adrienne Burgess,
Fatherhood Reclaimed, 1997

For a long time practical fatherly care [in art] was represented by Jesus' adoptive father St Joseph, and the development of his persona tells us a great deal about what was
considered right and proper for earthly fathers. In the
fifteenth century there are many illustrations of Joseph's
gentle domesticity. In pictures and engravings he is shown
drying the Baby Jesus' nappies and feeding him from a bowl
of milk. By the seventeenth century, childcare has ceased to
be his province (he is now shown protecting Mary and
working to keep her and the child), but in the occasional
painting or engraving he still holds the baby, who is softly
touching his face. As time passes Joseph's domestic involvement vanishes and, by the eighteenth century, he is portrayed
as a religious contemplative, praying or studying alone. So
it came about that fathers, in all their aspects, were rele-
gated to Heaven, elevated or reduced (depending on your
point of view) to one-dimensional lawgivers, in the image
of whom earthly fathers were to make themselves.

⌒

On the Birth of His Son

Su Tung-P'o, 1036–1101

Families, when a child is born,
Want it to be intelligent.
I, through intelligence,
Having wrecked my whole life,
Only hope the baby will prove
Ignorant and stupid.
Then he will crown a tranquil life
by becoming a Cabinet Minister.

Early Morning Feed

From Peter Redgrove, *Poems 1954–1987*

The father darts out on the stairs
To listen to that keening
In the upper room, for a change of note
That signifies distress, to scotch disaster,
The kettle humming in the room behind.

He thinks, on tiptoe, ears a-strain,
The cool dawn rising like the moon:
'Must not appear and pick him up;
He mustn't think he has me springing
To his beck and call,'
The kettle rattling behind the kitchen door.

He has him springing
A-quiver on the landing –
For a distress-note, a change of key,
To gallop up the stairs to him
To take him up, light as a violin,
And stroke his back until he smiles.
He sidles in the kitchen
And pours his tea . . .

And again stands hearkening
For milk cracking the lungs.
There's a little panting,
A cough: the thumb's in: he'll sleep,
The cup of tea cooling on the kitchen table.

Can he go in now to his chair and think
Of the miracle of breath, pick up a book,
Ready at all times to take it at a run
And intervene between him and disaster,
Sipping his cold tea as the sun comes up?

He returns to bed
And feels like something, with the door ajar,
Crouched in the bracken, alert, with big eyes
For the hunter, death, disaster.

My Baby

Song sung by Charlie Bakus at the San Francisco
Minstrels Opera House, *c.* 1880

I'm the father of an infant,
Baby mine, baby mine;
He won't let me rest an instant,
Baby mine, baby mine;
He won't do a thing he's bid,
How I wish that I was rid
Of that awful sassy kid,
Baby mine, baby mine,
Of that awful sassy kid,
Baby mine.

At my meals I have to hold him,
Baby mine, baby mine;
But I never dare to scold him,
Baby mine, baby mine;
My face he'll surely scratch,
And the tablecloth he'll snatch,
All my crockery goes smash,

Baby mine, baby mine,
All my crockery goes smash.
Baby mine, baby mine.

In my hair he often lingers,
Baby mine, baby mine;
With molasses on his fingers,
Baby mine, baby mine;
You ought to hear him roar,
While I have to walk the floor,
Oh, I'd like to break his jaw,
Baby mine, baby mine.
Yes, I'd like to break his jaw,
Baby mine.

Forever Young

Bob Dylan, song written for his infant son,
Jacob, 1972

May God bless and keep you always. May your wishes
all come true.
May you always do for others, and let others do for you.

May you build a ladder to the stars and climb on every rung.
And, may you stay forever young.

May you grow up to be righteous. May you grow up to be true.
May you always know the truth and see the light
surrounding you.

May you always be courageous, stand upright and be strong.
And, may you stay forever young.

Forever young. Forever young. May you stay forever young.

May your hands always be busy. May your feet always be
swift.
May you have a strong foundation when the winds of
changes shift.

May your heart always be joyful. May your song always
  be sung.
And, may you stay forever young.

Forever young. Forever young. May you stay forever young.

↶

Long time coming; the history of Father's Day

From *The Modernisation of Fatherhood*,
Ralph LaRossa, 1997

Although neither Father's Day nor Mother's Day were immediately embraced, and while each had their opponents, when the two were given their official sendoffs (in 1910 and 1908, respectively), Mother's Day took off more like a rocket, while Father's Day took off . . . well, more like a rock.

By 1911, three years after the West Virginia and Pennsylvania celebrations, every state in the nation was observing Mother's Day. Two years later, Congress voted to make Mother's Day a national holiday. In 1914, Woodrow Wilson issued a presidential proclamation 'legalising and immortalising' the second Sunday in May for generations to come.

No similar groundswell of support emerged for Father's Day. As I said, President Wilson did participate, if only from afar, in the Father's Day festivities that took place in Spokane, Washington, in 1916. Also, President Coolidge did encourage the states to organise their own Father's Day celebrations in 1924. But Coolidge (and Harding before him) did not accede to Harry Meek's request that Father's Day be made a federal holiday.

Congress also did not follow its 1913 resolution for Mother's Day with an equivalent resolution for Father's Day – at least not immediately. It was not until 1971 – fifty-eight years after Mother's Day received its imprimatur – that Congress finally saw fit to pass a bill in favour of Father's Day. In response, President Richard Nixon issued, in 1972, a proclamation ('In Witness Whereof . . .') asking everyone in the country to make the third Sunday in June 'an occasion for renewal of the love and gratitude we bear to our fathers'.

↶

The contrariness of early fatherhood

From Charles Jennings, *Father's Race*, 1999

The feeling of *being a father*, though: that was terrific. Away from any sort of social pressure or middle-class ritual – in fact, on my own, whenever possible, without even the distracting presence of the baby – it was a fantastic sensation. I had to restrain myself from grabbing passers-by in the street and shaking them and shouting in their faces, *I'm a father! Complete! Not firing blanks! My biological destiny fulfilled!* Obviously, part of this was relief that mother and child were okay and that the ordeal prefigured by Kitzinger and the others was over. But a lot of it was also late-developer exhilaration at having stepped beyond what I was before and into that real world of children and grown-ups and responsibility which I'd glimpsed a year earlier.

On the other hand, I got appalling mood swings – mood swings which every father of my acquaintance has suffered from, even though they haven't always chosen to use the phrase *mood swing* with its attendant static crackle of female unreliability: the way your feelings change from something moderated by the adult world to something ungovernable, unknowable, violently self-contradictory.

Nappies epitomise this contradictory state in the first year. Indeed, they provide a nice physical correlative for the whole new-baby period. There is a whole nappy culture out there. I know this because, working at home, there is no way I could escape the burden of nappy-changing. And the first time you deal with a nappy full of impacted crap (a bit like ten-week-old *tapenade*), it is a life-altering encounter. Your emotions when you come face to face with it are something you could never anticipate, unless you work in a hospital or on a pig farm. The whole thing is so powerfully real, so much in the present, that it borders on Zen. I can still remember the first time I changed a nappy. I was bubbling with a mixture of dread at what I might do to my newborn son by mistake and at what I might find inside the nappy when I undid it. The sun was shining and the room was overheated and there was an unfamiliar smell of medication from all the ointments and lotions we had lying around, just in case. Although I'd been acting out the caring man bit quite keenly up to now, I'd ruthlessly avoided nappies, using a system of weak excuses and outright refusals. So Susie had had to strong-arm me into it the first time, lots of threats and grievance. I held my breath, leaned forward and gripped the tabs. It can't have been anything but completely depressing for Alistair, trapped on the table with this scowling, grimacing face bearing down on him, one of his beloved parents looking as if he was peering into a road accident. And then I gripped a bit tighter. And I made one of those decisions which freeze time, in which you can hear the blood roar in your ears in the moment before you act. I thought – I don't know what I thought. I thought that something was going to explode across the ceiling and the walls. That I was going to be calcified in crap like one of those objects people leave in limestone stalactite caves to be turned into stone. I pulled. And then it turned out to be a false alarm – I mean, it was just pee rather than anything worse. God, I was relieved. 'Well *that's* all right!' I shouted at the little chap. '*That* I can deal with!' He must have thought I was mad.

Some of the images I keep with me from my nappy-changing years will live for ever in my mind, precisely because of the way they symbolise the contrariness of early fatherhood. You have, for instance, the unnatural loveliness of the baby's bottom, clagged up with the kind of stuff you normally wipe from the sole of your shoe, in a nexus of beauty and squalor; you have the desire to purify and care for your child, warring with an equal desire to forget the whole thing, or even wander away somewhere and puke; you have your paternal joy at seeing how fit and strong your kid is, fighting with your rage at the little bastard's refusal to lie still and *just get changed*.

⌒

A great nuisance

From Samuel Butler, *The Way of All Flesh*,
written 1873–4

The birth of his son opened Theobald's eyes to a good deal which he had but faintly realised hitherto. He had had no idea how great a nuisance a baby was. Babies come into the world so suddenly at the end, and upset everything so terribly when they do come: why cannot they steal in upon us with less of a shock to the domestic system? His wife, too, did not recover rapidly from her confinement; she remained an invalid for months; here was another nuisance and an expensive one, which interfered with the amount which Theobald liked to put by out of his income against, as he said, a rainy day, or to make provision for his family if he should have one. Now he was getting a family, so that it became all the more necessary to put money by, and here was the baby hindering him. Theorists may say what they like about a man's children being a continuation of his own identity, but it will generally be found that those who talk this way have no children of their own. Practical family men know better.

About twelve months after the birth of Ernest there came a second, also a boy, who was christened Joseph, and in less than twelve months afterwards, a girl, to whom was given the name of Charlotte. A few months before this girl was born Christina paid a visit to the John Pontifexes in London, and, knowing her condition, passed a good deal of time at the Royal Academy exhibition looking at the types of female beauty portrayed by the Academicians, for she had made up her mind that the child this time was to be a girl. Alethea warned her not to do this, but she persisted, and certainly the child turned out plain, but whether the pictures caused this or no I cannot say.

Theobald had never liked children. He had always got away from them as soon as he could, and so had they from him; oh, why, he was inclined to ask himself, could not children be born into the world grown-up? If Christina could have given birth to a few full-grown clergymen in priest's orders – of moderate views, but inclining rather to Evangelicalism, with comfortable livings and in all respects facsimiles of Theobald himself – why, there might have been more sense in it; or if people could buy ready-made children at a shop of whatever age and sex they liked, instead of always having to make them at home and to begin at the beginning with them – that might do better, but as it was he did not like it. He felt as he had felt when he had been required to come and be married to Christina – that he had been going on for a long time quite nicely, and would much rather continue things on their present footing. In the matter of getting married he had been obliged to pretend he liked it; but times were changed, and if he did not like a thing now, he could find a hundred unexceptionable ways of making his dislike apparent.

It might have been better if Theobald in his younger days had kicked more against his father: the fact that he had not done so encouraged him to expect the most implicit obedience from his own children. He could trust himself, he said (and so did Christina), to be more lenient than perhaps his father had been to himself; his danger, he said (and so again did Christina), would be rather in the direction of being too indulgent; he must be on his guard against this, for no duty could be more important than that of teaching a child to obey its parents in all things.

He had read not long since of an Eastern traveller, who, while exploring somewhere in the more remote parts of Arabia and Asia Minor, had come upon a remarkably hardy, sober, industrious little Christian community – all of them in the best of health – who had turned out to be the actual living descendants of Jonadab, the son of Rechab; and two men in European costume, indeed, but speaking English with a broken accent, and by their colour evidently Oriental, had come begging to Battersby soon afterwards, and represented themselves as belonging to this people; they had said they were collecting funds to promote the conversion of their fellow tribesmen to the English branch of the Christian religion. True, they turned out to be impostors, for when he gave them a pound and Christina five shillings from her private purse, they went and got drunk with it in the next village but one to Battersby; still, this did not invalidate the story of the Eastern traveller. Then there were the Romans – whose greatness was probably due to the wholesome authority exercised by the head of a family over all its members. Some Romans had even killed their children; this was going too far, but then the Romans were not Christians, and knew no better.

The practical outcome of the foregoing was a conviction in Theobald's mind, and if in his, then in Christina's, that it was their duty to begin training up their children in the way they should go, even from their earliest infancy. The first signs of self-will must be carefully looked for, and plucked up by the roots at once before they had time to grow. Theobald picked up this numb serpent of a metaphor and cherished it in his bosom.

Before Ernest could well crawl he was taught to kneel; before he could well speak he was taught to lisp the Lord's Prayer, and the general confession. How was it possible that these things could be taught too early? If his attention flagged or his memory failed him, here was an ill weed which would grow apace, unless it were plucked out immediately, and the only way to pluck it out was to whip him, or shut him up in a cupboard, or dock him of some of the small pleasures of childhood. Before he was three years old he could read and, after a fashion, write. Before he was four he was learning Latin, and could do rule of three sums.

Hector and son

From Homer, *The Iliad, c.* eighth century BC,
translated by Alexander Pope

Thus having spoke, th'illustrious Chief of *Troy*
Stretch'd his fond Arms to clasp the lovely Boy.
The Babe clung crying to his Nurse's Breast,
Scar'd at the dazling Helm, and nodding Crest.
With secret Pleasure each fond Parent smil'd,
And *Hector* hasted to relieve his Child,
The glitt'ring Terrors from his Brows unbound,
And plac'd the beaming Helmet on the Ground.
Then kist the Child, and lifting high in Air,
Thus to the Gods prefer'd a Father's Pray'r.
    O Thou! whose Glory fills th' Ætherial Throne,
And all ye deathless Pow'rs! protect my Son!
Grant him, like me, to purchase just Renown,
To guard the *Trojans*, to defend the Crown,
Against his Country's Foes the War to wage,
And rise the *Hector* of the future Age!
So when triumphant from successful Toils,
Of Heroes slain he bears the reeking Spoils,
Whole Hosts may hail him with deserv'd Acclaim,
And say, This Chief transcends his Father's Fame:
While pleas'd amidst the gen'ral Shouts of *Troy*,
His Mother's conscious Heart o'erflows with Joy.
He spoke, and fondly gazing on her Charms
Restor'd the pleasing Burden to her Arms;

Rising late and playing with A-ts'ui, aged two

Po Chu-i, 772–846

All the morning I have lain perversely in bed;
Now at dusk I rise with many yawns.
My warm stove is quick to get ablaze;
At the cold mirror I am slow in doing my hair.
With melted snow I boil fragrant tea;
Seasoned with curds I cook a milk-pudding.
At my sloth and greed there is no one but me to laugh;
My cheerful vigour none but myself knows.
The taste of my wine is mild and works no poison;
The notes of my harp are soft and bring no sadness.
To the Three Joys in the book of Mencius
I have added the fourth of playing with my baby-boy.

Fatherhood, from the German

Les Murray, *Collected Poems*, 1998

Becoming a father, that is no
Achievement. Being one is, though.

2

Fathers and Sons

Little Boy Lost

William Blake, 1757–1827

Father! father! where are you going?
O do not walk so fast.
Speak, father, speak to your little boy,
Or else I shall be lost.

A Parental Ode to My Son, Aged Three Years and Five Months

Thomas Hood, 1837

Thou happy, happy elf!
(But stop – first let me kiss away that tear)
Thou tiny image of myself!
(My love, he's poking peas into his ear!)
Thou merry, laughing sprite!
With spirits feather-light.
Untouched by sorrow and unsoiled by sin –
(Good heavens, the child is swallowing a pin!)

Thou tricksy Puck!
With antic toys so funnily bestuck.
Light as the singing bird that wings the air –
(The door! the door! he'll tumble down the stair!)
Thou darling of thy sire!
(Why, Jane, he'll set his pinafore a-fire!)
Thou imp of mirth and joy!
In love's dear chain so strong and bright a link.
Thou idol of thy parents – (Drat the boy!
There goes my ink!)

Thou cherub! – but of earth:
Fit playfellow for Fays, by moonlight pale,

In harmless sport and mirth.
(That dog will bite him if he pulls its tail!)
Thou human humming-bee, extracting honey
From every blossom in the world that blows.
Singing in Youth's Elysium every sunny –
(Another tumble! – that's his precious nose!)

Thy father's pride and hope!
(He'll break the mirror with that skipping-rope!)
With pure heart newly stamped from Nature's mint
(Where *did* he learn that squint?)
Thou young domestic dove!
(He'll have that jug off, with another shove!)
Dear nursling of the hymeneal nest!
(Are those torn clothes his best?)
Little epitome of man!
(He'll climb upon the table, that's his plan!)
Touched with the beauteous tints of dawning life –
(He's got a knife!)

Thou enviable being!
No storms, no clouds, in thy blue sky foreseeing.
Play on, play on.
My elfin John!
Toss the light ball – bestride the stick –
(I knew so many cakes would make him sick!)
With fancies buoyant as the thistledown.
Prompting the face grotesque, and antic brisk.
With many a lamblike frisk –
(He's got the scissors, snipping at your gown!)

Thou pretty opening rose!
(Go to your mother, child, and wipe your nose!)
Balmy, and breathing music like the South.
(He really brings my heart into my mouth!)
Fresh as the morn, and brilliant as its star –
(I wish that window had an iron bar!)
Bold as the hawk, yet gentle as the dove –
(I tell you what, my love.
I cannot write, unless he's sent above!)

Nettles

From Vernon Scannell, *Collected Poems 1950–1993*

My son aged three fell in the nettle bed.
'Bed' seemed a curious name for those green spears,
That regiment of spite behind the shed:
It was no place for rest. With sobs and tears
The boy came seeking comfort and I saw
White blisters beaded on his tender skin.
We soothed him till his pain was not so raw.
At last he offered us a watery grin,
And then I took my billhook, honed the blade
And went outside and slashed in fury with it
Till not a nettle in that fierce parade
Stood upright any more. And then I lit
A funeral pyre to burn the fallen dead.
But in two weeks the busy sun and rain
Had called up tall recruits behind the shed:
My son would often feel sharp wounds again.

Teaching a son to walk

The Baal Shem Tov, 1698–1760

When a father sets out to teach his little son to walk, he stands
in front of him and holds his two hands on either side of the
child, so that he cannot fall, and the boy goes toward his father
between his father's hands. But the moment he is close to his
father, he moves away a little and holds his hands farther apart,
and he does this over and over, so that the child may learn to
walk.

Roughhousing rules ok

National Fatherhood Initiative, USA

New research suggests that little boys who are lucky enough to have fathers who roughhouse with them are actually better at controlling their aggression than those whose dads do no roughhouse with them. That's because if the little boy gets too rough and starts to hit or bite, Dad tells him to cool it. In this way, the little boy learns how to control – not act out – his aggressive impulses.

~~

Play fellow

A letter from Richard Steele to his wife,
16 March 1717

Your Son at the present writing is mighty well employed in Tumbling on the Floor of the room and Sweeping the sand with a Feather. He grows a most delightfull Child, and very full of Play and Spiritt. He is also a very great Scholar. He can read His Primer, and I have brought down my Virgil. He makes most shrewd remarks upon the Pictures. We are very intimate Friends and Play fellows. He begins to be very ragged and I hope I shall be pardoned if I equip Him with new Cloaths and Frocks or what Mrs Evans and I shall think for His Service.

~~

The main event

From Charles Jennings, *Father's Race*, 1999

The first time I found myself at a nursery-school sports day, I actually managed to butch it out and refused to have anything to do with the fathers' event. I stood my ground at the edge of the track, smirking uneasily. Fortunately, there were a couple of weaklings there with me (crippled by holiday accidents or squash games) so I got away with it. The second year, though, absolutely *every* father who'd turned up volunteered for the long-distance race, right round the perimeter of the borrowed cricket pitch on which the games were taking place. There was a lot of vicious joshing, a lot of evil-natured *How are you, David? You feeling UP TO IT?*, a certain amount of glancing spitefully in my direction. I had nowhere to hide. All the mums rounded on me (the deviant father, always around to collect his son) and jeered me up to the starting line. The other dads were already pulling off their shiny loafers and loosening their ties and smoothing back their hair and gazing down the grass track with a murderous fixity. Some of them had evidently been waiting for this moment for some time. I could tell that they had been practising. I tried to get into the mood by hitching up my socks and wiping my spectacles, but instead of fearsome competitiveness, nothing much entered my heart except dread. It was one of those calm, slightly sultry English summer days, a good day for lying on your back and staring thoughtfully at the sky. I thought I might be sick. The headmistress of the Montessori nursery said *Go* and immediately a pack of grunting men shot past me and ran off into the distance, their ties flying out behind them, their heels flashing in the sunshine.

I found myself right at the back, alongside a very old man — a late father, or possibly even a grandfather. His thinning grey hair flapped around on his crown. He looked into the distance with watery eyes. 'God,' he said, 'I must be mad.' We trudged round for a while, until it dawned on me that even he was moving slightly faster than I was. Another minute went by and the gap between us grew wider, and then he had deserted me and I was alone, stumbling along, the distance between me and the rest of them widening until they were two-thirds of a lap ahead of me, in a three-lap race. I struggled and sweated and groaned for air as I tried to close the margin between me and the old man (that affirming lard I had been carrying since Alistair was born coming back to haunt me), but he got further and further away, closer and closer to the rolling, jostling backs of the fit men, leagues away. Eventually, after they had all crossed the finish line, I was still yards off, lurching along, nearly in tears.

But then a wonderful thing happened. Alistair, who'd been watching with the rest of the children, coralled into a fairy ring

next to the teachers, took pity on my state, ran up beside me
and jogged along, making encouraging remarks. 'I thought I'd
keep you company,' he said. And he did. I don't know whether
I was more ashamed for myself for being a fat turd, or for Alistair
for having to be seen with a father like me. But at the same time,
and more than either, I loved him for being generous and compa-
niable and brave. He saved that day from being one of those
memories that cause me to yelp with uncontainable embarrassment in public whenever I suffer a flashback – and turned it
instead into something bathed in a glow of fondness and hope.
At last I staggered and wheezed over the line, to a smattering of
sarcastic applause and ironical *well dones* from the nastier-minded
teachers, while Alistair gave my hand a squeeze. I can't tell you
how grateful I was to him for being there, and I still feel grateful
to him, just thinking about it now. I hope his kids will do the
same for him one day. It's typical of everything to do with children, that while some situations can – out of the blue – turn into
disasters when emotions get out of control or when expectations
get unmanageable, disasters such as this one can just as abruptly
be filled with love and gratitude.

Nothing spared

From Ivan Turgenev, *Fathers and Sons*, 1862

'I ought to tell you, I . . . idolise my son . . .
    '. . . And I don't only idolise him, Arkady Nikolaich, I am
proud of him, and the height of my ambition is that some day
there will be the following lines in his biography: "The son of a
simple army-doctor, who was, however, capable of divining his
greatness betimes, and spared nothing for his education . . ."'
The old man's voice broke.

That's my pateras!

From Barry Strauss, *Fathers and Sons in Athens*,
1997

We find another example of paternal pride in Xenophon's
Symposium, a Socratic dialogue with the dramatic date of 421.
The guests of honour at the drinking party in the home of Kallias
in Piraeus are Lykon and his teenage son Autolykos. Father and
son recline next to each other on a couch at the symposium.
Famous for his good looks, Autolykos had just won the prize
in the pankration (a combination of boxing and wrestling) at
the Panathenaic games, and Kallias wanted to become his lover.
The conversation at the symposium turned to the question of
what possession or accomplishment each guest most prided
himself in having. When it was Lykon's turn to answer, he
responded, 'Don't you all know that it is my son?' (Xen. *Symp.*
3.12). One of the guests suggests snidely that what Autolykos
is proud of, on the other hand, is his prize. But Autolykos pipes
up with the reply that no, indeed, what he is proud of is his
father! Up to this point Autolykos had been sitting demurely
beside his father, while the other guests reclined; it was customary
for adult males alone to recline at an Athenian party. Now,
Autolykos underlines his respect by reclining beside his father
on the dining couch, a gesture perhaps even of affection and
ease, perhaps even a manly gesture: children were not expected
to speak at a symposium, but Autolykos' remark had delighted
the audience (3.12–13). As syrupy as the scene is, as 'goody-
two-shoes' as Autolykos is, the smitten Kallias is overcome, and
blurts out that Lykon is the richest man in the world; Lykon
agrees, naturally (Xen. *Symp.* 3.13).

A mystical estate

From *Ulysses* by James Joyce, 1922

Fatherhood, in the sense of conscious begetting, is unknown to man. It is a mystical estate, an apostolic succession, from only begetter to only begotten On that mystery and not on the madonna which the cunning Italian intellect flung to the mob of Europe the church is founded and founded irremovably because founded, like the world, macro and microcosm, upon the void. Upon incertitude, upon unlikelihood, *Amor matris*, subjective and objective genitive, may be the only true thing in life. Paternity may be a legal fiction. Who is the father of any son that any son should love him or he any son?

A Boy Named Sue

Song popularised by Johnny Cash, 1958

My daddy left home when I was three/ And he didn't leave much to ma and me/ Just this old guitar and an empty bottle of booze. Now, I don't blame him 'cause he run and hid/ But the meanest thing that he ever did/ Was before he left, he went and named me 'Sue'.

Well, he must o' thought that it was quite a joke/ And it got a lot of laughs from a' lots of folk/ It seems I had to fight my whole life through/ Some gal would giggle and I'd get red/ And some guy'd laugh and I'd bust his head/ I tell ya, life ain't easy for a boy named 'Sue'.

Well, I grew up quick and I grew up mean/ My fist got hard and my wits got keen/ I'd roam from town to town to hide my shame/ But I made me a vow to the moon and stars/ That I'd search the honky-tonks and bars/ And kill that man that give me that awful name.

Well, it was Gatlinburg in mid-July/ And I just hit town and my throat was dry/ I thought I'd stop and have myself a brew/ At an old saloon on a street of mud/ There at a table, dealing stud/ Sat the dirty, mangy dog that named me 'Sue'.

Well, I knew that snake was my own sweet dad from a worn-out picture that my mother'd had/ And I knew that scar on his cheek and his evil eye/ He was big and bent and gray and old/ And I looked at him and my blood ran cold/ And I said: 'My name is Sue! How do you do! Now you gonna die!!'

Well, I hit him hard right between the eyes/ And he went down but, to my surprise/ He come up with a knife and cut off a piece of my ear/ But I busted a chair right across his teeth/ And we crashed through the wall and into the street/ Kicking and a' gouging in the mud and the blood and the beer.

I tell ya, I've fought tougher men/ But I really can't remember when/ He kicked like a mule and he bit like a crocodile/ I heard him laugh and then I heard him cuss/ He went for his gun and I pulled mine first/ He stood there lookin' at me and I saw him smile.

And he said: 'Son, this world is rough/ And if a man's gonna make it, he's gotta be tough/ And I know I wouldn't be there to help ya along/ So I give ya that name and I said goodbye; I knew you'd have to get tough or die/ And it's that name that helped to make you strong.'

He said: 'Now you just fought one hell of a fight/ And I know you hate me, and you got the right/ To kill me now, and I wouldn't blame you if you do/ But ya ought to thank me, before I die, For the gravel in ya guts and the spit in ya eye/ Cause I'm the son-of-a-bitch that named you "Sue".'

I got all choked up and I threw down my gun/ And I called him my pa, and he called me his son/ And I come away with a different point of view/ And I think about him, now and then/ Every time I try and every time I win/ And if I ever have a son, I think I'm gonna name him Bill or George! Anything but Sue! I still hate that name!

What makes a father's love distinct?

From David Blankenhorn, *Fatherless America*, 1995

This conditional nature of paternal sponsorship – I am a good father if my children become good adults – often means that a father's love is qualitatively different from a mother's love. This difference takes us to the heart of the matter. Compared to a mother's love, a father's love is frequently more expectant, more instrumental, and significantly less unconditional.

For the child, from the beginning, the mother's love is an unquestioned source of comfort and the foundation of human attachment. But the father's love is almost always a bit farther away, more distant and contingent. Compared to the mother's love, the father's must frequently be sought after, deserved, earned through achievement. My mother loves me unconditionally because I am her child. My father loves me, but he tends to make me work for it. Lucky is the child who receives both varieties of parental love.

'This is a poem to my son Peter'

Peter Meinke, 1932–

this is a poem to my son Peter
whom I have hurt a thousand times
whose large and vulnerable eyes
have glazed in pain at my ragings
thin wrists and fingers hung
boneless in despair, pale freckled back
bent in defeat, pillow soaked
by my failure to understand.
I have scarred through weakness
and impatience your frail confidence forever
because when I needed to strike
you were there to be hurt and because
I thought you knew
you were beautiful and fair
your bright eyes and hair

but now I see that no one knows that
about himself, but must be told
and retold until it takes hold
because I think anything can be killed
after a while, especially beauty
so I write this for life, for love, for
you, my oldest son Peter, age 10,
going on 11.

⌒

Boy tyrannus

From Plutarch *c.* 46–*c.* 120, *Themistocles*

Themistocles used to say of his son (who bullied his mother and, through her, himself) that he was the most powerful person in Greece. The Athenians controlled the rest of Greece, he himself controlled the Athenians, the boy's mother controlled him, and the boy controlled his mother.

⌒

The Judgement

By Franz Kafka, written during the night of
22–23 September 1912

George was amazed at how dark his father's room was, even on that sunny morning. What a shadow it cast, that high wall beyond the narrow courtyard! His father was sitting by the window, in a corner of the room that was adorned with various mementoes of George's late mother; he was reading the newspaper, holding it up to his eyes at an angle in an attempt to compensate for some deficiency in his eyesight. On the table stood the remains of his breakfast, not much of which appeared to have been consumed.

'Ah, George!' his father said, coming across the room towards him. His heavy dressing-gown fell open as he walked, the flaps swirling about him – 'He's still a giant, my father,' George said to himself.

Then he said, 'It's intolerably dark in here.'

'It's dark, all right,' his father replied.

'And you have the window shut?'

'I prefer it that way.'

'It's really warm outside,' said George, as if following up his earlier remark. He took a seat.

His father cleared the breakfast things away and put them on top of a cupboard.

'I just wanted to tell you,' George went on, following the old man's movements with a forlorn look, 'that I've sent word of my engagement to Petersburg after all.' He pulled the letter out of his pocket a little way; then let it drop back.

'Why to Petersburg?' his father asked.

'To my friend, *you* know,' said George, looking his father in the eye. 'He's not at all like this in the office,' he was thinking, 'sitting there so four-square with his arms across his chest!'

'Quite. Your friend,' his father said with emphasis.

'But I told you, Father, how I didn't want to tell him of my engagement at first. Purely out of consideration, for no other reason. You know yourself how difficult he is. What I said to myself was, he may hear about my engagement from someone else, though it's hardly likely in view of the solitary life he leads – I can't help that – but he's not going to hear about it from me.'

'And now you've changed your mind, is that it?' his father inquired, putting his huge newspaper down on the window-sill, placing his spectacles on top of it, and covering the spectacles with his hand.

'Yes, now I've changed my mind. If he's a good friend of mine, I said to myself, then my being happily engaged will make him happy too. That's why I no longer had any hesitation in notifying him of the fact. But before I posted the letter I wanted to tell you what I'd done.'

'George,' his father said, pulling his toothless mouth into a broad slit, 'listen to me! You've come to me with this thing because you want to talk it over with me. That does you credit, no doubt about it. But it's no good, in fact it's less than no good, if you're not going to tell me the whole truth. I don't want to stir up things that have no place here. Since the death of your beloved mother certain not very nice things have been happening. Maybe there's a time for them too, and maybe that time comes sooner than we expect. A great deal escapes me in the office, though perhaps not because it's kept from me – the last thing I'm trying to suggest is that things are being kept from me – but I haven't the strength any more, my memory is beginning to go, and I no longer have an eye for all the little details. This is simply nature taking its course for one thing, and for another, Mummy's death hit me much harder than it did you. But as long as we're on the subject of this letter, promise me one thing, George: don't try to hoodwink me. It's a trifle, it's not worth bothering about, so don't try to hoodwink me. Do you really have this friend in Petersburg?'

George stood up in embarrassment. 'Never mind about my friends. A thousand friends could never take the place of my father. Do you know what I think? You don't look after yourself enough. Old age is demanding its due. I can't do without you in the office, you know that as well as I do, but if the business should ever start undermining your health I'd shut up shop for good tomorrow. I'm not having that. No, we're going to have to start a new regimen for you. Radically new, I mean. Here you are, sitting in the dark, when in the living-room it would be lovely and light for you. You peck at your breakfast instead of building yourself up properly. You sit around with the window shut when fresh air would do you so much good. No, Father, no! I'll get the doctor round and we'll do exactly what he says. We'll swap rooms: you move into the front room and I'll come in here. There'll be no difference as far as you're concerned because we'll move all your things over too. But there's time enough for all that. You go back to bed for a bit now; you've got to take things easy. Here, I'll help you get undressed. I can, you know. Or would you like to go in the front room now? You can have my bed for the time being. In fact that would be a very sensible arrangement.'

George was standing right beside his father, whose head of shaggy white hair had sunk to his breast.

'George,' his father said softly, not moving.

George immediately knelt down beside his father; he looked into his father's weary face and into the huge pupils staring out at him from the corners of his father's eyes.

'You have no friend in Petersburg. You've always liked to have your little joke, even with me. How should you have a friend there, of all places! I find that too much to believe.'

'Think back for a moment, Father,' George said, heaving the

old man out of his chair and, as he stood there in a really extremely weak condition, pulling off his dressing-gown. 'Nearly three years ago now my friend came here to see us. You didn't particularly like him, I remember. On at least two occasions I disowned him in conversation with you, although he was sitting in my room at the time. I could understand your dislike of him perfectly well; my friend has his peculiarities. But then there was that other time when you got on with him very well. I was really proud of the fact that you listened to him, nodded at what he said, and asked questions. Think back – you must remember. He was telling us those incredible stories about the Russian Revolution. About how for example on a business trip to Kiev he had become involved in a disturbance and seen a priest up on a balcony cut a large, bleeding cross in the flat of his hand, hold the hand in the air, and shout to the crowd. You've even recounted the story yourself on occasion.'

In the meantime George had managed to lower his father into his chair again, carefully remove the woollen trousers he wore over his linen pants, and pull off his socks. Seeing the not particularly clean state of his father's underwear, he reproached himself for having neglected to ensure that his father changed his clothes whenever necessary. He and his fiancée had not yet discussed in so many words how they were going to arrange his father's future; they had tacitly assumed that he would stay on in the old flat by himself. Now, however, George resolved on the spur of the moment to take his father with him when he set up house. In fact, on second thought, it looked as if the care and attention he planned to give his father there might almost come too late.

He picked his father up and carried him into bed. An awful feeling came over him as he became aware during the few steps to the bed that his father, curled up in his arms, was playing with the watch chain at his lapel. So firmly did his father grasp the watch chain that for a moment George was unable to put him to bed.

Once he was in bed, however, everything seemed to be fine. He arranged the bedclothes himself, pulling the quilt unusually high over his shoulders. He looked up at George in a not unfriendly fashion.

'You do remember him, don't you?' George asked, nodding encouragingly.

'Am I covered up now?' asked his father, as if he could not tell whether his feet were adequately covered.

'See, you like it in bed,' said George, tucking the quilt in around him.

'Am I covered up?' his father asked again. He seemed to be particularly interested in what the answer would be.

'Don't worry, you're well covered up.'

'No, I'm not!' his father shouted, slamming the answer down on the question, and he threw the quilt back with such force that for a moment it opened out completely in flight. He stood up in bed, one hand pressed lightly to the ceiling. 'You wanted to cover me up, you scoundrel, I know you did, but I'm not covered up yet. If it's my last ounce of strength it's enough for you – more than enough for you. I know your friend, all right. A son after my own heart, he'd have been. That's why you've been deceiving him all these years, isn't it? Why else? Do you think I haven't wept for him? That's why you shut yourself in your office – the boss is busy, no one's to disturb him – purely in order to write your lying notes to Russia. But luckily for your father he doesn't need anyone to teach him to see through his son. And now that you thought you'd got the better of him, so much so that you could plant your bottom down on him and he wouldn't move, what does my high and mighty son do but decide to get married!'

George looked up at this terrifying vision of his father. The friend in Petersburg, whom his father suddenly knew so well, affected him as never before. He thought of him, lost in the depths of Russia. He saw him at the door of his empty, looted shop against a background of smashed-up shelving, ransacked stock, and bent gas brackets, barely able to stand. Why had he had to go so far away?

'Look at me, will you!' his father shouted, and George almost distractedly ran over to the bed to take everything in but came to a halt halfway there.

'Because she hauled up her skirts,' his father began in a slimy falsetto, 'because she hauled up her skirts like this, the filthy bitch,' and by way of illustration he lifted the hem of his night-shirt so high that the war wound on his thigh was exposed, 'because she hauled up her skirts like this and like this and like this you had to have a go at her, and to make sure you can have your way with her undisturbed you defile your mother's memory, betray your friend, and stick your father in bed where he can't budge. Well, can he budge or can't he?'

And he stood without holding on at all and kicked his legs in the air. His eyes blazed with insight.

George was now standing in a corner, as far away from his father as possible. A long time ago he had made up his mind to keep a really close watch on everything lest he should ever, by some devious means, either from behind or from above, be caught by surprise. He recalled his long-forgotten resolution and promptly forgot it, like drawing a short thread through the eye of a needle.

'But the friend isn't betrayed after all!' his father shouted, and a wagging forefinger corroborated this. 'I was his locum tenens here.'

'Playactor!' George could not refrain from shouting; realising his mistake he immediately, though too late – there was a glazed look in his eyes – bit his tongue so hard that he doubled up in pain.

'Of course I've been playacting! Hah, that's just the word for it! What other consolation was left to your old widowed father? Tell me – and for the space of your answer be my living son still – what else was left to me in my little back room, persecuted by disloyal staff, an old man to the marrow of my bones? And my son went about rejoicing, clinching deals that I had set up, giddying himself with pleasure, and departing from his father's presence with the opaque face of a man of honour! Do you think I didn't love you – having fathered you?'

'Now he's going to lean forward,' George thought. 'If only he'd fall and smash to pieces!' The words went hissing through his head.

His father leant forward but did not fall. Since George did not approach as he had expected, he straightened up again.

'Stay where you are, I don't need you! You think you still have the strength to come over here and are just holding back because you want to. Well, don't delude yourself! I'm still the stronger by far. On my own I might have had to stand down, but Mother has left me her strength. I'm in business with your friend in a big way; I've got your customer right here in my pocket!'

'He's even got pockets in his nightshirt!' George said to himself, thinking that he could make him look ridiculous in the eyes of the whole world by this remark. He only thought it for a moment, because he always forgot everything.

'Just you take your fancy woman on your arm and come up

and see me! I'll swat her away from your side for you, you'll see
if I don't!'

George made a face as if he did not believe it. His father simply
nodded, driving home the truth of his words, in the direction of
George's corner.

'You made me laugh today, coming to ask whether you should
write to your friend about your engagement! He knows everything, stupid, he knows everything! I wrote to him myself, because
you forgot to take my writing things away. That's why he hasn't
been here for years. He knows everything a hundred times better
than you do yourself. He screws your letter up unread in his left
hand while holding up my letters to read in his right!'

He waved an arm about enthusiastically above his head. 'He
knows everything a thousand times better!' he yelled.

'Ten thousand times!' George said to poke fun at his father,
but even before the words had left his lips they had a deadly
serious sound.

'For years I've been waiting for you to come along with that
question! Do you think I care about anything else? Do you think
I read the papers? Here!' And he threw George a sheet of newspaper that had somehow got carried into bed with him. An old
newspaper with a name George did not begin to recognise.

'The time it's taken you to grow up! Your mother had to die,
she was not to see the joyful day, your friend's going to rack and
ruin in Russia, he looked as if he was on his last legs three years
ago, and you can see for yourself the state I'm in! You've got
eyes, haven't you?'

'So you've been trying to catch me out!' cried George.

Sympathetically his father observed, 'You wanted to say that
before, probably. Now it's completely out of place.'

And in a louder voice: 'So now you know what else there was
apart from you; up to now you only knew about yourself! You
were an innocent child, to tell the truth – though to tell the whole
truth you were the devil incarnate! Therefore know: I hereby
sentence you to death by drowning!'

George felt himself thrust from the room, the thud with which
his father fell on the bed behind him still echoing in his ears. On
the stairs, which he took at a rush as if descending an inclined
plane, he surprised his cleaning lady, who was going up to tidy
the flat after the night. 'Jesus!' she cried, hiding her face in her

apron, but he had already gone. Out of the door he shot, his momentum carrying him across the road to the water's edge. He clutched the railing as a hungry man will clutch at food.

He vaulted over it, expert gymnast that he had been in his boyhood days, much to his parents' pride. Still holding on with weakening grip, he glimpsed a bus through the bars, knew it would easily cover the noise of his fall, called softly, 'Dear parents, I did love you, always,' and let himself drop.

Crossing the bridge at that moment was a simply endless stream of traffic.

⌒

What will daddy say?

From Sophocles, *Ajax*, written *c.* 440 BC

AJAX: With what face shall I appear before my father
Telamon? How will he find heart to look
On me, stripped of my championship in war,
That mighty crown of fame that once was his?
No, that I dare not. Shall I then assault
Troy's fortress, and alone against them all
Achieve some glorious exploit and then die?
No, I might gratify the Atreidae thus.
That must not be. Some scheme let me devise
Which may prove to my aged sire that I,
His son, at least by nature am no coward.

⌒

Sons, what things you are

William Shakespeare, *Henry IV, Part 2*
(Act IV, Scene 5), *c.* 1597

KING HENRY: See, sons, what things you are!
How quickly nature falls into revolt
When gold becomes her object!
For this the foolish over-careful fathers

Have broke their sleep with thoughts, their
   brains with care,
Their bones with industry;
For this they have engrossed and pil'd up
The canker'd heaps of strange-achieved gold:
For this they have been thoughtful to invest
Their sons with arts and martial exercises:
When, like the bee, tolling from every flower
The virtuous sweets,
Our things with wax, our mouths with honey
   pack'd.
We bring it to the hive: and, like the bees,
Are murder'd for our pains. This bitter taste
Yield his engrossments to the ending father.

Repentance

Moliere [Jean-Baptiste Poquelin], 1622–73

How easily a father's tenderness is recalled and how quickly a
son's offences vanish at the slightest word of repentance.

Father's pride

From the memoir of a schoolboy, Mesopotamia,
c. 2000 BC

Arriving at school in the morning I recited my tablet, ate my
lunch, prepared my new tablet, wrote it, finished it, then they
assigned me my oral work . . . When school was dismissed, I
went home, entered the house, and found my father sitting there.
I told my father of my written work, then recited my tablet to
him, and my father was delighted.

The Toys

Coventry Patmore, 1823–96

My little Son, who looked from thoughtful eyes,
And moved and spoke in quiet grown-up wise,
Having my law the seventh time disobeyed,
I struck him, and dismissed
With hard words and unkissed,
– His Mother, who was patient, being dead.
Then, fearing lest his grief should hinder sleep,
I visited his bed,
But found him slumbering deep,
With darkened eyelids, and their lashes yet
From his late sobbing wet.
And I, with moan,
Kissing away his tears, left others of my own;
For on a table drawn beside his head,
He had put, within his reach,
A box of counters and a red-veined stone,
A piece of glass abraded by the beach,
And six or seven shells,
A bottle with bluebells,
And two French copper coins, ranged there with careful art,
To comfort his sad heart.
So when that night I prayed
To God, I wept, and said:
Ah, when at last we lie with trancéd breath,
Not vexing Thee in death,
And Thou rememberest of what toys
We made our joys,
How weakly understood
Thy great commanded good,
Then fatherly not less
Than I whom Thou has moulded from the clay,
Thou'lt leave Thy wrath, and say,
'I will be sorry for their childishness.'

All children should be equal in the eyes of the father

Advice from Jean-Jacques Rousseau's *Emile*, 1762

A father has no choice and ought to have no preferences in the family God gives him. All his children are equally his children; he owes to them all the same care and the same tenderness. Whether they are crippled or not, whether they are sickly or robust, each of them is a deposit of which he owes an account to the hand from which he receives it; and marriage is a contract made with nature as well as between the spouses.

A *liberal allowance*

From *Brief Lives* by John Aubrey, 1626–97

Sir William Platers, Knight, was a Cambridgeshire Gentleman . . . He was temperate and thriftie as to all other things. He had only one Sonne, who was handsome and ingeniose, and whome he cultivated with all imaginable care and Education, and knowing that he was flesh and blood, tooke care himselfe to provide sound and agreable females for him. He allowed his son liberally but enjoyned him still temperance, and to sett-downe his expences, e.g. Item for a semel tetegit [single session] 20s [£1].

Older and wiser

Mark Twain, 1835–1910

When I was a boy of fourteen, my father was so ignorant I could hardly stand to have the old man around. But when I got to be twenty-one, I was astounded at how much the old man had learned in seven years.

My Son, My Executioner

Donald Hall, 1954

My son, my executioner.
I take you in my arms,
Quiet and small and just astir,
And whom my body warms.

Sweet death, small son, our instrument
Of immortality.
Your cries and hungers document
Our bodily decay.

We twenty-five and twenty-two,
Who seemed to live forever,
Observe enduring life in you
And start to die together.

On an Old Photograph of My Son

From Raymond Carver, *A New Path to the Waterfall*, 1989

It's 1974 again, and he's back once more. Smirking,
a pair of coveralls over a white tee-shirt,
no shoes. His hair, long and blond, falls
to his shoulders like his mother's did
back then, and like one of those young Greek
heroes I was just reading about. But
there the resemblance ends. On his face
the contemptuous expression of the wise guy,
the petty tyrant. I'd know that look anywhere.
It burns in my memory like acid. It's
the look I never hoped I'd live to see
again. I want to forget that boy
in the picture – that jerk, that bully!

What's for supper, mother dear? Snap to!
Hey, old lady, jump, why don't you? Speak
when spoken to. I think I'll put you in

a headlock to see how you like it. I like
it. I want to keep you on
your toes. Dance for me now. Go ahead,
bag, dance. I'll show you a step or two.
Let me twist your arm. Beg me to stop, beg me
to be nice. Want a black eye? You got it!

Oh, son, in those days I wanted you dead
a hundred – no, a thousand – different times.
I thought all that was behind us. Who in hell
took this picture, and
why'd it turn up now,
just as I was beginning to forget?
I look at your picture and my stomach cramps.
I find myself clamping my jaws, teeth on edge, and
once more I'm filled with despair and anger.
Honestly, I feel like reaching for a drink.
That's a measure of your strength and power, the fear
and confusion you still inspire. That's
how mighty you once were. Hey, I hate this
photograph. I hate what became of us all.
I don't want this artefact in my house another hour!
Maybe I'll send it to your mother, assuming
she's still alive somewhere and the post can reach
her this side of the grave. If so, she'll have
a different reaction to it, I know. Your youth and
beauty, that's all she'll see and exclaim over.
My handsome son, she'll say. My boy wonder.
She'll study the picture, searching for her likeness
in the features, and mine. (She'll find them, too.)
Maybe she'll weep, if there are any tears left.
Maybe – who knows? – she'll even wish for those days
back again! Who knows anything anymore?

But wishes don't come true, and it's a good thing.
Still, she's bound to keep your picture out
on the table for a while and make over you
for a time. Then, soon, you'll go
into the big family album along with the other crazies –
herself, her daughter and me, her former husband. You'll be
safe in there, cheek to jowl with all your victims. But don't
worry, my boy – the pages turn, my son. We all
do better in the future.

⌒

The son of my father

From *Sherwood Anderson's Memoirs*, 1942

A boy wants something very special from his father. You are always hearing it said that fathers want their sons to be what they feel they cannot themselves be but I tell you it also works the other way. I know that, as a small boy, I wanted my father to be a certain thing he was not, could not be. I wanted him to be a proud silent dignified one. When I was with other small boys and he passed along the street, I wanted to feel in my breast the glow of pride.

'There he is. That is my father.'

But he wasn't such a one. He couldn't be. It seemed to me then that he was always showing off. Let's say someone in our town had got up a show. They were always doing it. At that time it would have been the GAR, the Grand Army of the Republic. They did it to raise some money to help pay the rent of their hall.

So they had a show, the druggist in it, the fellow who clerked in the shoe store. A certain horse doctor was always in such shows in our town and, to be sure, a lot of women and girls. They got as many in it as they could so that all of the relatives of the actors would come. It was to be, of course, a comedy.

And there was my father. He had managed to get the chief comedy part. It was, let's say, a Civil War play and he was a comic Irish soldier. He had to do the most absurd things. They thought he was funny, but I didn't think so.

I thought he was terrible. I didn't see how Mother could stand it. She even laughed with the others. It may be that I also would have laughed if it hadn't been my father.

Or there was a parade, say on the Fourth of July or on Decoration Day. He'd be in that too. He'd be right at the front of it. He had got himself appointed Grand Marshal or some such office, had got, to ride in the parade, a white horse hired from a livery stable.

He couldn't ride for shucks. He fell off the horse and everyone hooted with laughter but he did not care. He even seemed to like it. I remember one such occasion when he had done something ridiculous, and right out on the main street too, when I couldn't stand it. I was with some other boys and they were laughing and shouting at him and he was shouting back to them and having as good a time as they were. I ran away. There was an alleyway back of the stores on Main Street and I ran down that. There were some sheds, back of the Presbyterian church, where country people stabled horses during church on Sundays and I went in there. I had a good long cry.

And then there came a certain night. Mother was away from home when Father came in and he was alone. He'd been off somewhere for two or three weeks. He found me alone in the house.

He came silently into the house and it was raining outside. It may be there was church that night and that Mother had gone. I was alone and was sitting in the kitchen. I had a book before me and was sitting and reading by the kitchen table.

So in came my father. He had been walking in the rain and was very wet. He sat and looked at me and I was startled for, on that night, there was on his face the saddest look I have ever seen on a human face. For a long time he sat looking at me, not saying a word.

And then something happened to me.

There are times when a boy is so sad, he doesn't quite know why, that he thinks he can hardly bear to go on living. He thinks he'd rather die. The sadness comes mostly when it has been raining or it comes in the fall when the leaves fall off the trees. It isn't anything special. It is just sadness.

So there was Father on the rainy summer night. He was sad and looking at him made me sad. He sat for a time, saying nothing, his clothes dripping. He must have been walking a long time in the rain. He got up out of his chair.

'You come on, you come with me,' he said.

I got up and went with him out of the house. I was filled with wonder but, although he had suddenly become like a stranger to me, I wasn't afraid. We went along a street. At that time we lived in a little yellow frame house, quite far out at the edge of our town. It was a house we hadn't lived in very long. We had moved a lot. Once I heard my mother say to my father, 'Well, I guess we'll have to be moving,' she said. She said we were back three months on our rent and that there wasn't any money to pay it with. She didn't scold. She even laughed. She just took it as a fact that when the rent got far behind we had to move.

I was walking with my father and we went out of the town. We were on a dirt road. It was a road that led up a little hill, past fields and strips of woodland, and went on over the hill and down into a little valley, about a mile out of town, to where there was a pond. We walked in silence. The man who was always talking had stopped talking.

I didn't know what was up and had the queer feeling that I was with a stranger. I don't know now whether or not my father intended it so. I don't think he did.

The pond at the edge of the town was quite large. It was a place where a creek had been dammed and was owned by a man who sold ice in our town. We were there at the edge of the pond. We had come in silence. It was still raining hard and there were flashes of lightning followed by thunder. We were on a grassy bank at the pond's edge, when my father spoke, and in the darkness and rain his voice sounded strange. It was the only time during the evening that he did speak to me.

'Take off your clothes,' he said and, still filled with wonder, I began to undress. There was a flash of lightning and I saw that he was already naked.

And so naked we went into the pond. He did not speak or explain. Taking my hand he led me down to the pond's edge and pulled me in. It may be that I was too frightened, too full of a feeling of strangeness to speak. Before that night my father had never seemed to pay any attention to me.

'And what is he up to now?' I kept asking myself that question. It was as though the man, my father I had not wanted as father, had got suddenly some kind of power over me.

I was afraid and then, right away, I wasn't afraid. We were in the pond in darkness. It was a large pond and I did not swim very well but he had put my hand on his shoulder. Still he did not speak but struck out at once into the darkness.

He was a man with very big shoulders and was a powerful swimmer. In the darkness I could feel the movement of his muscles. The rain poured down on us and the wind blew and there were the flashes of lightning followed by the peals of thunder.

And so we swam, I will never know for how long. It seemed hours to me. We swam thus in the darkness to the far edge of the pond and then back to where we had left our clothes. There was the rain on our faces. Sometimes my father turned and swam on his back and when he did he took my hand in his large powerful one and moved it over so that it rested always on his shoulder and sometimes as we swam thus I could look into his face. There would be a flash of lightning and I could see his face clearly.

It was as it was when he had come earlier into the kitchen where I sat reading the book. It was a face filled with sadness. There would be the momentary glimpse of his face and then again the darkness, the wind and the rain. In me there was a feeling I had never known before that night.

It was a feeling of closeness. It was something strange. It was as though there were only we two in the world. It was as though I had been jerked suddenly out of myself, out of a world of the schoolboy, out of a world in which I was ashamed of my father, out of a place where I had been judging my father.

He had become blood of my blood. I think I felt it. He the stronger swimmer and I the boy clinging to him in the darkness. We swam in silence and in silence we dressed, in our wet clothes, and went back along the road to the town and our house.

It had become a strange house to me. There was the little porch at the front where on so many nights my father had sat with the men. There was the tree by the spring and the shed at the back. There was a lamp lighted in the kitchen and when we came in, the water dripping from us, there was my mother. She was as she had always been. She smiled at us. I remember that she called us 'boys'. 'What have you boys been up to?' she asked, but my father did not answer. As he had begun the evening's experience with me in silence so he ended it. He turned and looked at me and then he went, I thought with a new and strange dignity, out of the room.

He went to his room to get out of his wet clothes and I climbed the stairs to my own room. I undressed in darkness and got into bed. I was still in the grip of the feeling of strangeness that had taken possession of me in the darkness in the pond. I couldn't sleep and did not want to sleep. For the first time I had come to know that I was the son of my father. He was a storyteller as I was to be. It may be that on the night of my childhood I even laughed a little softly there in the darkness in my bed in the room. If I did, I laughed knowing that, no matter how much as a storyteller I might be using him, I would never again be wanting another father.

⌒

So there!

A boy writes to his father, Greece, *c.* 300

Theon to his father Theon, greeting. Thank you for not taking me to town with you. If you won't take me with you to Alexandria I won't write you a letter or speak to you or say goodbye to you; and if you go to Alexandria I won't take your hand nor greet you again. That is what will happen if you won't take me. Mother said to Archelaos, 'He drives me crazy: take him.' Thank you for sending me presents . . . Send for me, *please*. If you don't I won't eat, I won't drink; there now!

⌒

The old chestnut

From Oliver Goldsmith, *The Good Natur'd Man*, 1768

LEONTINE: An only son, sir, might expect more indulgence
CROAKER: An only father, sir, might expect more obedience

⌒

The Father and the Son

David Citino, 1947–

I nick my chin while shaving;
my son bares his wrist,
searches for the rustiest blade,
sorrow pooling in his eyes.

I scold; he thrusts his hand
into ice, fire, calls himself
'Forever Second Best', climbs
the cross, singing 'It is finished.'

I grow comic; he invents love,
the erection, children.
He watches as I go ashen,
fall backwards into the casket.

We trade places; I bring flowers,
light memory's candles with
his last breath. We trade places.
This goes on forever and ever.

The prestige of the father

From Simone de Beauvoir, *The Second Sex*, 1949

The life of the father has a mysterious prestige: the hours he
spends at home, the room where he works, the objects he has
around him, his pursuits, his hobbies, have a sacred character.
He supports the family, and he is the responsible head of the
family. As a rule his work takes him outside, and so it is through
him that the family communicates with the rest of the world: he
incarnates that immense, difficult and marvellous world of adven-
ture; he personifies transcendence, he is God.

'As long as my dad was there'

News report in *The Daily Telegraph*, August 2000

A boy was saved from drowning when a plaster cast on his fractured arm wedged him above the waterline after he fell down a
narrow outlet pipe.

Seven-year-old Sean Herman spent 40 minutes trapped inside
the shaft as the tidal waters began to rise around him.

He was freed when his father and a fireman managed to lasso a rope on to the wrist of his uninjured arm and pull him out.

Sean had broken his left arm when he fell while climbing a fence.

Wayne Herman, 28, his father, took him and his two-year-old sister Courtney fishing at Smith's Dock, North Shields, North Tyneside, on Sunday.

Sean disappeared when he stepped into some undergrowth behind him and fell 12ft down the concealed outlet pipe.

Rescuers believe his plaster cast prevented him falling a further 15ft down the pipe at the abandoned dry dock.

Mr Herman, a merchant seaman, said: 'If ever there was a lucky break it was this one. The cast was sticking out at a funny angle and added that extra vital inch that wedged him in the pipe.'

Another angler ran over and Mr Herman asked him to call the fire brigade as he grabbed a rope from a boat. He tied a slip knot which he lowered down to his son, who grabbed it in his teeth.

Mr Herman said: 'I told him to keep calm but that it was very important he got his good arm free . . . I managed to lasso his wrist and pulled the slip knot tight, so at least I had him secure . . . and held the rope and made sure he didn't slip below the waterline.

'It must have taken about 20 minutes for the fire brigade to arrive but it felt like an eternity. I could see his little face looking up at me and he was calling "Please get me out, Daddy."'

A fireman joined him and they were able gradually to hoist Sean up until he emerged from the pipe. Mr Herman said: 'We had to act quickly because of the tide but thankfully we managed to get him out before the water level rose any further.'

Sean, who suffered cuts and bruises, was taken to hospital for a check-up. He said: 'I was scared but I knew as long as my dad was there I would be all right.'

⌒

'Dads ought to have their whack sometimes'

From a letter by Edward Burne-Jones, 1861, shortly after his marriage

I want my dad to come and live near me: business doesn't answer and he grows old [he was 59], and a little cottage twelve miles out of London seems a good idea. Next year I hope it can be managed – by then I shall be out of debt and getting on a bit. Dads ought to have their whack sometimes; it's very dull to be a dad and have a son cutting about and enjoying himself and still be working on drearily. I shall hate it when I'm a dad.

An aperitif for the world of men

From Kirk Douglas, *The Ragman's Son*, 1988

I loved my father but I hated him, too. He was a ragman who drove a horse and wagon and couldn't read or write. But to me he was big. He was strong. He was a man. I didn't know what I was. But I wanted to be accepted by him, to be given a pat on the back. I would walk past the saloon at night, its curtains raised high on the tall windows so that no young boy could peer over them. I'd hear my father's voice in there, in that roaring accent, regaling his drunken cronies with some story about things that had happened in Russia; I'd hear them all burst into laughter. It was the world of men. No women were allowed, and I wasn't allowed either. I kept waiting for my father to take me by the hand into the world of men.

Once he gave me just a taste of it, a tease. One hot summer day, Pa took me by the hand and led me into a saloon. I can see it so clearly, the streaks of brilliant sunlight streaming through the window and then the black shadows in contrast . . . just like the movie sets that I would later play in. No one was there but the bartender. My father bought me a glass of loganberry. Nectar of the gods! I was in the world of men for a brief moment, even though the men had not yet arrived. But I was in their habitat. Later on, I would be in those settings often with Burt Lancaster or John Wayne. It always made me smile, because it seemed to me that we were all still children pretending to be in the world of men.

Anecdote for Fathers

William Wordsworth, 1798

I have a boy of five years old;
His face is fair and fresh to see;
His limbs are cast in beauty's mould,
And dearly he loves me.

One morn we strolled on our dry walk,
Our quiet home all full in view,
And held such intermitted talk
As we are wont to do.

My thoughts on former pleasures ran;
I thought of Kilve's delightful shore,
Our pleasant home when spring began,
A long, long year before.

A day it was when I could bear
Some fond regrets to entertain;
With so much happiness to spare,
I could not feel a pain.

The green earth echoed to the feet
Of lambs that bounded through the glade,
From shade to sunshine, and as fleet
From sunshine back to shade.

Birds warbled round me – and each trace
Of inward sadness had its charm;
Kilve, thought I, was a favoured place,
And so is Liswyn farm.

My boy beside me tripped, so slim
And graceful in his rustic dress!
And, as we talked, I questioned him,
In very idleness.

'Now tell me, had you rather be,'
I said, and took him by the arm,
'On Kilve's smooth shore, by the green sea,
Or here at Liswyn farm?'

In careless mood he looked at me,
While still I held him by the arm,
And said, 'At Kilve I'd rather be
Than here at Liswyn farm.'

'Now, little Edward, say why so:
My little Edward, tell me why.' –
'I cannot tell, I do not know.' –
'Why, this is strange,' said I;

'For here are woods, hills smooth and warm:
There surely must some reason be
Why you would change sweet Liswyn farm
For Kilve by the green sea.'

At this my boy hung down his head,
He blushed with shame, nor made reply;
And three times to the child I said,
'Why, Edward, tell me why?'

His head he raised – there was in sight,
It caught his eye, he saw it plain –
Upon the house-top, glittering bright,
A broad and gilded vane.

Then did the boy his tongue unlock,
And eased his mind with this reply:
'At Kilve there was no weather-cock;
And that's the reason why.'

O dearest, dearest boy! my heart
For better lore would seldom yearn,
Could I but teach the hundredth part
Of what from thee I learn.

Boxing lesson

From *The Autobiography of Benvenuto Cellini*, 1558–62

When I was already about three years old my grandfather Andrea was still alive and over a hundred. One day they were changing a cistern pipe when a large scorpion which they had not noticed crawled out of it, slipped to the ground, and scuttled away under a bench. I caught sight of it, ran over, and picked the thing up. It was so big that when I had it in my little hand its tail hung out at one end and both its claws at the other. They say that laughing happily I ran up to my grandfather and said: 'Look, grandpapa, look at my lovely little crab.' He recognised what it was and almost dropped dead from shock and anxiety. Then he tried to coax me into giving it to him, but the more he did so the more I screamed tearfully, refusing to give it to anyone.

My father was also in the house and, hearing the noise, he ran in to see what it was all about. He was so terror-stricken that his mind refused to work and he could not think up any way of stopping the poisonous creature from killing me. Then his eyes fell on a pair of scissors and he managed to wheedle me into letting him snip off the scorpion's tail and claws. When the danger was past he regarded it as a good omen.

Another time, when I was about five, my father was sitting alone in one of our small rooms, singing and playing his viol. Some washing had just been done there and a good log fire was still burning. It was very cold, and he had drawn near the fire. Then, as he was looking at the flames, his eye fell on a little animal, like a lizard, that was running around merrily in the very hottest part of the fire. Suddenly realising what it was, he called my sister and myself and showed it to us. And then he gave me such a violent box on the ears that I screamed and burst into tears. At this he calmed me as kindly as he could and said: 'My dear little boy, I didn't hit you because you had done wrong. I only did it so that you will never forget that the lizard you saw in the fire is a salamander, and as far as we know for certain no one has ever seen one before.'

Then he kissed me and gave me a little money.

Rebel son without a pause

From the diary of Reverend Ralph Josselin

Oct. 9 [1669]: A sad morning with John, his stout heart outwardly submitted(,) I forgave him and god I hope mee.

Nov. 29 [1669]: John tooké his clothes and mony and in the morning unknown to any of us. or without a line to tell what he aimed at went away. Lord let him not outrun thy mercy. I will daily seeke to god to keepe him. to breake his heart and deliver him from his own evill mind, and save his soule. lord heare prayer. hasten an houre of love for him for Christs sake.

Feb. 4 [1670]: faire and dry. John returned, but lord change his heart, make us wise to win him to thee, god good in his word, lord owne us for thine

Feb. 12: A good day in my affectionate strivings to recover sinners out of Satans and their hearts snare, my soule yearned over John. oh Lord overcome his heart in obedience to thee.

Feb. 19: A sad wecke with John, his carriage intolerable. uncertain what to resolve. Lord direct mee. a day of comfort in the word, though troubles in my house. 26. came home opportunely to save a cow cast. found John within, but as I dreamed high and proud so he was(,) cast him lord down as that cow that he may rise up again.

Mar. 12: Sad with my sons as to their trades, and sadder nearer mee. the lord helpe mee, for I stand alone as to all helpe and comfort, but from thee. god carries on my outward affaires beyond expectations(.) a sweet raine

Mar. 19: John rid away, carried some things with him. without taking his leave of mee.

Mar. 22: god in mercy looke after him

Crime and punishment

Deuteronomy 21: 18–22

18 ¶ If a man have a stubborn and rebellious son, which will not obey the voice of his father, or the voice of his mother, and *that*, when they have chastened him, will not hearken unto them:

19 Then shall his father and his mother lay hold on him, and bring him out unto the elders of his city, and unto the gate of his place;

20 And they shall say unto the elders of his city. This our son *is* stubborn and rebellious, he will not obey our voice; *he is* a glutton, and a drunkard.

21 And all the men of his city shall stone him with stones, that he die: so shalt thou put evil away from among you; and all Israel shall hear, and fear.

Off with his hand

Code of Hammurabi, Babylon, eighteenth century BC

If a son has struck his father, they shall cut off his hand.

The elephant's tale

Dr Wade F. Horn, *The Washington Times*, 1999

Recently, the National Fatherhood Initiative released a television public service announcement recounting the true story of the consequence when a group of young male elephants was transported from one wild game preserve in Africa to another without also transporting older bull elephants with them.

Without the presence of older male elephants, this group of juvenile elephants began to do something elephants just don't do in the wild – they began marauding in bands, wantonly killing other animals. This pack of 'wilding' juvenile elephants especially liked to harass white rhinos – chasing them over great distances, throwing sticks at them and finally stomping them to death.

It was only after a group of adult male elephants was transported into the game preserve that this delinquent and violent behaviour stopped.

How did this happen? Did the older elephants bring the younger males together to express their feelings? No. They started to enforce the rules. In no uncertain terms, the older males began to discipline the younger elephants. Quickly, the younger males fell back into line. There hasn't been a report of a single murderous elephant since.

If we want to prevent future tragedies such as the Littleton school massacre, we have to take a lesson from the elephants. Little boys, like juvenile elephants, need the presence of adult males who monitor their behaviour and enforce the rules. And in doing so, we also have to give them opportunities to express their maleness and desire for meaning in ways that don't involve worshipping Adolf Hitler or Marilyn Manson.

Boys will be boys. Whether they grow up to be well-socialised, decent men is up to us.

Father knows best (even when you're forty)

From Blake Morrison's *And When Did You Last See Your Father?*, 1985

He isn't drinking, isn't eating. He wears his trousers open at the waist, held up not by a belt but by pain and swelling. He looks like death, but he is not dead and won't be for another four weeks. He has driven down from Yorkshire to London. He has made it against the odds. He is still my father. He is still here.

'I've brought some plants for you.'

'Come and sit down first, Dad, you've been driving for hours.'

'No, best get them unloaded.'

It's like Birnam Wood coming to Dunsinane, black plastic bags and wooden boxes blooming in the back seat, the rear window, the boot: herbs, hypericum, escallonia, cotoneaster, ivies, potentillas. He directs me where to leave the different plants – which will need shade, which sun, which shelter. Like all my father's presents, they come with a pay-off. He will not leave until he has seen every one of them planted: 'I know you. And I don't want them drying up.'

We walk round the house, the expanse of rooms, so different from the old flat. 'It's wonderful to see you settled at last,' he says, and I resist telling him that I'm not settled, have never felt less settled in my life. I see his eyes taking in the little things to be done, the leaky taps, the cracked paint, the rotting window-frames.

'You'll need a new switch unit for the mirror light – the contact has gone, see.'

'Yes.'

'And a couple of two-inch Phillips screws will solve this.'

'I've got some. Let's have a drink now, eh?'

'What's the schedule for tomorrow?' he asks, as always, and I'm irritated, as always, at his need to parcel out the weekend into a series of tasks, as if without a plan of action it wouldn't be worth his coming, not even to see his son or grandchildren. 'I don't think I'll be much help to you,' he says, 'but I'll try.' By nine-thirty he is in bed and asleep.

I wake him next day at nine, unthinkably late, with a pint-mug of tea, unthinkably refused. After his breakfast of strawberry Complan he comes round the house with me, stooped and crouching over his swollen stomach. For once it's me who is going to have to do the hammering and screwing. We go down to the hardware shop in Greenwich, where he charms the socks off the black assistant, who gives me a shrug and a pat at the end, as if to say, 'Where'd you get a dad like this from?' Back home again, he decides that the job for him is to get the curtains moving freely on their rails. 'You know the best thing for it?' he says. 'Furniture polish. Get me a can of it and I'll sort it out for you.' He teeters on a wooden kitchen stool at each of the windows in the house, his trousers gaping open, and sprays polish on the rails and wipes it over with a dirty rag. His balance looks precarious, and I try to talk him down, but he is stubborn.

'No, it needs doing. And every time you pull the curtains from now on, you can think of me.'

I ask him about the operation: is he apprehensive?

'No point in being. They have to have a look. I expect it's an infarct, and they'll be able to cure that, but if not . . . well, I've had a good life and I've left everything in order for you.'

'I'd rather you than order.'

'Too true.'

I make sure there are only two light but time-consuming jobs for us. The first is to fix a curtain pole across the garden end of the kitchen, over the glazed door, and we spend the best part of two hours bickering about the best way to do this: there's a problem on the left-hand side because the kitchen cupboards finish close to the end wall, six inches or so, and you can't get an electric drill in easily to make the holes for the fixing bracket. The drill keeps sheering off, partly because I'm unnerved by him standing below, drawing something on the back of an envelope. I get down and he shows me his plan: a specially mounted shelf in the side wall to support the pole rather than a fixing bracket for it on the end. Sighing and cursing, I climb back up and follow his instructions in every detail – not just the size of screws and Rawlplugs needed, but how to clasp the hammer.

'Hold it at the end, you daft sod, not up near the top.'

'Christ, Dad, I'm forty-one years old.'

'And you still don't know how to hold a hammer properly – or a screwdriver.' Infuriatingly, his plan works – the shelf mounting, the pole, the curtain, all fine. I try not to give him the satisfaction of admitting it.

We bicker our way into the next room and the other job: to hang the chandelier he once gave me, inherited from Uncle Bert. At some point in the move, many of the glass pieces have become separated, and now, in the dim November light behind the tall sash-window, we spend the afternoon working out where they belong, reattaching them with bits of wire, and then strengthening the candelabra from which they dangle. 'This really needs soldering,' he says, meaning that he will find an alternative to soldering, since to solder would mean going out and spending money on a soldering iron when he has a perfectly good one at home. I watch him bowed over the glass diamonds, with pliers and fractured screw-threads and nuts and bits of wire: the improviser, the amateur inventor. I think of all the jobs he's done for me down the years, and how sooner or later I'll have to learn to do them for myself. The metal clasps joining glass ball to glass ball are like the clasps on his King Edward cigar boxes, and like those on his old student skeleton, Janet, whom we'd joined together once, bone to bone.

'I think that's it,' he says, attaching a last bauble. 'Three pieces missing, but no one will notice.' He stands at the foot of the stepladder, holding the heavy chandelier while I connect the two electrical wires to the ceiling rose, tighten the rose-cover and slip the ring-attachment over the dangling hook. He lets go tentatively – 'Gently does it' – unable to believe, since he has not done the fixing himself, that the chandelier will hold. It holds. We turn the light on, and the six candle-bulbs shimmer through the cage of glass, the prison of prisms. 'Let there be light,' my dad says, the only time I can ever remember him quoting anything. We stand there gawping upward for a moment, as if we had witnessed a miracle, or as if this were a grand ballroom, not a suburban dining-room, and the next dance, if we had the courage to take part in it, might be the beginning of a new life. Then he turns the switch off and it's dark again and he says: 'Excellent. What's the next job, then?'

$\sim$

The good father, he ain't heavy

From Maureen Green, *Goodbye Father*, 1976

Though a boy seems to need his father most in the years before five, the rest of his childhood also contributes to the man he ultimately becomes. And folk wisdom has always to some extent recognised this. Growing up alongside a father who talks to him, takes a constant interest in him, makes decisions that his son is aware of, sets some limits to what his son may or may not do, gets his son to work with him on jobs and play with him in sports, enriches and smooths the transition from young child to adolescent. If his father knows how to praise and encourage rather than criticise and undermine, he will learn all the faster. The 'heavy father', pompous and authoritarian, seems simply to put his son off.

$\sim$

Thoughtlessness

Harry Graham, the inventor of 'ruthless rhymes',
1874–1936

I never shall forget my shame
To find my son had forged my name.
If he'd had any thought for others
He might at least have forged his mother's.

~~

The ungrateful son

From *Grimm's Fairy Tales*, 1812–22

A man and his wife were once sitting by the door of their house,
and they had a roasted chicken set before them, and were about
to eat it together. Then the man saw that his aged father was
coming, and hastily took the chicken and hid it, for he would
not permit him to have any of it. The old man came, took a
drink, and went away. Now the son wanted to put the roasted
chicken on the table again, but when he took it up, it had become
a great toad, which jumped into his face and sat there and never
went away again, and if any one wanted to take it off, it looked
venomously at him as if it would jump in his face, so that no
one would venture to touch it. And the ungrateful son was forced
to feed the toad every day, or else it fed itself on his face; and
thus he went about the world knowing no rest.

~~

The prodigal son

The Gospel According to Saint Luke, 17: 11–32

11 ¶And he said, A certain man had two sons:
12 And the younger of them said to *his* father, Father, give me
the portion of goods that falleth *to me*. And he divided unto
them *his* living.

13 And not many days after the younger son gathered all together, and took his journey into a far country, and there wasted his substance with riotous living.

14 And when he had spent all, there arose a mighty famine in that land; and he began to be in want.

15 And he went and joined himself to a citizen of that country; and he sent him into his fields to feed swine.

16 And he would fain have filled his belly with the husks that the swine did eat: and no man gave unto him.

17 And when he came to himself, he said, How many hired servants of my father's have bread enough and to spare, and I perish with hunger!

18 I will arise and go to my father, and will say unto him, Father, I have sinned against heaven, and before thee,

19 And am no more worthy to be called thy son: make me as one of thy hired servants.

20 And he arose, and came to his father. But when he was yet a great way off, his father saw him, and had compassion, and ran, and fell on his neck, and kissed him.

21 And the son said unto him, Father, I have sinned against heaven, and in thy sight, and am no more worthy to be called thy son.

22 But the father said to his servants, Bring forth the best robe, and put *it* on him; and put a ring on his hand, and shoes on *his* feet:

23 And bring hither the fatted calf, and kill *it*; and let us eat, and be merry:

24 For this my son was dead, and is alive again; he was lost, and is found. And they began to be merry.

25 Now his elder son was in the field: and as he came and drew nigh to the house, he heard musick and dancing.

26 And he called one of the servants, and asked what these things meant.

27 And he said unto him. Thy brother is come; and thy father hath killed the fatted calf, because he hath received him safe and sound.

28 And he was angry, and would not go in: therefore came his father out, and entreated him.

29 And he answering said to *his* father, Lo, these many years do I serve thee, neither transgressed I at any time thy command-

ment: and yet thou never gavest me a kid, that I might make merry with my friends:

30 But as soon as this thy son was come, which hath devoured thy living with harlots, thou hast killed for him the fatted calf.

31 And he said unto him, Son, thou art ever with me, and all that I have is thine.

32 It was meet that we should make merry, and be glad: for this thy brother was dead, and is alive again; and was lost, and is found.

The toughest thing in the world

William Carlos Williams writes to his son Bill,
in July 1942 and July 1944

That relationship between father and son is one of the toughest things in the world to break down. It seems so natural and it is natural – in fact it's inevitable – but it separates as much as it joins. A man wants to protect his son, wants to teach him the things he, the father, has learned or thinks he has learned. But it's exactly that which a child resents. He wants to know but he wants to know on his own – and the longer the paternal influence lasts the harder it is to break down and the more two individuals who should have much in common are pushed apart. Only a sudden enforced break can get through that one.

But I've sweated over wanting to do and say the right thing concerning you boys. Certain things stick in my mind – I just didn't do the right thing and I suffered for it. Once when you were a little kid some question of veracity came up between you and Elsie, that goofy girl we had here. I should have known that you were just a baby but I lost my temper, insisting one of you was lying when I should have known, if I had thought for a moment, that it wasn't you. Or if it was, then what the hell anyway? It might have been from fear – no doubt of me. Then one day at the close of Watty's camp in Maine you were in some sort of a canoe race and were about to win when someone quite unfairly cut you out and you cried. I like a God-damned fool laughed at you. Why? Just to hide my own embarrassment. You looked at me and said, 'It was my only chance to win anything!' I tell you that hurt. I've never forgotten it. Such are a father's inner regrets. Stupid enough. And what in the hell is a parent to do when an older child is tormented by a younger child, finally smears his younger tormentor and then comes up for punishment? I've never solved that one. I've done many more seriously stupid things than those mentioned – but I wanted so hard to give you the best.

On the other hand, when you say you've got so much more in the bank than some of the men you have to deal with, I feel that what we did for you wasn't too bad. The same for what you say about the kitten and the spiders. That you can get the good out of such trivia is a tribute to your mind which I have always respected and which I'm glad to see maintaining itself with distinction in the situation in which you are placed. I don't know what kind of a father I was but in things like that at least something 'took' of what I intended and that it wasn't all beside the point.

You say you'd like to see my book of poems. What the hell? Let 'em go. They are things I wrote because to maintain myself in a world much of which I didn't love I had to fight to keep myself as I wanted to be. The poems are me, in much of the faulty perspective in which I have existed in my own sight – and nothing to copy, not for anyone even so much as to admire. I have wanted to link myself up with a traditional art, to feel that I was developing individually it might be, but along with that, developing still in the true evolving tradition of the art. I wonder how much I have succeeded there. I haven't been recognised and I doubt that my technical influence is good or even adequate.

However, this is just one more instance of the benefits to be gained by breaking entirely with the father–son hook-up. It was logical for you not to have looked at my poems – or only casually to look at them. You had me in my own person too strongly before you to need that added emphasis. You did the right thing and I never cared a damn. Now, separated from me by distance and circumstance, it may after all be permissible for you to look at the poems. Not to do anything more than to enjoy them, man to man, if you can get any enjoyment out of them, I'll send them. I have a gold-edged copy reserved for you, one of the de luxe copies, but I'll not send that. Look, if you care to, at whatever

I have done as if you had never known me. That's the only way for a father and son to behave toward each other after the son's majority has been reached. Then, if you still find something to cherish, it will be something worthwhile.

*

Proud of you, Bill, real proud of you. A father follows the course of his son's life and notes many things of which he has not the privilege to speak. He sees, of course, his own past life unfolding – with many variations, naturally. Sees moments when he'd like to speak a word of warning or commendation – places where he himself went wrong or made a difficult decision that was profitable later. And all the time he can't say much.

He can't say anything largely because he realises that in the present case, the case of his son's life, a new and radically different individual is facing life, that the life he faces is different from the life the older man knew when he was young. But mostly he can't speak because – he can't. It would do no good. Likewise he can't praise, much as he'd like to.

My Papa's Waltz

Theodore Roethke, *Selected Poems*, 1969

The whiskey on your breath
Could make a small boy dizzy;
But I hung on like death:
Such waltzing was not easy.

We romped until the pans
Slid from the kitchen shelf;
My mother's countenance
Could not unfrown itself.

The hand that held my wrist
Was battered on one knuckle;
At every step you missed
My right ear scraped a buckle.

You beat time on my head
With a palm caked hard by dirt,
Then waltzed me off to bed
Still clinging to your shirt.

⌇

Fatherwards

From *Iron John*, Robert Bly, 1993

It takes a while for a son to overcome these early negative views of the father. The psyche holds on tenaciously to these early perceptions. Idealisation of the mother or obsession with her, liking her or hating her, may last until the son is thirty, or thirty-five, forty. Somewhere around forty or forty-five a movement toward the father takes place naturally – a desire to see him more clearly and to draw closer to him. This happens unexplainably, almost as if on a biological timetable.

A friend told me how that movement took place in his life. At about thirty-five, he began to wonder who his father really was. He hadn't seen his father in about ten years. He flew out to Seattle, where his father was living, knocked on the door, and when his father opened the door, said, 'I want you to understand one thing. I don't accept my mother's view of you any longer.'

'What happened?' I asked.

'My father broke into tears, and said, "Now I can die."' Fathers wait. What else can they do?

⌇

The ghost of Achilles seeks news of his son and father

From Homer's *The Odyssey*, Book II, in which Odysseus enters 'the infernal regions' Translated by William Cowper, 1792

But come – speak to me of my noble boy;
Proceeds he, as he promis'd, brave in arms,

Or shuns he war? Say also, hast thou heard
Of royal Peleus? shares he still respect
Among his num'rous Myrmidons, or scorn
In Hellas and in Phthia, for that age
Predominates in his enfeebled limbs?
For help is none in me; the glorious sun
No longer sees me such, as when in aid
Of the Achaians I o'erspread the field
Of spacious Troy with all their bravest slain.
Oh might I, vigorous as then, repair
For one short moment to my father's house,
They all should tremble; I would shew an arm,
Such as should daunt the fiercest who presumes
To injure *him*, or to despise his age.

Achilles spake, to whom I thus replied.
Of noble Peleus have I nothing heard;
But I will tell thee, as thou bidd'st, the truth
Unfeign'd of Neoptolemus thy son;
For him, myself, on board my hollow bark
From Scyros to Achaia's host convey'd.
Oft as in council under Ilium's walls
We met, he ever foremost was in speech,
Nor spake erroneous; Nestor and myself
Except, no Grecian could with him compare.
Oft, too, as we with battle hemm'd around
Troy's bulwarks, from among the mingled crowd
Thy son sprang foremost into martial act,
Inferior in heroic worth to none.
Beneath him num'rous fell the sons of Troy
In dreadful fight, nor have I pow'r to name
Distinctly all, who by his glorious arm
Exerted in the cause of Greece, expired.
Yet will I name Eurypylus, the son
Of Telephus, an Hero whom his sword
Of life bereav'd, and all around him strew'd
The plain with his Cetean warriors, won
To Ilium's side by bribes to women giv'n.
Save noble Memnon only, I beheld
No Chief at Ilium beautiful as he.
Again, when we within the horse of wood
Framed by Epeüs sat, an ambush chos'n
Of all the bravest Greeks, and I in trust

Was placed to open or to keep fast-closed
The hollow fraud; then, ev'ry Chieftain there
And Senator of Greece wiped from his cheeks
The tears, and tremors felt in ev'ry limb;
But never saw I changed to terror's hue
His ruddy cheek, no tears wiped *he* away,
But oft he press'd me to go forth, his suit
With pray'rs enforcing, griping hard his hilt
And his brass-burthen'd spear, and dire revenge
Denouncing, ardent, on the race of Troy.
At length, when we had sack'd the lofty town
Of Priam, laden with abundant spoils
He safe embark'd, neither by spear or shaft
Aught hurt, or in close fight by faulchion's edge,
As oft in war befalls, where wounds are dealt
Promiscuous at the will of fiery Mars.
So I; then striding large, the spirit thence
Withdrew of swift Æacides, along
The hoary mead pacing, with joy elate
That I had blazon'd bright his son's renown.

3

Daddy's Girl

Beattie is Three

Adrian Mitchell, *Heart on the Left: Poems 1953–84*

> At the top of the stairs
> I ask for her hand. OK.
> She gives it to me.
> How her fist fits my palm.
> A bunch of consolation.
> We take our time
> Down the steep carpetway
> As I wish silently
> That the stairs were endless.

Devotion

From Honoré de Balzac, *Old Goriot*, 1834

Goriot's unreflecting devotion and touchy, easily alarmed, protective love for his daughters was so well known that one day one of his competitors, who wanted to make him leave the Exchange in order to have the field to himself, told him that Delphine had just been knocked down by a cab. The vermicelli-maker, his face ghastly pale, left the Exchange at once. He was ill for several days as a result of the shock of this false alarm and the reaction from it. If he did not make this man feel the weight of his murderous fist he yet drove him from the Corn Exchange, forcing him into bankruptcy at a crisis in his affairs.

Naturally his two daughters were spoiled: their education was not subject to the dictates of common sense. Goriot was worth more than sixty thousand francs a year and spent barely twelve hundred on himself; his sole pleasure was to gratify his daughters' whims. The best masters were engaged to endow them with the accomplishments which are the hallmark of a good education; they had a chaperon – luckily for them she was a woman of intelligence and good taste; they rode; they kept their carriage; they lived like the mistresses of a rich old lord; they had only to express a wish for something, however costly, to see their father rush to give it to them, and he asked nothing in return but a kiss. Goriot raised his daughters to the rank of angels, and so of necessity above himself. Poor man! He even loved them for the pain they caused him.

To My Daughter

Stephen Spender, 1909–95

Bright clasp of her whole hand around my finger,
My daughter, as we walk together now.
All my life I'll feel a ring invisibly
Circle this bone with shining: when she is grown
Far from today as her eyes are already.

Foster father

From *Silas Marner*, 1861, by George Eliot

Silas Marner's determination to keep the 'tramp's child' was matter of hardly less surprising and iterated talk in the village than the robbery of his money. That softening of feeling towards him which dated from his misfortune, that merging of suspicion and dislike in a rather contemptuous pity for him as lone and crazy, was now accompanied with a more active sympathy, especially amongst the women. Notable mothers, who knew what it was to keep children 'whole and sweet'; lazy mothers, who knew what it was to be interrupted in folding their arms and scratching their elbows by the mischievous propensities of children just firm on their legs, were equally interested in conjecturing how a lone man would manage with a two-year-old child on his hands, and

were equally ready with their suggestions: the notable chiefly
telling him what he had better do, and the lazy ones being
emphatic in telling him what he would never be able to do.

Among the notable mothers, Dolly Winthrop was the one
whose neighbourly offices were the most acceptable to Marner,
for they were rendered without any show of bustling instruction.
Silas had asked her what he should do about getting some clothes
for the child.

'Eh, Master Marner,' said Dolly, 'there's no call to buy, no more
nor a pair o' shoes; for I've got the little petticoats as Aaron wore
five years ago, and it's ill spending the money on them baby-clothes,
for the child 'ull grow like grass i' May, bless it – that it will.'

And the same day Dolly brought her bundle, and displayed to
Marner, one by one, the tiny garments in their due order of succession, most of them patched and darned, but clean and neat as
fresh-sprung herbs. This was the introduction to a great ceremony
with soap and water, from which baby came out in new beauty,
and sat on Dolly's knee, handling her toes and chuckling and
patting her palms together with an air of having made several
discoveries about herself, which she communicated by alternate
sounds of 'gug-gug-gug', and 'mammy'. The 'mammy' was not
a cry of need or uneasiness: Baby had been used to utter it without
expecting either sound or touch to follow.

'Anybody 'ud think the angils in heaven couldn't be prettier,'
said Dolly, rubbing the golden curls and kissing them. 'And to
think of its being covered wi' them dirty rags; but there's Them
as took care of it, and brought it to your door, Master Marner.
The door was open, and it walked in over the snow, like as if it
had been a little starved robin. Didn't you say the door was open?'

'Yes,' said Silas, meditatively. 'Yes – the door was open. The
money's gone I don't know where, and this is come from I don't
know where.'

'I think you're in the right on it to keep the little un, Master
Marner, seeing as it's been sent to you, though there's folks as
thinks different. You'll happen be a bit moithered with it while
it's so little; but I'll come, and welcome, and see to it for you.
I've a bit o' time to spare most days, for when one gets up betimes
i' the morning, the clock seems to stan' still tow'rt ten, afore it's
time to go about the victual. So, as I say, I'll come to see to the
child for you, and welcome.'

'Thank you . . . kindly,' said Silas, hesitating a little, 'I'll be glad if you'll tell me things. But,' he added, uneasily, leaning forward to look at Baby with some jealousy, as she was resting her head backward against Dolly's arm, and eyeing him contentedly from a distance – 'But I want to do things for it myself, else it may get fond o' somebody else, and not fond o' me. I've been used to fending for myself in the house – I can learn, I can learn.'

'Eh, to be sure, I've seen men as are wonderful handy with children. You see this goes first, next the skin,' proceeded Dolly, taking up the little shirt, and putting it on.

'Yes,' said Marner, docilely, bringing his eyes very close that they might be initiated in the mysteries; whereupon Baby seized his head with both her small arms, and put her lips against his face with purring noises.

'See there,' said Dolly, with a woman's tender tact, 'she's fondest o' you. She wants to go o' your lap, I'll be bound. Go, then: take her, Master Marner; you can put the things on, and then you can say as you've done for her from the first of her coming to you.'

Marner took her on his lap, trembling with an emotion mysterious to himself, at something unknown dawning on his life. Thought and feeling were so confused within him, that if he had tried to give them utterance, he could only have said that the child was come instead of the gold – that the gold had turned into the child. He took the garments from Dolly, and put them on under her teaching; interrupted, of course, by Baby's gymnastics.

'There, then! why, you take to it quite easy, Master Marner,' said Dolly; 'but what shall you do when you're forced to sit in your loom? For she'll get busier and mischievouser every day – she will, bless her. It's lucky as you've got that high hearth i'stead of a grate, for that keeps the fire more out of her reach; but if you've got anything as can be spilt or broke, or as is fit to cut her fingers off, she'll be at it – and it is but right you should know.'

Silas meditated a little while in some perplexity. 'I'll tie her to the leg o' the loom,' he said at last – 'tie her with a good long strip o' something.'

'Well, mayhap that'll do, as it's a little gell, for they're easier persuaded to sit i' one place nor the lads. I know what the lads are; for I've had four – four I've had, God knows – and if you was to take and tie 'em up, they'd make a fighting and a crying as if you was ringing pigs. But I'll bring you my little chair, and some bits o' red rag and things for her to play wi'; an' she'll sit and chatter to 'em as if they was alive. Eh, if it wasn't a sin to the lads to wish 'em made different, bless 'em, I should ha' been glad for one of 'em to be a little gell; and to think as I could ha' taught her to scour, and mend, and the knitting, and everything. But I can teach 'em this little un, Master Marner, when she gets old enough.'

'But she'll be *my* little un,' said Marner, rather hastily. 'She'll be nobody else's.'

⌒

Cocooned in her father's shirt

From a letter by Thomas Meauty, 1632

Now I pray, give me leave to ask you a question, and that is, How you like my little girl . . . ? I must tell you that she hath been lapt in the skirts of her father's shirt, for she is beloved where she comes, and I love her very well, and so doth she me; and yet sometimes I can whip [smack] her and love her too. You must excuse me for using this language, for when I cannot see my children it does me good to talk of them.

⌒

My girl

From Laurie Lee, *Two Women*, 1983

As she grew and changed, I was increasingly wondering what this new girl could be, with her ecstatic adorations and rages. The beaming knife-keen awakening, cracking the dawn like an egg, her furies at the small frets of living, the long fat slumbers, almost continental in their reaches, the bedtimes of chuckles, private jokes and languors.

And who was I to her? The rough dark shadow of pummelling games and shouts, the cosy frightener, the tossing and swinging arms, lifting the body to the highest point of hysteria before lowering it back again to the safe male smell.

But she was my girl now, the second force in my life, and with

her puffed, knowing eyes, forever moving with colour and light,
she was well aware of it.

⌒

A *nineteenth-century father writes from*
a business trip

Thomas Hood to his daughter, 23 October 1837

MY DEAR FANNY,
I hope you are as good still as when I went away – a comfort to
your good mother and a kind playfellow to your little brother. Mind
you tell him my horse eats bread out of my hand, and walks up to
the officers who are eating, and pokes his nose into the women's
baskets. I wish I could give you both a ride. I hope you liked your
paints; pray keep them out of Tom's way, as they are poisonous. I
shall have rare stories to tell you when I come home; but mind,
you must be good till then, or I shall be as mute as a stockfish.
Your mama will show you on the map where I was when I wrote
this [Halle]; and when she writes will let you put in a word.

Now God bless you, my dear little girl, my pet, and think of
your

Loving Father,
THOMAS HOOD.

⌒

Listen up

From the diary of Cotton Mather, America, 1698,
when his daughter was four

I took my little daughter Katy into my Study and then I told my
child I am to dye Shortly and shee must, when I am Dead, remember
Everything I now said unto her. I set before her the sinful Condition
of her Nature, and I charged her to pray in Secret Places every
Day. That God for the sake of Jesus Christ would give her a New
Heart. I gave her to understand that when I am taken from her
she must look to meet with more humbling Afflictions than she
does now she has a Tender Father to provide for her.

⌒

Like father, like daughter

The author William Godwin writes to his author
daughter, Mary Shelley

Tuesday, 18 February [1823]
Do not, I entreat you, be cast down about your worldly circumstances. You certainly contain within yourself the means of your
subsistence. Your talents are truly extraordinary. *Frankenstein* is
universally known, and though it can never be a book for vulgar
reading, is everywhere respected. It is the most wonderful work
to have been written at twenty years of age that I ever heard of.
You are now five and twenty, and, most fortunately, you have
pursued a course of reading, and cultivated your mind, in a
manner the most admirably adapted to make you a great and
successful author. If you cannot be independent, who should be?

Your talents, as far as I can at present discern, are turned for
the writing of fictitious adventures.

If it shall ever happen to you to be placed in sudden and urgent
want of a small sum, I entreat you to let me know immediately;
we must see what I can do. We must help one another.

Your affectionate Father,
William Godwin

A runaway daughter

From *The Vicar of Wakefield*, Oliver Goldsmith,
1776

The next morning we missed our wretched child at breakfast, where
she used to give life and cheerfulness to us all. My wife . . .
attempted to ease her heart by reproaches. 'Never,' cried she, 'shall
that vilest stain of our family again darken these harmless doors.
I will never call her daughter more. No, let the strumpet live with
her vile seducer: she may bring us to shame, but she shall never
more deceive us.'

'Wife,' said I, 'do not talk thus hardly: my detestation of her
guilt is as great as yours; but ever shall this house and this heart

be open to a poor returning repentant sinner. The sooner she returns from her transgressions, the more welcome shall she be to me. For the first time the very best may err; art may persuade, and novelty spread out its charm. The first fault is the child of simplicity, but every other the offspring of guilt. Yes, the wretched creature shall be welcome to this heart and this house, though stained with ten thousand vices. I will again hearken to the music of her voice, again will I hang fondly on her bosom, if I find but repentance there. My son, bring hither my Bible and my staff: I will pursue her, wherever she is; and though I cannot save her from shame, I may prevent the continuance of iniquity.'

Affection but Not Seduction

From Majorie Leonard, 'Fathers and Daughters',
International Journal of Psychoanalysis, 1981

A father can be not there enough, which leads a girl to idealise her father and men, or to endow them with immensely sadistic or punitive characteristics – or can be there too much (be too possessive, seductive, or identified with their daughter), requiring her to develop defensive measures against involvement with him and with men. Fathers . . . must be able to make themselves available as a heterosexual love object and to offer affection without being seduced by their daughters' fantasies or seducing them with their own.

Freudian electricity

From 'Sugar Daddy' by Angela Carter, 1983

He is still capable of surprising me. He recently prepared an electric bed for my boyfriend, which is the sort of thing a doting father in a Scots ballad might have done had the technology been available at the time. We knew he'd put us in separate rooms – my father is a Victorian, by birth – but not that he'd plug the metal base of Mark's bed into the electric-light fitment. Mark noticed how the bed throbbed when he put his hand on it and disconnected every plug in sight. We ate breakfast, next morning, as if nothing untoward had happened, and I should say, in the context of my father's house, it had not. He is an enthusiastic handyman, with a special fascination with electricity, whose work my mother once described as combining the theory of Heath Robinson with the practice of Mr Pooter.

All the same, the Freudian overtones are inescapable. However unconsciously, as if *that* were an excuse, he'd prepared a potentially lethal bed for his daughter's lover. But let me not dot the i's and cross the t's. His final act of low, emotional cunning (another Highland characteristic) is to have lived so long that everything is forgiven, even his habit of referring to the present incumbent by my first husband's name, enough to give anybody a temporary feeling.

'That you are my daughter shouldn't do you any harm, either'

Sigmund Freud to his daughter Mathilde,
19 March 1908

I think you probably associate the present minor complaint with an old worry about which I should very much like to talk to you for once. I have guessed for a long time that in spite of all your common sense you fret because you think you are not good-looking enough and therefore might not attract a man. I have watched this with a smile, first of all because you seem quite attractive enough to me, and secondly because I know that in reality it is no longer physical beauty which decides the fate of a girl, but the impression of her whole personality. Your mirror will inform you that there is nothing common or repellent in your features, and your memory will confirm the fact that you have managed to inspire respect and sympathy in any circle of human beings. And as a result I have felt perfectly reassured about your future so far as it depends on you, and you have every reason to feel the same. That you are my daughter shouldn't do you any harm, either. I know that finding a respected name and a warm atmosphere in her home was decisive in my choice of a wife, and there are certain to be others who think as I did when I was young.

⟿

More reveals his daughters' goods

From John Aubrey's *Brief Lives*, written *c.* 1690

Sir Thomas More, Lord Chancellour:
  Memorandum that in his *Utopia*, his lawe is that the young people are to see each other stark-naked before marriage. Sir [William] Roper, of . . . ('tis by Eltham in Kent), came one morning pretty early to my Lord, with a proposall to marry one of [his] daughters. My Lord's daughters were then both together a bed in a truckle-bed in their father's chamber asleep. He carries Sir [William] into the chamber, and takes the sheet by the corner and suddenly whippes it off. They lay on their backs, and their smocks up as high as their arme pitts; this awakened them, and immediately they turned on their bellies. Quoth Sir William Roper, 'I have seen both sides', and so gave a patt on her buttock, he made choice of, sayeing, 'Thou art mine.'
  Here was all the trouble of the wooeing.

⟿

Independent fortune

From *The Journal of Eliza Weeton*, 1824

My father was for some time captain of a merchantman in the African slave trade, but the American war breaking out, he was next commissioned . . . to command a vessel carrying a Letter of Marque [i.e., orders to attack enemy vessels and win prize money]. In this vessel he sailed, and in the course of his voyage took many prizes. He returned, and was loaded with congratulations for his successful bravery. During this period, my mother had brought him three children; Edward, the eldest, who died at 3fi years old; next myself, born on Christmas Day, 1776, and christened by the name of Nelly. My father being out on a voyage when I was born, my mother was at a loss what name to give me; but knowing that the ship Nelly in which he was sailing, was a great favourite of his, she thought to win his affection for me by naming me after it, as she had heard him say that he could wish his children to be all boys. When he returned, and she told him this, he expressed himself as very sorry that she should have been hurt by what he said; declaring that he loved me as much as Edward (who was only 11 months older than I); but, he said, unless a father can provide independent fortunes for his daughters, they must either be mop squeezers, or mantua makers, whereas sons can easily make their way in the world.

⌒

A father suckled by his daughter

E. Cobham Brewer, *Dictionary of Phrase and Fable*, 1870

Euphra'sia, the Grecian daughter, so [by suckling him] preserved the life of Evander, her aged father.

Xantip'pe so preserved the life of her father Cimo'nos in prison. The guard, marvelling the old man held out so long, set a watch and discovered the fact. Byron alludes to these stories in his *Childe Harold.*

> 'There is a dungeon, in whose dim, drear light
> What do I gaze on? . . .
> An old man, and a female young and fair,
> Fresh as a nursing mother, in whose vein
> The blood is nectar . . .
> Here youth offers to old age the food,
> The milk of his own gift: – it is her sire
> To whom she renders back the debt of blood . . .
> Drink, drink and live, old ma! heaven's realm holds no such
>   tide.'

Byron: *Childe Harold*, iv: 148, 150

⌒

The fall

From a 'Short Digest of a Long Novel'
by Budd Schulberg, 1953

It was just before Christmas and she was sitting on her little chair, her lips pressed together in concentration, writing a last-minute letter to Santa Claus. The words were written in some language of her own invention but she obligingly translated as she went along.

> Dear Santa, I am a very good girl and everybody likes me. So please don't forget to bring me a set of dishes, a doll that goes to sleep and wakes up again, and a washing machine. I need the washing machine because Raggedy Ann's dress is so dirty.

After she had finished her letter, folded it, and asked him to address it, he tossed her up in the air, caught her and tossed her again, to hear her giggle. 'Higher, Daddy, higher,' she instructed. His mind embraced her sentimentally: she is a virgin island in a lewd world. She is a winged seed of innocence blown through the wasteland. If only she could root somewhere. If only she could grow like this.

'Let me down, Daddy,' she said when she decided that she had indulged him long enough, 'I have to mail my letter to Santa.'

'But didn't you see him this afternoon?' he asked. 'Didn't you ask for everything you wanted? Mommy said she took you up to meet him and you sat on his lap.'

'I just wanted to remind him,' she said. 'There were so many other children.'

He fought down the impulse to laugh, because she was not something to laugh at. And he was obsessed with the idea that to hurt her feelings with laughter was to nick her, to blemish the perfection.

'Daddy can't catch me-ee,' she sang out, and the old chase was on, following the pattern that had become so familiar to them, the same wild shrieks and the same scream of pretended anguish at the inevitable result. Two laps around the dining-room table was the established course before he caught her in the kitchen. He swung her up from the floor and set her down on the kitchen table. She stood on the edge, poised confidently for another of their games. But this was no panting, giggling game like tag or hide-and-seek. This game was ceremonial. The table was several feet higher than she was. 'Jump, jump, and Daddy will catch you,' he would challenge. They would count together, *one, two* and on *three* she would leap out into the air. He would not even hold out his arms to her until the last possible moment. But he would always catch her. They had played the game for more than a year and the experience never failed to exhilarate them. You see, I am always here to catch you when you are falling, it said to them, and each time she jumped, her confidence increased and their bond deepened.

They were going through the ceremony when the woman next door came in with her five-year-old son, Billy. 'Hello, Mr Steevers,' she said. 'Would you mind if I left Bill with you for an hour while I go do my marketing?'

'No, of course not, glad to have him,' he said and he mussed Billy's hair playfully. 'How's the boy, Billy?'

But his heart wasn't in it. This was his only afternoon of the week with her and he resented the intrusion. And then too, he was convinced that Billy was going to grow up into the type of man for whom he had a particular resentment. A sturdy, good-looking boy, big for his age, aggressively unchildlike, a malicious, arrogant, insensitive extrovert. I can just see him drunk and red-faced and pulling up girls' dresses at Legion Conventions, Mr Steevers would think. And the worst of it was, his daughter seemed blind to Billy's faults. The moment she saw him she forgot about their game.

'Hello, Billy-Boy,' she called and ran over to hug him.

'I want a cookie,' said Billy.

'Oh, yes, a cookie; some animal crackers, Daddy.'

She had her hostess face on and as he went into the pantry, he could hear the treble of her musical laughter against the premature baritone of Billy's guffaws.

He swung open the pantry door with the animal crackers in his hand just in time to see it. She was poised on the edge of the table. Billy was standing below her, as he had seen her father do. 'Jump and I'll catch you,' he was saying.

Smiling, confident and unblemished, she jumped. But no hands reached out to break her flight. With a cynical grin on his face, Billy stepped back and watched her fall.

Watching from the doorway, her father felt the horror that possessed him the time he saw a parachutist smashed like a bug on a windshield when his chute failed to open. She was lying there, crying, not so much in pain as in disillusionment. He ran forward to pick her up and he would never forget the expression on her face, the *new* expression, unchildlike, unvirginal, embittered.

'I hate you, I hate you,' she was screaming at Billy through hysterical sobs.

Well, now she knows, thought her father, the facts of life. Now she's one of us. Now she knows treachery and fear. Now she must learn to replace innocence with courage.

She was still bawling. He knew these tears were as natural and as necessary as those she shed at birth, but that could not overcome entirely the heavy sadness that enveloped him. Finally, when he spoke, he said, a little more harshly than he had intended, 'Now, now, stop crying. Stand up and act like a big girl. A little fall like that can't hurt you.'

Alice in the White House

Theodore Roosevelt, 1858–1919, 26th President
of the USA

I can do one of two things. I can be president of the United States or I can control Alice. I cannot possibly do both.

Golden Bells

Po Chu-i, 772–846

When I was almost forty
I had a daughter whose name was Golden Bells.
Now it is just a year since she was born;
She is learning to sit and cannot yet talk.

Ashamed, – to find that I have not a sage's heart:
I cannot resist vulgar thoughts and feelings.
Henceforward I am tied to things outside myself:
My only reward, – the pleasure I am getting now.
If I am spared the grief of her dying young,
Then I shall have the trouble of getting her married.
My plan for retiring and going back to the hills
Must now be postponed for fifteen years!

⌐⌐

Fathers and daughters in Ancient Greece

From *The Supplicants* by Euripides, *c.* 422 BC

For naught is there more sweet to an aged sire
Than a daughter's love; our sons are made of sterner
Stuff, but less winning are their caresses.

⌐⌐

Mary be good

Lyric by Irving Berlin, 1888–1989

Mary Ellin, Mary Ellin
Is her Daddy's girl.
It must be understood
Only when she is good
Is Mary Ellin, Mary Ellin
Her Daddy's girl.

⌐⌐

The earth father

From D. H. Lawrence, *The Rainbow*, 1915

At Eastertime one year, she helped him to set potatoes. It was the first time she had ever helped him. The occasion remained as a picture, one of her earliest memories. They had gone out

soon after dawn. A cold wind was blowing. He had his old
trousers tucked into his boots, he wore no coat nor waistcoat,
his shirt-sleeves fluttered in the wind, his face was ruddy and
intent, in a kind of sleep. When he was at work he neither
heard nor saw. A long, thin man, looking still a youth, with a
line of black moustache above his thick mouth, and his fine
hair blown on his forehead, he worked away at the earth in
the grey first light, alone. His solitariness drew the child like a
spell.

The wind came chill over the dark-green fields. Ursula ran up
and watched him push the setting-peg in at one side of his ready
earth, stride across, and push it in the other side, pulling the line
taut and clear upon the clods intervening. Then with a sharp
cutting noise the bright spade came towards her, cutting a grip
into the new, soft earth.

He struck his spade upright and straightened himself.

'Do you want to help me?' he said.

She looked up at him from out of her little woollen bonnet.

'Ay,' he said, 'you can put some taters in for me. Look – like
that – these little sprits standing up – so much apart, you see.'

And stooping down he quickly, surely placed the spritted potatoes in the soft grip, where they rested separate and pathetic
on the heavy cold earth.

He gave her a little basket of potatoes, and strode himself to
the other end of the line. She saw him stooping, working towards
her. She was excited, and unused. She put in one potato, then
rearranged it, to make it sit nicely. Some of the sprits were
broken, and she was afraid. The responsibility excited her like
a string tying her up. She could not help looking with dread
at the string buried under the heaped-back soil. Her father
was working nearer, stooping, working nearer. She was overcome by her responsibility. She put potatoes quickly into the
cold earth.

He came near.

'Not so close,' he said, stooping over her potatoes, taking some
out and rearranging the others. She stood by with the painful
terrified helplessness of childhood. He was so unseeing and confident, she wanted to do the thing and yet she could not. She stood
by looking on, her little blue overall fluttering in the wind, the
red woollen ends of her shawl blowing gustily. Then he went

down the row, relentlessly, turning the potatoes in with his sharp spade-cuts. He took no notice of her, only worked on. He had another world from hers.

She stood helplessly stranded on his world. He continued his work. She knew she could not help him. A little bit forlorn, at last she turned away, and ran down the garden, away from him, as fast as she could go away from him, to forget him and his work.

He missed her presence, her face in her red woollen bonnet, her blue overall fluttering. She ran to where a little water ran trickling between grass and stones. That she loved.

When he came by he said to her:

'You didn't help me much.'

The child looked at him dumbly. Already her heart was heavy because of her own disappointment. Her mouth was dumb and pathetic. But he did not notice, he went his way.

﹏

By Duty Divided

William Shakespeare, *Othello* (Act I, Scene 3),
c. 1604

DESDEMONA:	My noble father,
	I do perceive here a divided duty:
	To you I am bound for life and education;
	My life and education both do learn me
	How to respect you; you are lord of all my duty,
	I am hitherto your daughter: but here's my husband:
	And so much duty as my mother show'd
	To you, preferring you before her father,
	So much I challenge, that I may profess
	Due to the Moor my lord.
BRABANTIO:	God bu'y, I ha' done:
	Please it your grace, on to the state affairs;
	I had rather to adopt a child than get it.
	Come hither, Moor:
	I here do give thee that with all my heart,
	Which, but thou hast already, with all my heart

I would keep from thee. For your sake, jewel,
I am glad at soul I have no other child,
For thy escape would teach me tyranny,
To hang clogs on 'em. I have done, my lord.

⮌

The Grief of Lear

From *History of the Kings of Britain*
by Geoffrey of Monmouth, *c.* 1120

Some long time after, when Lear began to wax more sluggish
by reason of age, the aforesaid dukes, with whom and his two
daughters he had divided Britain, rebelled against him and took
away from him the realm and the kingly power which up to
that time he had held right manfully and gloriously. Howbeit,
concord was restored, and one of his sons-in-law, Maglaunus,
duke of Albany, agreed to maintain him with threescore knights,
so that he should not be without some semblance of state. But
after that he had sojourned with his son-in-law two years, his
daughter Goneril began to wax indignant at the number of his
knights, who flung gibes at her servants for that their rations
were not more plentiful. Whereupon, after speaking to her
husband, she ordered her father to be content with a service of
thirty knights and to dismiss the other thirty that he had. The
king, taking his in dudgeon, left Maglaunus, and betook him to
Henvin, duke of Cornwall, unto whom he had married his other
daughter. Here, at first, he was received with honour, but a year
had not passed before discord again rose betwixt those of the
king's household and those of the duke's, insomuch as that
Regan, waxing indignant, ordered her father to dismiss all his
company save five knights only to do him service. Her father,
beyond measure aggrieved thereat, returned once more to his
eldest daughter, thinking to move her to pity and to persuade
her to maintain himself and his retinue. Howbeit, she had never
renounced her first indignation, but swore by all the gods of
Heaven that never should he take up his abode with her save
he contented himself with the service of a single knight and were
quit of all the rest. Moreover, she upbraided the old man for

that, having nothing of his own to give away, he should be minded to go about with such a retinue; so that finding she would not give way to his wishes one single tittle, he at last obeyed and remained content with one knight only, leaving the rest to go their way. But when the remembrance of his former dignity came back unto him, bearing witness to the misery of the estate to which he was now reduced, he began to bethink him of going to his youngest daughter oversea. Howbeit, he sore misdoubted that she would do nought for him, seeing that he had held her, as I have said, in such scanty honour in the matter of her marriage. Natheless, disdaining any longer to endure so mean a life, he betook him across the Channel into Gaul. But when he found that two other princes were making the passage at the same time, and that he himself had been assigned but the third place, he brake forth into tears and sobbing, and cried aloud: 'Ye destinies that do pursue your wonted way marked out by irrevocable decree, wherefore was it your will ever to uplift me to happiness so fleeting? For a keener grief it is to call to mind that lost happiness than to suffer the presence of the unhappiness that cometh after. For the memory of the days when in the midst of hundreds of thousands of warriors I went to batter down the walls of cities and to lay waste the provinces of mine enemies is more grievous unto me than the calamity that hath overtaken me in the meanness of mine estate, which hath incited them that but now were grovelling under my feet to desert my feebleness. O angry fortune! will the day ever come wherein I may requite the evil turn that hath thus driven forth the length of my days and my poverty? O Cordelia, my daughter, how true were the words wherein thou didst make answer unto me, when I did ask of thee how much thou didst love me! For thou saidst: "So much as thou hast, so much art thou worth, and so much do I love thee." So long, therefore, as I had that which was mine own to give, so long seemed I of worth unto them that were the lovers, not of myself but of my gifts. They loved me at times, but better loved they the presents I made unto them. Now that the presents are no longer forthcoming, they too have gone their ways. But with what face, O thou dearest of my children, shall I dare appear before thee? I who, wroth with thee for these thy words, was minded to marry thee less honourably than thy sisters, who, after all the kindnesses I have conferred upon them have allowed me to become an outcast and a beggar?'

Landing at last, his mind filled with these reflections and others of a like kind, he came to Karitia, where his daughter lived, and waiting without the city, sent a messenger to tell her into what indigence he had fallen, and to beseech his daughter's compassion inasmuch as he had neither food nor clothing. On hearing the tidings, Cordelia was much moved and wept bitterly. When she made inquiry how many armed men he had with him, the messenger told her that he had none save a single knight, who was waiting with him without the city. Then took she as much gold and silver as was needful and gave it unto the messenger, bidding him take her father to another city, where he should bathe him, clothe him, and nurse him, feigning that he was a sick man. She commanded also that he should have a retinue of forty knights well appointed and armed, and that then he should duly announce his arrival to Aganippus and herself. The messenger accordingly forthwith attended King Lear into another city, and hid him there in secret until that he had fully accomplished all that Cordelia had borne him on hand to do.

~~

To Her Father

Mehetabel Wright, 1697–1750

In vain, mistaken Sir, you boast
Your Frown can give me lasting Pain;
Your Rigour, when you threaten most,
Attempts to wound my Peace in vain.

With transient Grief you may oppress
A Mind that greater Griefs can bear.
To make Unkindness past Redress,
Your child must *love*, as well as *fear*!

If your kind Hand had fixt me sure
From Want and Shame's impending Harms
Or lodg'd my ripen'd Bloom, secure,
Within some worthy Husband's Arms:

Or when you saw me circled round
With ills that vex and shorten Life,
Had once your dear Condolence found
My sufferings when a wretched Wife;

Altho' *I* was not worth your *Love,*
Had *you* a Parent's *Care* exprest;
Or by one tender Action strove
To make the Life you gave me blest;

How should I mourn had this been so!
How ill your Rage I should endure!
But *gentler Hands* must give the Blow,
Which *rankles,* and *admits no Cure.*

If any Hand a Stroke could send
To vanquish and undo me quite;
'Tis where the *Guardian, Father, Friend,*
And ev'ry kinder name unite.

From such a Sire, rever'd an Age,
A *Look,* perchance, or *Word unkind,*
Might wound beyond your utmost Rage,
With ev'ry faithless Friend combin'd.

The shocks that must on Life attend,
We firmly bear, or shun their Pow'r:
But hard Reproaches from a Friend
Will *torture* to our *latest Hour.*

Refrain your needless Rages then:
Your Anger touches me no more
Than *needless wounds* on dying Men,
Who felt the *mortal pang* before.

As Caesar, bay'd by cruel Foes,
Dauntless, awhile defers his Fate:
He bears, or wards, repeated Blows;
Nor deigns to sink beneath their Weight,

Till, wounded in the tend'rest Part,
He finds his Life not worth his Care:

His hand disdains to guard his Heart,
And ev'ry Stab is welcome there.

~

Daddy

Sylvia Plath, 1932–63

You do not do, you do not do
Any more, black shoe
In which I have lived like a foot
For thirty years, poor and white,
Barely daring to breathe or Achoo.

Daddy, I have had to kill you.
You died before I had time –
Marble-heavy, a bag full of God,
Ghastly statue with one grey toe
Big as a Frisco seal

And a head in the freakish Atlantic
Where it pours bean green over blue
In the waters off beautiful Nauset.
I used to pray to recover you.
Ach, du.

In the German tongue, in the Polish town
Scraped flat by the roller
Of wars, wars, wars.
But the name of the town is common.
My Polack friend

Says there are a dozen or two.
So I never could tell where you
Put your foot, your root,
I never could talk to you.
The tongue stuck in my jaw.

It stuck in a barb wire snare.
Ich, ich, ich, ich,
I could hardly speak.

I thought every German was you.
And the language obscene

An engine, an engine
Chuffing me off like a Jew.
A Jew to Dachau, Auschwitz, Belsen.
I began to talk like a Jew.
I think I may well be a Jew.

The snows of the Tyrol, the clear beer of Vienna
Are not very pure or true.
With my gypsy ancestress and my weird luck
And my Taroc pack and my Taroc pack
I may be a bit of a Jew.

I have always been scared of *you*,
With your Luftwaffe, your gobbledygoo.
And your neat moustache
And your Aryan eye, bright blue.
Panzer-man, panzer-man, O You –

Bit my pretty red heart in two.
I was ten when they buried you.
At twenty I tried to die
And get back, back, back to you.
I thought even the bones would do.

But they pulled me out of the sack,
And they stuck me together with glue,
And then I knew what to do.
I made a model of you,
A man in black with a Meinkampf look

And a love of the rack and the screw.
And I said I do, I do.
So daddy, I'm finally through.
The black telephone's off at the root,
The voices just can't worm through.

If I've killed one man, I've killed two –
The vampire who said he was you
And drank my blood for a year,
Seven years, if you want to know.
Daddy, you can lie back now.

There's a stake in your fat black heart
And the villagers never liked you.
They are dancing and stamping on you.
They always *knew* it was you.
Daddy, daddy, you bastard, I'm through.

Charmed

From the diary of James Boswell

4 January 1776:
. . . In the afternoon I was quite charmed with Veronica [his daughter]. She could now sing a number of tunes: Carrickfergus, O'er the Water to Charlie, Johnnie McGill, Wee Willy Gray, Nancy Dawson, Paddy Wake, Ploughman Laddie, Brose and Butter, O'er the Hills and Far Away. It was really extraordinary that a child not three years old should have such a musical memory, and she sung with a sweet voice and fine ear (if that expression be just). She could speak a great many words, but in an imperfect manner: 'Etti me see u picture' (Let me see your picture.) She could not pronounce 'f'. 'I heed.' (I'm feared. English, I'm afraid.) She rubbed my sprained ankle this afternoon with rum, with care and tenderness. With eager affection I cried, 'God bless you, my dearest little creature.' She answered, 'Od bess u, Papa.' Yet she loved her mother more than me, I suppose because her behaviour to her was more uniform.

The pillar tumbles

From *The Sibling Society* by John Bly, 1996

During our eighteenth century, the American father was thought of as the stone and roof-pillar of the family. The Puritan household in 1750 was set up so that it paralleled the Puritan State. Older men ran both. The service involved, for many fathers, more power than love; and it would be wrong to be sentimental or nostalgic about those families.

We are talking not of the wisdom of father-power but merely of the extent of it. If we look at a family in, say, Salem, Massachusetts, in 1750, the father was the Navigator in social waters; he was the Moral Teacher and Spiritual Comforter; he was the Earner, who brought in the income and kept the family alive; he was the Hearer of Distress as well; cares were brought to the mother and then to him. People imagined the family as a Hebraic unit, as if the children were all children of God, and the house a tiny house of Abraham.

But this arrangement soon faltered. When the West opened up, fathers and prospective fathers headed there. Many factories opened in New England. The father's eyes turned outward toward opportunity, factories, and long days; and the mother became the sole confidant of the children.

⌣

The value of a daughter

From William Faulkner, *Absalom, Absalom!*, 1936

Son. Intrinsic val . . . Emotional val. plus 100% times nil plus val. crop. Emotional val. 100% times increase yearly for each child plus intrinsic val. plus liquid assets plus working acquired credit . . . Daughter and you could maybe even have seen the question mark after it and the other words even: *daughter? daughter? daughter?* trailing off not because thinking trailed off, but on the contrary, thinking stopping right still then, backing up a little and spreading like when you lay a stick across a trickle of water, spreading and rising slow around him in whatever place it was that he could lock the door to and sit quiet . . .

⌣

The four ways in which fatherhood makes children richer

From David Blankenhorn, *Fatherless America*, 1995

Fatherhood is a social role that obligates men to their biological offspring. For two reasons, it is society's most important role for men. First, fatherhood, more than any other male activity, helps men to become good men: more likely to obey the law, to be good citizens, and to think about the needs of others. Put more abstractly, fatherhood bends maleness – in particular, male aggression – toward prosocial purposes. Second, fatherhood privileges children. In this respect, fatherhood is a social invention designed to supplement maternal investment in children with paternal investment in children.

Paternal investment enriches children in four ways. First, it provides them with a father's physical protection. Second, it provides them with a father's money and other material resources. Third, and probably most important, it provides them with what might be termed paternal cultural transmission: a father's distinctive capacity to contribute to the identity, character, and competence of his children. Fourth, and most obviously, paternal investment provides children with the day-to-day nurturing – feeding them, playing with them, telling them a story – that they want and need from both of their parents. In virtually all human societies, children's well-being depends decisively upon a relatively high level of paternal investment.

Indeed, many anthropologists view the rise of fatherhood as the key to the emergence of the human family and, ultimately, of human civilisation.

'Fathers imprint girls for sexual adequacy'

From Alex Comfort, *The Listener*, 1973

The greater a woman's conviction that love objects are not dependable, and must be held onto, the poorer her capacity for full response. This may come about through loss of a father, or childhood deprivation of the father's role. Some degree of parental seduction at the unconscious level seems to be necessary for human females to establish full function. Deprived of a stable father-figure, the non-orgasmic seem to be unable to face the blurring of personal boundaries which goes with full physiological orgasm. It looks as though sexual response in women is based on pre-sexual learning, and of a specific kind . . . This very important finding about the attitudinal basis of sexual contentment ought to be a salutary check on the idea of fatherless upbringing as a contribution to Women's Lib, an idea which no primatologist would regard with favour. Fathers are there to imprint girls for sexual adequacy.

A Prayer for My Daughter

W. B. Yeats, June 1919

Once more the storm is howling, and half hid
Under this cradle-hood and coverlid
My child sleeps on. There is no obstacle
But Gregory's wood and one bare hill
Whereby the haystack and roof-levelling wind,
Bred on the Atlantic, can be stayed;
And for an hour I have walked and prayed
Because of the great gloom that is in my mind.

I have walked and prayed for this young child an hour
And heard the sea-wind scream upon the tower,
And under the arches of the bridge, and scream
In the elms above the flooded stream;
Imagining in excited reverie
That the future years had come,

Dancing to a frenzied drum,
Out of the murderous innocence of the sea.

May she be granted beauty and yet not
Beauty to make a stranger's eye distraught,
Or hers before a looking-glass, for such,
Being made beautiful overmuch,
Consider beauty a sufficient end,
Lose natural kindness and maybe
The heart-revealing intimacy
That chooses right, and never find a friend.

Helen being chosen found life flat and dull
And later had much trouble from a fool,
While that great Queen, that rose out of the spray,
Being fatherless could have her way
Yet chose a bandy-leggèd smith for man.
It's certain that fine women eat
A crazy salad with their meat
Whereby the Horn of Plenty is undone.

In courtesy I'd have her chiefly learned;
Hearts are not had as a gift but hearts are earned
By those that are not entirely beautiful;
Yet many, that have played the fool
For beauty's very self, has charm made wise,
And many a poor man that has roved,
Loved and thought himself beloved,
From a glad kindness cannot take his eyes.

May she become a flourishing hidden tree
That all her thoughts may like the linnet be,
And have no business but dispensing round
Their magnanimities of sound,
Nor but in merriment begin a chase,
Nor but in merriment a quarrel.
O may she live like some green laurel
Rooted in one dear perpetual place.

My mind, because the minds that I have loved,
The sort of beauty that I have approved,
Prosper but little, has dried up of late,
Yet knows that to be choked with hate

May well be of all evil chances chief.
If there's no hatred in a mind
Assault and battery of the wind
Can never tear the linnet from the leaf.

An intellectual hatred is the worst,
So let her think opinions are accursed.
Have I not seen the loveliest woman born
Out of the mouth of Plenty's horn,
Because of her opinionated mind
Barter that horn and every good
By quiet natures understood
For an old bellows full of angry wind?

Considering that, all hatred driven hence,
The soul recovers radical innocence
And learns at last that it is self-delighting,
Self-appeasing, self-affrighting,
And that its own sweet will is Heaven's will;
She can, though every face should scowl
And every windy quarter howl
Or every bellows burst, be happy still.

And may her bridegroom bring her to a house
Where all's accustomed, ceremonious;
For arrogance and hatred are the wares
Peddled in the thoroughfares.
How but in custom and in ceremony
Are innocence and beauty born?
Ceremony's a name for the rich horn,
And custom for the spreading laurel tree.

⌒

And never lose it

Amos Bronson Alcott to his daughter Anna, 1839

This is your birthday. You have now lived eight years with your
father and mother, six years with your loving sister Louisa, and
almost four years with your sweet little sister Elizabeth. Your
father knows how much you love him. . . . He wants to see his

little girl kind and gentle, and sweet-tempered, as fragrant as the flowers in springtime, and as beautiful as they are when the dew glitters on them in the morning dew.

Do you want to know how you can be so beautiful and sweet? It is easy. Only try, with all your resolution, to mind what that silent teacher in your breast says to you: that is all.

A birthday is a good time to begin anew: throwing away the old habits, as you would old clothes, and never putting them on again. Begin, my daughter, today, and when your next birthday shall come, how glad you will be that you made the resolution. Resolution makes all things new. . . .

When you were a few weeks old, you smiled on us. I sometimes see the same look and the same smile on your face, and feel that my daughter is yet good and pure. O keep it there, my daughter, and never lose it.

Thank heaven for a little girl

From *Angela's Ashes*, Frank McCourt, 1996

When Dad comes home from looking for a job he holds Margaret and sings to her:

> *In a shady nook one moonlit night*
> *A leprechaun I spied.*
> *With scarlet cap and coat of green*
> *A cruiskeen by his side.*
> *'Twas tick tock tick his hammer went*
> *Upon a tiny shoe.*
> *Oh, I laugh to think he was caught at last,*
> *But the fairy was laughing, too.*

He walks around the kitchen with her and talks to her. He tells her how lovely she is with her curly black hair and the blue eyes of her mother. He tells her he'll take her to Ireland and they'll walk the Glens of Antrim and swim in Lough Neagh. He'll get a job soon, so he will, and she'll have dresses of silk and shoes with silver buckles.

The more Dad sings to Margaret the less she cries and as the days pass she even begins to laugh. Mam says, Look at him trying to dance with that child in his arms, him with his two left feet. She laughs and we all laugh.

The twins cried when they were small and Dad and Mam would say Whisht and Hush and feed them and they'd go back to sleep. But when Margaret cries there's a high lonely feeling in the air and Dad is out of bed in a second, holding her to him, doing a slow dance around the table, singing to her, making sounds like a mother. When he passes the window where the streetlight shines in you can see tears on his cheeks and that's strange because he never cries for anyone unless he has the drink taken and he sings the Kevin Barry song and the Roddy McCorley song. Now he cries over Margaret and he has no smell of drink on him.

Mam tells Minnie MacAdorey, He's in heaven over that child. He hasn't touched a drop since she was born. I should've had a little girl a long time ago.

Och, they're lovely, aren't they? says Minnie. The little boys are grand, too, but you need a little girl for yourself.

My mother laughs, For myself? Lord above, if I didn't nurse her I wouldn't be able to get near her the way he wants to be holding her day, and night.

Minnie says it's lovely, all the same, to see a man so charmed with his little girl for isn't everyone charmed with her?

Everyone.

⌇⌇

Papa Love Baby

Stevie Smith, 1902–71

My mother was a romantic girl
So she had to marry a man with his hair in curl
Who subsequently became my unrespected papa,
But that was a long time ago now.

What folly is it that daughters are always supposed to be
In love with papa. It wasn't the case with me

I couldn't take to him at all
But he took to me
What a sad fate to befall
A child of three.

I sat upright in my baby carriage
And wished mama hadn't made such a foolish marriage.
I tried to hide it, but it showed in my eyes unfortunately
And a fortnight later papa ran away to sea.

He used to come home on leave
It was always the same
I could not grieve
But I think I was somewhat to blame.

Lap girl

From Naomi Mitchison, *Small Talk: Memories of an Edwardian Childhood*, 1973

Of course there were areas of safety; nothing could get at me if I curled up on my father's lap, holding on to his ear with one thumb tucked into it. He had a big brown moustache and a wide Haldane nose with a small lump on it which I liked. When he kissed me it was rough and tickly. Across his front was a gold watch chain with a big tick-tock watch on the end. In my own children's time it also had a chocolate tree which flowered into silver-paper-covered chocolates. All about him was safe.

Poem for Jane

Vernon Scannell, *Selected Poems*, 1971

So many catalogues have been
Compiled by poets, good and bad,
Of qualities that they would wish

To see their infant daughters wear;
Or lacking children they have clad
Others' daughters in the bright
Imagined garments of the flesh,
Prayed for jet or golden hair
Or for the inconspicuous
Homespun of the character
That no one ever whistles after.

Dear Jane, whatever I may say
I'm sure approving whistles will
Send you like an admiral on
Ships of welcome in a bay
Of tender waters where the fish
Will surface longing to be meshed
Among the treasure of your hair.
And as for other qualities
There's only one I really wish
To see you amply manifest
And that's a deep capacity
For loving; and I long for this
Not for any lucky one
Who chances under your love's sun
But because, without it, you
Would never know completely joy
As I know joy through loving you.

⌒

First Lesson

Philip Booth, 1922–

Lie back, daughter, let your head
be tipped back in the cup of my hand.
Gently, and I will hold you. Spread
your arms wide, lie out on the stream
and look high at the gulls. A dead-
man's float is face down. You will dive
and swim soon enough where this tidewater
ebbs to the sea. Daughter, believe
me, when you tire on the long thrash

to your island, lie up, and survive.
As you float now, where I held you
and let go, remember when fear
cramps your heart what I told you:
lie gently and wide to the light-year
stars, lie back, and the sea will hold you.

4

The Sins of the Father

Study of a figure in a landscape

From Paul Durcan, *Daddy, Daddy*, 1990

– Did your bowels move today?
– Yes, Daddy.
– At what time did your bowels move today?
– At eight o'clock, Daddy.
– Are you sure?
– Yes, Daddy.
– Are you sure that your bowels moved today?
– I am, Daddy.
– Were you sitting down in the long grass?
– I was, Daddy.
– Are you telling me the truth?
– I am, Daddy.
– Are you sure you are not telling me a lie?
– I am, Daddy.
– You are sure that your bowels moved today?
– I am, Daddy, but please don't beat me, Daddy.
Don't be vexed with me, Daddy.
I am not absolutely sure, Daddy.
– Why are you not absolutely sure?
– I don't know, Daddy.
– What do you mean you don't know?
– I don't know what bowels are, Daddy.
– What do you think bowels are?
– I think bowels are wheels, Daddy.
Black wheels under my tummy, Daddy,
– Did your black wheels move today?
– They did, Daddy.
– Then your bowels definitely did move today.
– Yes, Daddy.
– You should be proud of yourself.
– Yes, Daddy.
– Are you proud of yourself?
– Yes, Daddy.
– Constipation is the curse of Cain.

– Yes, Daddy.
– You will cut and reap the corn today.
– Yes, Daddy.
– Every day be sure that your bowels move.
– Yes, Daddy.
– If your bowels do not move, you are doomed.
– Yes, Daddy.
– Are you all right?
– No, Daddy.
– What in the name of the Mother of God
And the dead generations is the matter with you?
– I want to go to the toilet, Daddy.
– Don't just stand there, run for it.
– Yes, Daddy.
– Are you in your starting blocks?
– Yes, Daddy.
– When I count to three, leap from your starting blocks.
– I can't, Daddy.
– Can't can't.
– Don't, Daddy, don't, Daddy, don't, Daddy, don't.

A bad temper on a Sunday evening

From Samuel Butler, *The Way of all Flesh*, 1903

I was there on a Sunday, and observed the rigour with which the young people were taught to observe the Sabbath: they might not cut out things, nor use their paint box on a Sunday, and this they thought rather hard because their cousins the John Pontifexes might do these things. Their cousins might play with their toy train on Sunday, but though they had promised that they would run none but Sunday trains, all traffic had been prohibited. One treat only was allowed them – on Sunday evenings they might choose their own hymns.

In the course of the evening they came into the drawing-room and as an especial treat were to sing some of their hymns to me instead of saying them, so that I might hear how nicely they sang. Ernest was to choose the first hymn and he chose one about some people who were to come to the sunset tree. I am no botanist, and do not know what kind of a tree a sunset tree is, but the words began, 'Come, come, come: come to the sunset tree for the day is past and gone.' The tune was rather pretty and had taken Ernest's fancy, for he was unusually fond of music and had a sweet little child's voice which he liked using. He was, however, very late in being about to sound a hard C or K, and instead of saying 'Come,' he said 'tum, tum, tum'.

'Ernest,' said Theobald from the armchair in front of the fire where he was sitting with his hands folded before him, 'don't you think it would be very nice if you were to say "come" like other people, instead of "tum"?'

'I do say tum,' replied Ernest, meaning that he had said 'come'.

Theobald was always in a bad temper on Sunday evening. Whether it is that they are as much bored with their day as their neighbour, or whether they are tired, or whatever the cause may be, clergymen are seldom at their best on Sunday evening: I had already seen signs that evening that my host was cross, and was a little nervous at hearing Ernest say so promptly, 'I do say tum,' when his papa had said he did not say it as he should.

Theobald noticed the fact that he was being contradicted in a moment. He had been sitting in an armchair in front of the fire with his hands folded, doing nothing, but he got up at once and went to the piano.

'No Ernest, you don't,' he said: 'you say nothing of the kind, you say "tum" not "come". Now say "come" after me, as I do.'

'Tum,' said Ernest at once. 'Is that better?' I have no doubt he thought it was, but it was not.

'Now Ernest, you are not taking pains: you are not trying as you ought to do. It is high time you learned to say "come": why Joey can say "come", can't you, Joey?'

'Yeth I can,' replied Joey promptly, and he said something which was not far off 'come'.

'There, Ernest, do you hear that? There's no difficulty about it now, no shadow of difficulty. Now take your own time; think about it and say "come" after me.'

The boy remained silent for a few seconds and then said 'tum' again.

I laughed, but Theobald turned to me impatiently and said, 'Please do not laugh Overton, it will make the boy think it does not matter, and it matters a great deal'; then turning to Ernest he said, 'Now Ernest, I will give you one more chance, and if you don't say "come" I shall know that you are self-willed and naughty.'

He looked very angry and a shade came over Ernest's face, like that which comes upon the face of a puppy when it is being scolded without understanding why. The child saw well what was coming now, was frightened, and of course said 'tum' once more.

'Very well Ernest,' said his father, catching him angrily by the shoulder. 'I have done my best to save you but if you will have it so you will,' and he lugged the little wretch out of the room crying by anticipation. A few minutes more and we could hear screams coming from the dining-room across the hall which separated the drawing-room from the dining-room, and knew that poor Ernest was being beaten. 'I have sent him to bed,' said Theobald, as he returned to the drawing-room, 'and now, Christina, I think we will have the servants in to prayers,' and he rang the bell for them, red-handed as he was.

⌒

The philosophy of punishment

Aristophanes, *The Clouds,* c. 450 BC

PHIDIPPIDES: I will begin where you did interrupt me,
                 And first will ask, did you not beat me as a
                     child?
STREPSIADES: But that was out of love.
PHIDIPPIDES: 'Tis very right, tell men then, ought not I
                 To recompence your love with equall love;
                 If to be beaten be to be belov'd,
                 Why should I suffer stripes, and you have
                     none?

⌒

The no-praise man

From *The Journals of Anaïs Nin*, 1966–83
Nin writes about her childhood relationship
with her father

The child expected protectiveness, loyalty, comfort, attention, help, teaching, guidance, companionship. His failure to be reassuring, present even, accessible, approving, companionable, dictated the judgement. If I had known him as a playmate with whom roughhousing and games might be treacherous, dangerous even, and a matter of pitting one's energy and skills, or sharing adventures, he would have been my companion in dangerous experiences. Instead he became the awesome figure of the no-praise man, creating in me such a need of approval,

'Most fathers prefer DIY to their kids'

The Daily Telegraph, 1998

Most fathers prefer watching television or doing sport, hobbies and gardening to spending time with their children, claims a report published yesterday.

More than half of fathers surveyed spent less than five minutes a day one-to-one with their child. Fifteen per cent spent no time at all with their child on a weekday.

Fathers who did want closer relationships with their children blamed lack of time and work pressures as the most common barriers.

The NOP poll among 2,000 adults was commissioned by the charity Care for the Family in a study of attitudes to fatherhood.

Nearly half of all fathers would have liked to have changed the way they brought up their children.

The survey also found that fathers were more likely to spend time with a son than a daughter. Mr Rob Parsons, executive director of the charity, an off-shoot of Christian Action Research and Education – CARE – said: 'What I find staggering is that fathers prefer sports and hobbies, gardening, DIY, television, and then time with kids comes way down.

'I'm as sad for the fathers as I am for the kids. I think they will regret it.'

~

You shall not go to the ball

From H. G. Wells, *Ann Veronica*, 1909

'There are plenty of things a girl can find to do at home.'
'Until someone takes pity on me and marries me?'
He raised his eyebrows in mild appeal. His foot tapped impatiently, and he took up the papers.
'Look here, father,' she said, with a change in her voice, 'suppose I won't stand it?'
He regarded her as though this was a new idea.
'Suppose, for example, I go to this dance?'
'You won't.'
'Well' – her breath failed her for a moment. 'How would you prevent it?' she asked.
'But I have forbidden it!' he said, raising his voice.
'Yes, I know. But suppose I go?'
'Now, Veronica! No, no. This won't do. Understand me! I forbid it. I do not want to hear from you even the threat of disobedience.' He spoke loudly. 'The thing is forbidden!'
'I am ready to give up anything that you show to be wrong.'
'You will give up anything I wish you to give up.'

~

The Stern Parent

From Harry Graham, *Ruthless Rhymes*, 1899

Father heard his Children scream,
So he threw them in the stream,
Saying, as he drowned the third,
'Children should be seen, *not* heard!

Lost fathers

From Jonathan Bradshaw *et al.*, *Absent Fathers*, 1999

It is difficult to produce reasonable estimates of the number of non-resident fathers in Britain. Certainly there are over two million and there could be as many as five million. Perhaps the best way to think about the scale of the experience of non-resident fathering is to note the fact that it is estimated that between a third and half of all children will experience a period of not living with both natural parents during their childhood. Each one of those children will have a non-resident parent and in most cases it will be the father.

⌒⌒

Bygones

From *Fredi, Shirl & The Kids: The Autobiography in Fable of Richard M. Elman*, 1972

People are always saying: WEREN'T YOU JUST A LITTLE AFRAID OF FREDI & SHIRL?

OF MY FATHER . . . ?

YES.

MY LOVED ONES?

YES.

THOSE WHO WERE NEAR AND DEAR TO ME?

THEM TOO . . .

OF COURSE NOT. I WAS SCARED TO DEATH.

RICHARD WHY ARE YOU ALWAYS FLINCHING? ARE YOU AFRAID OF US?

I'M AFRAID NOT.

DON'T BE AFRAID RICHARD. WE DON'T WANT TO HURT YOU . . .

BUT YOU ALWAYS DO . . .

THAT'S JUST AN ACCIDENT.

WELL MAYBE YOU OUGHT TO BE MORE CAREFUL . . .

Fredi says, LOOK AT BIG SHOT RICHARD GIVING ADVICE. LISTEN TO HIM . . .

AFRAID SO.

RICHALEH, says Shirl, CAN'T WE JUST LET BYGONES BE BYGONES. IT'S NOT AS IF WE DIDN'T LOVE YOU.

I think about that one a minute. To Shirl letting bygones be bygones means I am not to remember all the times she gave me enemas and poured perfume on me and Fredi beat me with Mr Strap because, after all, I must have provoked them somehow, and it's not as if they didn't love me. On the other hand, it seems to me it's not as if they ever did . . .

AFTER ALL WE'VE DONE FOR YOU, Shirl says.

I TOLD YOU RIGHT FROM THE START SHIRL THAT KID WAS NO GOOD . . .

YOU SEE, I tell her, SEE WHAT I MEAN ABOUT HIM.

RICHALEH PLEASE BEHAVE.

YOU TOO!

I'LL KILL HIM. I'LL KILL HIM SHIRL FOR TALKING TO US LIKE THAT . . .

NOW DO YOU SEE WHAT YOU'VE DONE, Shirl says. YOU'VE MADE YOUR FATHER LOSE HIS TEMPER AND IT'S ALL YOUR FAULT.

The thing about growing up in an enlightened twentieth-century household like mine: if I was ever afraid of Fredi & Shirl I usually had good reasons.

⌒

Cuckolding thy own sonne

From 'The Father Hath Beguil'd the Sonne'
English ballad registered in 1629

4 For once on a day
    The young man did say:
    vnto his wise and aged dad,
    That twas his intent
    (Worse things to preuent)
    with marriage to make him glad:
    Me thinkes first quoth he,
    Your wife I might see,
    why will you hastily run:
    On such brittle ware?

Yet for all his care,
(old fox) he beguil'd his owne sonne.

5 The sonne told his father,
How that he had rather:
to haue in the same his consent,
So to haue a view
Of his Louer true,
the sonne with his father went:
And when they came there
The Lasse did appeare,
so faire and so louely a one,
That the old doting churle,
Fell in loue with the girle
and sought to beguile his owne sonne.

6 With such pleasant words
As to loue accords,
they all did depart for that season,
The honest young Lad,
Was ioyfull and glad:
his sweet-hart had shew'd him good reason,
The loue-sicke old man,
Did looke pale and wan,
and could to no pleasure be wonne,
By night and by day,
Still musing hee lay,
how he might beguile his owne sonne.

7 Yet none did mistrust,
A thing so vniust:
for he was neere threescore yeeres old:
Which yeeres one would thinke,
Should make a man shrinke,
when his vitall spirits are cold:
But now to be briefe,
That was all his griefe,
from loue all this mischiefe begun:
And nothing could serue,
His life to preserue,
but that vvhich must kill his owne sonne.

8 So once on a day,
When his sonne to make hay:

was gone a good mile from the house,
Away the old man,
Is gone to see *Nan,*
as briske as a body louse:
And with a bold face,
He told her his case,
and into what care he was runne,
Unless that she,
Would kindly agree,
to take him in stead of his sonne.

The second part, To the same tune.

9 She mused in mind,
   Such greeting to find,
   and thus vnto him shee said,
   Can such an old knaue,
   With one foot in the graue:
   set loue on a young tender maid,
   That hardly sixteene
   Cold winters had seene,
   sure such thing cannot be done:
   Nay more then all this
   You know what past is,
   tvvixt me and your onely sonne.

10 Sweet *Nan* quoth hee,
   Ne're dally with me,
   I loue thee as well as may be,
   And though I am old
   I haue siluer and gold
   to keepe thee as braue as a Lady,
   All my whole estate
   Upon thee shall wait,
   and whatsoere thou wouldst haue done,
   With gold in thy hand
   Thou shalt it command,
   if thou wilt take me instead of my sonne.

11 If me thou doe shun,
   In hope of my sonne
   then take him and ift be thy minde,
   But into the bargaine

Looke not for one farthing,
then be not with folly let blind,
For it lies in my power,
At this instant houre
(if thou say no it shall be done)
To giue all I haue,
Away from the knaue,
then take me and leaue off my sonne.

12 When she heard these words,
To him shee accords
vpon the same condition,
That of all his pelfe,
He should his owne selfe,
her set in full possession,
To which he agreed,
And gaue her a deed,
by which the poore Lad was vndone,
Unnaturally
To please his fancy,
he did dis-inherit his sonne.

13 These things being [said,]
And they both contriued,
by witnesse [conspires] so the Lad,
The old man home went
With hearty content,
reioycing at his courses bad,
And thus the next day,
He carryed away
the Lasse which with wealth he had won.
He maried was,
Twelue miles from the place,
thus the father beguil'd his own sonne.

14 The young-man with griefe,
Heard of this mischiefe
and blaming this monstrous part,
Before both their faces,
Unto their disgraces,
he stab'd himselfe to the heart:
The vnnaturall dad,
Ran presently mad:

repenting of what he had done,
He runs vp and downe,
From towne vnto towne,
and hourely calles on his sonne.

15 The faithlesse young wife,
Weary of her life,
(to thinke what folly befell)
Ran straight in all hast,
And headlong shee cast
herselfe in a deepe draw-well.
And there shee was found,
Next morning quite drown'd
these things for certaine were done,
Some sixe weekes agoe,
As many men know,
that knew both father and sonne.

16 Let euery good father
A warning here gather,
by this old mans punishment:
And let euery young Lasse,
(As in a glasse,)
looke on this disastrous euent;
For both were to blame,
And both suffer'd shame,
the old man yet liuing doth run
In mad franticke wise
And always he cryes,
for casting away his owne sonne.

Finis.

✑

'Father jailed for chaining up son'

A report in *The Daily Telegraph*, 1996

A father who chained his 15-year-old son to the wall of a garage after reaching 'the end of his tether' following years of unruly behaviour was jailed for three years yesterday.

A judge told the father, who cannot be named for legal reasons, that his action had been 'brutal and sadistic'.

The boy's mother was jailed for 15 months, suspended for two years, after the couple admitted child cruelty. Nottingham Crown Court was told that the father, aged 37, forced his son to eat two cigarettes in an attempt to stop him smoking.

Suspecting him of arson, he splashed paint-thinner on the boy and then chained his right wrist to a hook, leaving a cigarette lighter nearby.

The boy was freed by police who had been called by some of his friends to the lock-up garage in Warsop, Notts, which was padlocked and had a Rottweiler outside.

We have no bananas

From *Will This Do?*, Auberon Waugh, 1991

On one occasion, just after the war, the first consignment of bananas reached Britain. Neither I, my sister Teresa nor my sister Margaret had ever eaten a banana throughout the war, when they were unprocurable, but we had heard all about them as the most delicious taste in the world. When this first consignment arrived, the socialist government decided that every child in the country should be allowed one banana. An army of civil servants issued a library of special banana coupons, and the great day arrived when my mother came home with three bananas. All three were put on my father's plate, and before the anguished eyes of his children, he poured on cream, which was almost unprocurable, and sugar, which was heavily rationed, and ate all three. A child's sense of justice may be defective in many respects, and egocentric at the best of times, but it is no less intense for either. By any standards, he had done wrong. It would be absurd to say that I never forgave him, but he was permanently marked down in my estimation from that moment, in ways which no amount of sexual transgression would have achieved . . . From that moment, I never treated anything he had to say on faith or morals very seriously.

Take that, you little whelp!

From James Joyce, 'Counterparts', *Dubliners*, 1914

His tram let him down at Shelbourne Road and he steered his great body along in the shadow of the wall of the barracks. He loathed returning to his home. When he went in by the side-door he found the kitchen empty and the kitchen fire nearly out. He bawled upstairs:

'Ada! Ada!'

His wife was a little sharp-faced woman who bullied her husband when he was sober and was bullied by him when he was drunk. They had five children. A little boy came running down the stairs.

'Who is that?' said the man, peering through the darkness.

'Me, pa.'

'Who are you? Charlie?'

'No, pa. Tom.'

'Where's your mother?'

'She's out at the chapel.'

'That's right . . . Did she think of leaving any dinner for me?'

'Yes, pa. I—'

'Light the lamp. What do you mean by having the place in darkness? Are the other children in bed?'

The man sat down heavily on one of the chairs while the little boy lit the lamp. He began to mimic his son's flat accent, saying half to himself: '*At the chapel. At the chapel, if you please!*' When the lamp was lit he banged his fist on the table and shouted:

'What's for my dinner?'

'I'm going . . . to cook it, pa,' said the little boy.

The man jumped up furiously and pointed to the fire.

'On that fire! You let the fire out! By God, I'll teach you to do that again!'

He took a step to the door and seized the walking-stick which was standing behind it.

'I'll teach you to let the fire out!' he said, rolling up his sleeve in order to give his arm free play.

The little boy cried 'O, *pa!*' and ran whimpering round the table, but the man followed him and caught him by the coat.

The little boy looked about him wildly but, seeing no way of escape, fell upon his knees.

'Now, you'll let the fire out the next time!' said the man, striking at him vigorously with the stick. 'Take that, you little whelp!'

The boy uttered a squeal of pain as the stick cut his thigh. He clasped his hands together in the air and his voice shook with fright.

'O, pa!' he cried. 'Don't beat me, pa! And I'll . . . I'll say a *Hail Mary* for you . . . I'll say a *Hail Mary* for you, pa, if you don't beat me . . . I'll say a *Hail Mary* . . .'

I'll take you down a peg . . .

From Mark Twain, *The Adventures of Huckleberry Finn*, 1884

I had shut the door to. Then I turned around, and there he was. I used to be scared of him all the time, he tanned me so much. I reckoned I was scared now, too; but in a minute I see I was mistaken – that is, after the first jolt, as you may say, when my breath sort of hitched, he being so unexpected; but right away after I see I warn't scared of him worth bothering about.

He was most fifty, and he looked it. His hair was long and tangled and greasy, and hung down, and you could see his eyes shining through like he was behind vines. It was all black, no grey; so was his long, mixed-up whiskers. There warn't no colour in his face, where his face showed; it was white; not like another man's white, but a white to make a body sick, a white to make a body's flesh crawl – a tree-toad white, a fish-belly white. As for his clothes – just rags, that was all. He had one ankle resting on t'other knee; the boot on that foot was busted, and two of his toes stuck through, and he worked them now and then. His hat was laying on the floor – an old black slouch with the top caved in, like a lid.

I stood a-looking at him; he set there a-looking at me, with his chair tilted back a little. I set the candle down. I noticed the window was up; so he had clumb in by the shed. He kept a-looking me all over. By and by he says:

'Starchy clothes – very. You think you're a good deal of a big-bug, *don't* you?'

'Maybe I am, maybe I ain't,' I says.

'Don't you give me none o' your lip,' says he. 'You've put on considerable many frills since I been away. I'll take you down a peg before I get done with you. You're educated, too, they say – can read and write. You think you're better'n your father, now, don't you, because he can't? *I'll* take it out of you. Who told you you might meddle with such hifalut'n foolishness, hey? – who told you you could?'

'The widow. She told me.'

'The widow, hey? – and who told the widow she could put in her shovel about a thing that ain't none of her business?'

'Nobody never told her.'

'Well, I'll learn her how to meddle. And looky here – you drop that school, you hear? I'll learn people to bring up a boy to put on airs over his own father and let on to be better'n what *he* is. You lemme catch you fooling around that school again, you hear? Your mother couldn't read, and she couldn't write, nuther, before she died. None of the family couldn't before *they* died. *I* can't; and here you're a-swelling yourself up like this. I ain't the man to stand it – you hear? Say, lemme hear you read.'

I took up a book and begun something about General Washington and the wars. When I'd read about a half a minute, he fetched the book a whack with his hand and knocked it across the house. He says:

'It's so. You can do it. I had my doubts when you told me. Now looky here; you stop that putting on frills. I won't have it. I'll lay for you, my smarty; and if I catch you about that school I'll tan you good. First you know you'll get religion, too. I never see such a son.'

He took up a little blue and yaller picture of some cows and a boy, and says:

'What's this?'

'It's something they give me for learning my lessons good.'

He tore it up, and says:

'I'll give you something better – I'll give you a cowhide.'

He sat there a-mumbling and a-growling a minute, and then he says:

'*Ain't* you a sweet-scented dandy, though? A bed; and bedclothes; and a look'n' glass; and a piece of carpet on the floor – and your own father got to sleep with the hogs in the tanyard. I never see such a son. I bet I'll take some o' these frills out o' you before I'm done with you. Why, there ain't no end to your airs – they say you're rich. Hey? – how's that?'

'They lie – that's how.'

'Looky here – mind how you talk to me; I'm a-standing about all I can stand now – so don't gimme no sass. I've been in town two days, and I hain't heard nothing but about you bein' rich. I heard about it away down the river, too. That's why I come. You git me that money tomorrow – I want it.'

'I hain't got no money.'

'It's a lie. Judge Thatcher's got it. You git it. I want it.'

'I hain't got no money, I tell you. You ask Judge Thatcher; he'll tell you the same.'

'All right. I'll ask him; and I'll make him pungle, too, or I'll know the reason why. Say, how much you got in your pocket? I want it.'

'I hain't got only a dollar, and I want that to—'

'It don't make no difference what you want it for – you just shell it out.'

He took it and bit it to see if it was good, and then he said he was going downtown to get some whisky; said he hadn't had a drink all day. When he had got out on the shed he put his head in again, and cussed me for putting on frills and trying to be better than him; and when I reckoned he was gone he came back and put his head in again, and told me to mind about that school, because he was going to lay for me and lick me if I didn't drop that.

Next day he was drunk, and he went to Judge Thatcher's and bullyragged him, and tried to make him give up the money; but he couldn't, and then he swore he'd make the law force him.

The judge and the widow went to law to get the court to take me away from him and let one of them be my guardian; but it was a new judge that had just come, and he didn't know the old man; so he said courts mustn't interfere and separate families if they could help it; said he'd druther not take a child away from its father. So Judge Thatcher and the widow had to quit on the business.

That pleased the old man till he couldn't rest. He said he'd cowhide me till I was black and blue if I didn't raise some money for him. I borrowed three dollars from Judge Thatcher, and pap took it and got drunk, and went a-blowing around and cussing and whooping and carrying on; and he kept it up all over town, with a tin pan, till most midnight; then they jailed him, and the next day they had him before court, and jailed him again for a week. But he said *he* was satisfied; said he was boss of his son, and he'd make it warm for *him*.

When he got out the new judge said he was a-going to make a man of him. So he took him to his own house, and dressed him up clean and nice, and had him to breakfast and dinner and supper with the family, and was just old pie to him, so to speak. And after supper he talked to him about temperance and such things till the old man cried, and said he'd been a fool, and fooled away his life; but now he was a-going to turn over a new leaf and be a man nobody wouldn't be ashamed of, and he hoped the judge would help him and not look down on him. The judge said he could hug him for them words; so *he* cried, and his wife she cried again; pap said he'd been a man that had always been misunderstood before, and the judge said he believed it. The old man said that what a man wanted that was down was sympathy, and the judge said it was so; so they cried again. And when it was bedtime the old man rose up and held out his hand, and says:

'Look at it, gentlemen and ladies all; take a-hold of it; shake it. There's a hand that was the hand of a hog, but it ain't so no more; it's the hand of a man that's started in on a new life, and'll die before he'll go back. You mark them words – don't forget I said them. It's a clean hand now; shake it – don't be afeard.'

So they shook it, one after the other, all around, and cried. The judge's wife she kissed it. Then the old man he signed a pledge – made his mark. The judge said it was the holiest time on record, or something like that. Then they tucked the old man into a beautiful room, which was the spare room, and in the night some time he got powerful thirsty and clumb out on to the porch-roof and slid down a stanchion and traded his

new coat for a jug of forty-rod, and clumb back again and had
a good old time; and toward daylight he crawled out again,
drunk as a fiddler, and rolled off the porch and broke his left
arm in two places, and was most froze to death when somebody found him after sunup. And when they come to look at
that spare room they had to take soundings before they could
navigate it.

The judge he felt kind of sore. He said he reckoned a body
could reform the old man with a shot-gun, maybe, but he didn't
know no other way.

⌒

Pour encourager les autres

King George V, 1865–1935

⌒

What inconveniences do happen by the negligence of fathers?

From Plutarch, *The Morals,* c. AD 90, translated by
Sir Thomas Eliot, 1535

Often times I have thought much occasion of ill and corrupted
manners to be in such, which having children of their own, during
their infancy and tender youth commit them to good masters and
tutors, and as soon as they do enter into man's age, they abandon
them, and suffer them to live at their pleasure, wherein contrari-
wise in that entre and jeoperdous time more heed ought to be
taken of them, than when they were children. For men know
well that the defaults of children be of light importance, and
lightly redressed: as perchance it may hap, by negligence of tutors,
and lack of obedience. But the offences of them which be common
to perfect years be more grievous oftentimes and full of danger,
as riotous living consuming substance and inheritance, inordinate
and chargeable gaming, ingurgitations and surfeits, defloration
of maids, corrupting good women. These inconveniences ought

in time and speedily to be repressed. For the delicate flower of youth uneth may be preserved from the violence of bodily lust, unless he be bridelled, wherefore they which withstand not youth in their children: little foresee what liberty of imagination they give unto them to commit vice, wherefore wise fathers, having children, at that estate, and years will have to them a vigilante eye, that they may the rather induce them in to temperance, sometimes exhorting, another time menacing, other whiles desiring, in like wise counselling, efsoones promising, or other whiles alluring; sometimes declaring to them, what dangers and troubles themselves in youth have sustained: or how by virtue and sufferance they have attained both land and honour. For the two principal occasions of virtue be fear of pain and hope of reward: the one disposes a man to acts of honesty, the other maketh him slow to do ill . . .

Insensitivity

From Anny Thackeray, *Chapters from Some Memoirs*, 1894

I suppose the outer circuit of my own very limited wanderings must have been reached at the age of thirteen or thereabouts, when my father took me and my little sister for the grand tour of Europe. We had, of course, lived in Paris and spent our summers in quiet country places abroad with our grandparents, but this was to be something different from anything we had ever known before at St Germains or Montmorenci among the donkeys; Switzerland, and Venice, and Vienna, Germany and the Rhine! Our young souls thrilled with expectation. And yet those early feasts of life are not unlike the miracle of the loaves and the fishes; the twelve basketfuls that remain in after years are certainly even more precious than the feast itself.

We started one sleety summer morning. My father was pleased to be off, and we were enchanted. He had brought a grey wide-awake hat for the journey, and he had a new sketch book in his pocket, besides two smaller ones for us, which he produced as the steamer was starting. We sailed from London Bridge, and the decks were all wet and slippery as we came on board. We were scatter-brained little girls, although we looked demure enough in our mushroom hats and waterproofs. We also had prepared a travelling trousseau . . . which consisted I remember of a draught board, a large wooden work-box, a good many books, paint boxes, and other odds and ends: but I felt that whatever else might be deficient our *new bonnets* would bring us triumphantly out of every crisis. They were alike, but with a difference of blue and pink wreaths of acacia, and brilliant in ribbons to match, at a time when people affected less dazzling colours than they do now. Alas! for human expectations! When the happy moment came at last, and we had reached foreign parts and issued out of the hotel dressed and wreathed and triumphantly splendid, my father said 'My dear children go back and put those bonnets away in your box, and don't ever wear them any more!' How the sun shone as he spoke; how my heart sank under the acacia trees. My sister was eleven years old, and didn't care a bit; but at thirteen and fourteen one's clothes begin to strike root. I felt disgraced, beheaded of my lovely bonnet, utterly crushed, and I turned away to hide my tears.

⌒

'Now I don't like being touched in any way'

From *Behind Closed Doors* by Janine Turner, 1988

Dear Jan,

From an early age I remember my father touching me and hurting me. I thought that I had buried these memories until I had to sleep with Dave, my husband.

Now I'm married with two children, Mark who is 2fi, and Miranda who is nearly 10 months. But ever since I got married three years ago, I don't like any kind of relationship, from holding hands to sleeping with Dave. When he touches me it's like my father all over again when he forced me to sleep with him.

I feel so dirty. I hate Dave even looking at me, and will think up any excuse to sleep in the babies' room. I remember my father when he was drunk, beating and hurting me, touching me where I didn't like him to be, and I'm ashamed to be a woman.

I try losing weight to reduce my body so I don't look like a woman. The nightmares are all about Dad hurting me, and they upset me greatly. I've also produced a boy which I resent very much. Each time I see him, the anger inside me seems to boil to the surface. I don't like holding Mark. I get Dave to bath and change him when I can.

I'm finding it hard to overcome this anger as I find I'm now projecting the anger which was for my father onto Mark and Dave.

When my father died, I thought that it was all over. But the memories are with me as if it were happening now. Today. And while this is going on, I haven't been able to say goodbye to my father. I'm very confused. On the one hand I'm supposed to love my dad. But he hurt me. Now I don't like being touched in any way. I don't enjoy skin contact with my little boy or girl.

My life is so empty and I'm making it so unhappy for my husband and children. Please help me.

Sandra

⌒

A stricture against deadbeat dads, eighteenth-century version

From *Emile* by Jean-Jacques Rousseau, 1762

A father, when he engenders and feeds children, does with that only a third of his task. He owes to his species men; he owes to society sociable men; he owes to the state citizens. Every man who can pay this triple debt and does not do so is culpable, and more culpable perhaps when he pays it halfway. He who cannot fulfil the duties of a father has no right to become one. Neither poverty nor labours nor concern for public opinion exempts him from feeding his children and from raising them himself. Readers, you can believe me. I predict to whoever has vitals and neglects such holy duties that he will long shed bitter tears for his offence and will never find consolation for it.

⌒

Too late to play the role

From Kirk Douglas, *The Ragman's Son*, 1988

It took a minute for my eyes to adjust to the dimness of Boggi's and find him sitting at the bar. He was drinking his usual boilermaker, a shot of raw whiskey followed by a swallow of beer. The bartender recognised me and with great solicitude walked away, leaving me with my father.

'Hi, Pa.'

'Hullo.' He got up, kissed me on the mouth, Russian style. I was shocked to find I was taller than he. He always seemed such a huge man.

'How are you, Pa?'

A grunt.

I studied my father's face. He seemed a lot older. His moustache was gone. So was one of his front teeth, those that he had never brushed ('brushing made teeth loose,' he always said), those teeth that could take the cap off a bottle or chew glass. He used to gnash his teeth, grind them together and make a terrible sound. As I looked at him, I thought I'd hate to put those teeth to that test now. He still had all his hair, but it was completely grey. And he needed a shave, which was unlike him.

I never saw my father shave himself. We were poor, but he went to a barber to get shaved. Years later, I was in New York, at the barber's. I thought, My God, I'm a rich man. 'Give me a shave.' It was luxurious; I liked it. I can afford it. But that was the only time I did it.

After a long pause, 'I made a new movie, Pa.'

'Yeah?'

'*Champion.*'

'Yeah.'

Another long pause. 'Did you see it, Pa?'

'Yeah.'

'Did you like it?'

'Yeah.'

That was a pretty long conversation with Pa. He ordered another boilermaker. I gave him some money and left. I got in my waiting limousine, told the driver to take me to Albany.

Years later, I was told that my father went to see *Champion* with one of his drinking buddies. When I was being slaughtered by my opponent in the ring, my father covered his face with both hands. At the end of the fight, when I was finally winning, Pa got up and yelled in broken English, 'Issur, give it to him! Issur, give it to him!'

If only Pa could have said, 'Issur, give it to him,' when I was a kid. Pa covered his eyes when Kirk Douglas was bleeding make-up in a movie. But when Issur was being carried home, head bleeding for real, Pa was on the other side of the street, grumbling, 'That's what you get for playing.' He should have covered his eyes *then*. Years later, many people told me how Pa would brag about me. But it was too late to get that pat on the back when Pa was dead.

∽

Too *far*

From Mikal Gilmore's *Shot in the Heart: One Family's History of Murder*, 1994

Though I would later see indelible signs of my father's violence, I never experienced it in the unrestricted way that my brothers did. In fact, I remember being hit by my father on only one occasion. The cause of the spanking is vague – which only goes to support Frank's belief that all you truly carry away from such an incident is the bitterness of the punishment. I think I probably did something like drawing on a wall with a crayon or sassing my mother, and my father deemed that the act called for a whipping. I remember that he undressed me and stood me in front of him as he unbuckled his belt – a wide, black leather belt with a gleaming silver buckle – and pulled it from around his waist. This whole time he was telling me what my whipping was going to be like, how badly it was going to hurt. I remember I felt absolute terror in those moments – nobody had ever hit me before for any reason, and the dread of what was about to happen felt as fearful as the idea of death itself. My father was going to *hit* me, and it was going to hurt. It seemed horribly threatening – like the sort of thing I might not live through – and it also seemed horribly unjust.

My father doubled his belt over and held it in his hand. Then he sat down on his chair, reached out and took me by the arm and laid me across his lap. The next part is the only part I don't recall. I know I got whipped and that I cried out, but I can't remember a thing about the blows or the pain, or whether it was even truly bad. All I remember is that a few moments later I was standing in front of him again, this time held in my mother's embrace. 'That's enough, Frank,' she said. 'You've gone too far. You're not going to do to *this* one what you did to the others.' I stood there, looking at my father, rubbing my naked, sore butt, crying. I remember that what had really hurt me was that I felt I had lost my father's love, that the man I trusted most had hurt me in a way I had never expected. My father was smiling back at me – a smile that was meant to let me know that he was proud with what he had just done, that he enjoyed the power and the virtue of this moment. I looked back at him and I said: 'I hate you.'

I know it is the only time I ever said that to him in my life, and I cannot forget what those words did to his face. His smile fell – indeed, his whole face seemed to fall into a painful fear or sense of loss. He laid his belt on his desk and sat studying the floor, with a weary look of sadness.

My mother led me out of the room and dressed my nakedness.

↲

Provoke not

From the Epistle of Paul the Apostle to the Colossians, 3: 21

Fathers, provoke not your children to anger, lest they be discouraged

↲

Ten tips for fathers

Fatherhood USA, 1999

- **Be there.**
  Children want and need your physical presence, from infancy onward.
- **Listen.**
  Being there means more than being present physically.
- **Support your partner.**
  Work together on behalf of your child, even if you're not living together.
- **Learn to disagree appropriately with your partner.**
  Disagreement is a normal part of parenthood. It is how you resolve those differences that matters.
- **Get to know and be known to the people in your child's world.**
  Teachers, caregivers, doctors – all of them are an important part.
- **Get to know and be known to your children's friends and their parents.**
  If you have concerns about who your child is hanging out with, be sure to discuss this with your child.
- **Play with your children.**
  One of the best ways to learn about and develop a lasting connection with your children is to play with them – to enter their world.
- **Teach by example.**
  Children follow what you do more than what you say.
- **Discipline with love.**
  To discipline means to guide or lead out the best in your child, and that is best done with love.
- **Keep your sense of humour.**
  Nobody said fatherhood would be easy. If you can survive fatherhood, you can survive anything!

5

Experience

Things a Man Should Know about Fatherhood

Esquire magazine, 1999

Don't worry, your dad didn't know what he was doing, either.

No, no – not that Spock!

Second thought, maybe you should worry.

Never tell anybody that you and your wife are 'trying'.

We really don't need the visual, that's why.

Never tell anybody where your child was conceived, how long it took, or what song was playing.

Do not name your baby after cities, geographical points of interest, features of the solar system, seasons, plants, animals or current television stars.

Your child, at birth, already has a deeply complicated relationship with his mother, and, for the first year, you are only a curiosity.

For a couple of years after that, an amusement-park ride.

Then, a referee.

And finally, a bank.

If you want to subject your son to the unkindest cut, insist on a local anaesthetic, since many pediatricians don't bother to use one.

The anaesthetic is for the kid.

Baby gas is lessened with a good nipple connection during feeding, which decreases air intake.

Assuring that his lower lip is flipped out, not pursed, helps.

There is nothing wrong with thumb-sucking, which helps ease the pain of teething.

None the less, it probably ought to stop by kindergarten.

Diaper-rash remedy: expose baby's hydraulics to the air until dry. Soak baby's bottom in tepid water with a half-cup baking soda. Then Balmex. Or Lotrimin. Re-diaper.

You know how they say you'll get used to diapers? You won't.

Unless you wear them a lot . . .

The start of crawling: usually begins between six months and twelve months.

Standing: usually between nine and twelve months.

Walking: between twelve and fifteen months.

The onset of the above, as with all developmental skills, is hugely variable among individual children.

Avoid walkers, not only because they can be dangerous around stairs but because they don't require a child to balance and thus retard his walking progress.

Reason boys are better: they cannot get pregnant.

Reason girls are better: they're less likely to get arrested.

The threat of an unknown punishment is always more effective than a stated one.

Annals of great punishments: hang dolly from a noose!

That was a joke, Dad, a joke.

Annals of great punishments, for real: making him wash the car, clean the bathroom, and watch *The McLaughlin Group*.

You see, all great punishments should reduce the number of disagreeable tasks you would otherwise have to perform . . .

Your kids can develop an independent sense of good taste only if they're allowed to make their own mistakes in judgment.

Relax: lots of little boys want a Barbie and a dollhouse.

The first time you change your son's diaper and he pees all over you is not an accident. It's foreshadowing.

Children of too-strict parents are more likely to develop tics.

Let them take reasonable risks: a few scrapes in the long run are nothing compared with the scars left by hovering parents. Or tics.

In preparation for risks: a Red Cross first-aid course.

The most common cause of fatal injury among kids between five and nine involves cars, which is to say, hold their hands. And buckle them in.

Try to tuck them in every night, too . . .

Reason boys are better: they cost less, especially their clothes.

Reason girls are better: they're less likely to burn, slash or chew the clothes they have . . .

Dropping food on the floor is a new and delightful skill to a one-year-old, not a deliberate attempt to annoy you.

However small he or she might be, never underestimate an infant's ability to project chewed food over great distances.

The single most important thing a father can possess: Wet-Naps.

Now, more than ever, don't move into a place without laundry facilities.

Children's hobbies to nip quickly in the bud: drums, archery, matchbook collecting.

Beware your child's uncles, who will teach your kid dirty words, introduce him to liquor, and give him gifts of drums, archery sets and possibly matches.

It is, of course, your natural right to exert the above negative influences on your siblings' offspring.

You are under no obligation to tell children the truth.

Lying to children is, in fact, half the fun: 'Oh, that tree? That's a yellow-spotted spickle-gruber, of course.'

On the other hand, they do remember everything . . .

Your bedroom door gets a lock. Your teenage son's does not.

Lock or no, please knock before entering, as the disruption of a youth who is spanking his monkey will be twice as traumatic for you as it is for him.

Other doors to lock: those on the liquor cabinet.

There is only one reason for a teenager to burn incense, and we think you remember what it is . . .

Unfortunately, those books that say motherhood makes women desire more sex are referring to women who are not your wife.

No matter how wealthy you are, don't buy your kid a car – offer to match him.

Ditto for other adolescent big-ticket items; teach the little bastard some responsibility!

DNA tests are 99.9 per cent accurate, but check the ears to be absolutely sure.

Reason boys are better: boys start talking later than girls.

Reason girls are better: boys toilet-train later than girls.

The twos aren't always terrible.

Even if they are, take heart, as kids aged three to six generally believe their parents are the most amazing beings alive and wish to be exactly like them.

How scary is that?

Establishing savings accounts for your kids and requiring them to make regular monthly deposits teaches them how to eventually become J. R. Morgan.

The above could prove useful in your dotage . . .

Acceptable reading material: *Dr Seuss, Where the Wild Things Are, Harold and the Purple Crayon, Curious George* and any of the following by Roald Dahl – *James and the Giant Peach, Charlie and the Chocolate Factory* and *Danny the Champion of the World*.

Neither of the following by Roald Dahl: *Kiss Kiss* or *Switch Bitch* . . .

Some parents walk around naked in front of their children.

These parents should stop it.

Nearly all psychological problems result from feelings of worthlessness, which is to say, every now and then make sure that you tell your kid he's pretty great.

And never raise a hand to him. But being a good guy, you probably knew that.

The harder they play, the earlier they sleep.

Never turn down an invitation to play.

No toys that require batteries . . .

All in all, fatherhood is pretty terrific – filled with joy and triumph, promise and miracles – particularly other people's fatherhood.

You might think you know a lot about fatherhood, but not as much as you will when you're a grandfather.

If you're thinking that fatherhood means the end of life as you've known it, you, sir, are, of course, absolutely correct.

⌐⌐

The nighttime father-jitters

From Laurie Lee, *The Firstborn*, 1964

Here she is then, my daughter, here, alive, the one I must possess and guard. A year ago this space was empty, not even a hope of her was in it. Now she's here, brand new, with our name upon her: and no one will call in the night to reclaim her.

She is here for good, her life stretching before us, twenty-odd years wrapped up in that bundle; she will grow, learn to totter, to run in the garden, run back, and call this place home.

Or will she? Looking at those weaving hands and complicated ears, the fit of the skin round that delicate body, I can't indulge in the neurosis of imagining all this to be merely a receptacle for Strontium 90. The forces within her seem much too powerful to submit to a blanket death of that kind.

But she could, even so, be a victim of chance; all those quick lively tendrils seem so vulnerable to their own recklessness – surely she'll fall on the fire, or roll down some crevice, or kick herself out of the window?

I realise I'm succumbing to the occupational disease, the father-jitters or new-parenthood-shakes, expressed in: 'Hark, the child's screaming, she must be dying.' Or, 'She's so quiet, d'you think she's dead?'

As it is, my daughter is so new to me still that I can't yet leave her alone. I have to keep on digging her out of her sleep to make sure that she's really alive.

⌒

The pram-pusher's knack

From Vladimir Nabokov on bringing up baby in
Nazi Germany, from *Speak Memory: An
Autobiography Revisited*, 1964

You know, I still feel in my wrists certain echoes of the pram-pusher's knack, such as, for example, the glib downward pressure one applied to the handle in order to have the carriage tip up and climb the curb. First came an elaborate mouse-grey vehicle of Belgian make, with fat autoid tyres and luxurious springs, so large that it could not enter our puny elevator. It rolled on sidewalks in slow stately mystery, with the trapped baby inside lying supine, well covered with down, silk, and fur; only his eyes moved, warily, and sometimes they turned upward with one swift sweep of their showy lashes to follow the receding of branch-patterned blueness that flowed away from the edge of the half-cocked hood of the carriage, and presently he would dart a suspicious glance at my face to see if the teasing trees and sky did not belong, perhaps, to the same order of things as did rattles and parental humour. There followed a lighter carriage, and in this, as he spun

along, he would tend to rise, straining at his straps; clutching at
the edges; standing there less like the groggy passenger of a
pleasure boat than like an entranced scientist in a spaceship;
surveying the speckled skeins of a live, warm world; eyeing with
philosophic interest the pillow he had managed to throw over-
board; falling out himself when a strap burst one day. Still later
he rode in one of those small contraptions called strollers; from
initial springy and secure heights the child came lower and lower,
until, when he was about one and a half, he touched ground in
front of the moving stroller by slipping forward out of his seat
and beating the sidewalk with his heels in anticipation of being
set loose in some public garden. A new wave of evolution started
to swell, gradually lifting him again from the ground, when, for
his second birthday, he received a four-foot-long, silver-painted
Mercedes racing car operated by inside pedals, like an organ, and
in this he used to drive with a pumping, clanking noise up and
down the sidewalk of the Kurfürstendamm while from open
windows came the multiplied roar of a dictator still pounding
his chest in the Neander valley we had left far behind.

                    ↶

Henry Miller changes diapers

From *My Life and Times* by Henry Miller, 1971

My two children were a blessing. They weren't born at home –
we had no conveniences. There was no doctor in Big Sur, not
even a telephone nearby. From the time they were born, I was a
very happy man.

    When my children were very small I used to get up at night
to feed them. And much more. I changed their diapers too. In
those days, I didn't have a car; I would take the dirty diapers in
a bag, a big laundry bag, and walk six miles to the hot springs
(now taken over by Esalen) and wash them in that hot spring
water, then carry them home! Six miles! That's *one* thing I
remember about babies. For a time, after my wife left me, I was
there with the children alone. That's the hardest thing to ask a
man to do – take care of tots from three to five years of age,
bouncing with energy, and shut up with them in one room,

especially during the rains. In the winter when the rains came we were marooned. I fed them, changed their clothes, washed them, told them stories. I didn't do any writing. I couldn't. By noon every day I was exhausted! I'd say, 'Let's take a nap.' We'd get into bed, the three of us, and then they'd begin scrambling, screaming, fighting with each other. Finally I had to ask my wife to take them. As much as I loved them I couldn't handle the situation. It was something I'll never forget. That experience increased my respect for women, I guess. I realised what a tremendous job women have, married women, cooking meals, doing the laundry, cleaning house, taking care of children, and all that. This is something no man can understand or cope with no matter how hard his work may be.

The kids were fairly close together in age, two and a half years' difference. They fought all the time, like sworn enemies. Today, of course they're good friends.

When Val was able to toddle beside me, when she was about three years old, I took her into the forest every day for a long walk beside a narrow stream. I pointed out birds, trees, leaves, rocks, and told her stories. Then I'd pick her up and carry her on my shoulders. I'll never forget the first song I taught her. It was 'Yankee Doodle Dandy'. What joy, walking and whistling with this kid on my back. Anyone who hasn't had children doesn't know what life is. Yes, they were a great blessing.

⌒

'Restrain your mirth till you have children of your own'

Two scenes from Ancient Greece, as related in *The Percy Anecdotes*, 1821

The warlike Agesilaus was, within the walls of his own house, one of the most tender and playful of men. He used to join with his children in all their innocent gambols, and was once discovered by a friend, showing them how to ride upon a hobby-horse. When his friend expressed some surprise at beholding the great Agesilaus so employed, 'Wait,' said the hero, 'till you are yourself a father, and if you then blame me, I give you liberty to proclaim this act of mine to all the world.'

The grave Socrates was once surprised in nearly a similar situation by Alcibiades, and made nearly the same answer to the scoffs of that gay patrician. 'You have not,' said he, 'such reason as you imagine to laugh so, at a father playing with his child. You know nothing of that affection which parents have to their children; restrain your mirth till you have children of your own, when you will, perhaps, be found as ridiculous as I now seem to you to be.'

A wider arc

From *A Man Called Daddy* by Hugh O'Neill, 1996

Since I have been a father, the pendulum of my life swings through a wider arc. Before Josh and Rebecca, I rarely whispered and I rarely yelled. Now I do both all the time. Before Josh and Rebecca, I merely strode through the world like a man. Now I crawl, hunker, scramble, hop on one foot, often see the world from my hands and knees. Before Josh and Rebecca, I knew nothing about water slides. Now I hold several American records in the over-thirty-five division. Before Josh and Rebecca, I heard only the sound of my own voice. Now I sometimes hear the principal, asking to see me at my 'earliest possible convenience'. Now I always carry two small voices in my soul. Before Josh and Rebecca the world was plain. Now it's fancy, full of portents and omens, solemnity and awe.

Kitchen sink drama

From Fraser Harrison's *A Father's Diary*, 1985

Tonight Jack asked if he could 'help' me wash up, but the thought of water swilling all over the floor and having to rewash everything after he had finished seemed unbearable, so I curtly told him to play somewhere else. This was brutal and quite unnecessary: he would have been quite happy with two or three plastic cups and he is much better about spilling the water than he used to be. In any case, it is the work of a moment to clear up after him and I had nothing else to do.

'I won't make a mess,' he whined.

'That's not the point,' I shouted back at him. 'I just don't want you near the sink. Find something else to do.'

Stubbornly, he dragged over a chair and climbed up to the sink.

Get down, Jack,' I shouted again, in my most furious voice. He took no notice. I picked him up and thrust him, very forcefully, on to the floor.

He clutched his foot and howled, 'You've hurt me.'

Tilly came in to see what was happening.

'Daddy's being 'orrible to me,' he told her.

He got up and hit my legs as hard as he could with his clenched fist, swinging his arm in a mighty arc. I pushed him away. Snivelling, he joined Tilly in their playroom.

Five minutes later, perhaps even less, he ran in to show me how fast one of his cars could go: there was nothing in his manner, not the faintest hint or echo, to suggest that I had just been his mortal enemy.

I hate myself for these incidents. What they ask for is always so simple and small, so easily given. And by the same token, my reasons for refusing are so trivial, so mean. Usually, my reason simply amounts to not wanting to inconvenience myself or disrupt some pettifogging system I have set up. Not that I ever admit as much to them.

I hate the thought of slamming doors in their faces, closing down their world before they know how to explore it, instead of showing them new excitements, new marvels, which at their age can be done with next to no effort. They are of course splendidly resilient and shrug off my rebuffs to find some other amusement that does not require my permission or help. They accommodate, without much complaint, to whatever position they are faced with, no matter how unreasonable. None the less, we are all impoverished by my small-mindedness.

Growing Pain

Vernon Scannell, 1922–

The boy was barely five years old.
We sent him to the little school
And left him there to learn the names
Of flowers in jam jars on the sill
And learn to do as he was told.
He seemed quite happy there until
Three weeks afterwards, at night,
The darkness whimpered in his room.
I went upstairs, switched on his light,
And found him wide awake, distraught,
Sheets mangled and his eiderdown
Untidy carpet on the floor.
I said, 'Why can't you sleep? A pain?'
He snuffled, gave a little moan,
And then he spoke a single word:
'Jessica.' The sound was blurred.
'Jessica? What do you mean?'
'A girl at school called Jessica,
She hurts –' he touched himself between
The heart and stomach '– she has been
Aching here and I can see her.'
Nothing I had read or heard
Instructed me in what to do.
I covered him and stroked his head.
'The pain will go, in time,' I said.

Real men do childcare

Extracts from William Cobbett's *Advice to a Father*, 1830

249. It is, however, of the part which the husband has to act in participating in these cares and toils that I am now to speak. Let no man imagine that the world will despise him for helping to take care of his own child: thoughtless fools may attempt to ridicule; the unfeeling few may join in the attempt; but all whose

good opinion is worth having will applaud his conduct, and will, in many cases, be disposed to repose confidence in him on that very account. To say of a man that he is fond of his family is, of itself, to say that, in private life at least, he is a good and trustworthy man; aye, and in public life, too, pretty much; for it is no easy matter to separate the two characters; and it is naturally concluded that he who has been flagrantly wanting in feeling for his own flesh and blood will not be very sensitive towards the rest of mankind. There is nothing more amiable, nothing more delightful to behold, than a young man especially taking part in the work of nursing the children; and how often have I admired this in the labouring men in Hampshire! It is, indeed, generally the same all over England; and as to America, it would be deemed brutal for a man not to take his full share of these cares and labours.

250. The man who is to gain a living by his labour must be drawn away from home, or at least from the cradle-side, in order to perform that labour; but this will not, if he be made of good stuff, prevent him from doing his share of the duty due to his children. There are still many hours in the twenty-four that he will have to spare for this duty; and there ought to be no toils, no watchings, no breaking of rest imposed by this duty, of which he ought not to perform his full share, and that, too, without grudging. This is strictly due from him in payment for the pleasures of the married state. What right has he to the sole possession of a woman's person; what right to a husband's vast authority; what right to the honourable title and the boundless power of father: what right has he to all, or any of these, unless he can found his claim on the faithful performance of all the duties which these titles imply?

251. One great source of the unhappiness amongst mankind arises, however, from a neglect of these duties; but, as if by way of compensation for their privations, they are much more duly performed by the poor than by the rich. The fashion of the labouring people is this: the husband, when free from his toil in the fields, takes his share in the nursing, which he manifestly looks upon as a sort of reward for his labour. However distant from his cottage, his heart is always at that home towards which he is carried at night by limbs that feel not their weariness, being urged on by a heart anticipating the welcome of those who attend

him there. Those who have, as I so many hundreds of times have, seen the labourers in the woodland parts of Hampshire and Sussex coming at nightfall towards their cottage wickets laden with fuel for a day or two; whoever has seen three or four little creatures looking out for the father's approach, running in to announce the glad tidings, and then scampering out to meet him, clinging round his knees or hanging on his skirts; whoever has witnessed scenes like this, to witness which has formed one of the greatest delights of my life, will hesitate long before he prefer a life of ease to a life of labour; before he prefer a communication with children intercepted by servants and teachers to that communication which is here direct, and which admits not of any division of affection.

⌒

A Nottingham father's place is . . . ?

From John and Elizabeth Newson, *Patterns of Infant Care in an Urban Community*, 1965

Not unexpectedly, we found that some of the activities of child care were more popular than others with the fathers (see Table). Whereas 80 per cent were prepared to get the baby to sleep, for instance, only 57 per cent ever changed a nappy, and still fewer (39 per cent) ever gave him his bath.

The total of 68 per cent who, at least sometimes, take the baby out without the mother is perhaps surprising in view of the traditional reluctance of the Englishman to be seen pushing a pram; and this percentage does not include fathers who 'wouldn't mind doing it, but we always go out as a family'. Many fathers took all the young children out of the mother's way on a Saturday or Sunday morning, while she cleared up; and a large number, especially those living on new housing estates, regularly took the baby without its mother on a visit to the paternal grandmother in the older part of the city. One father, who lived on the new council estate outside the city, cycled the seven miles to his mother's terrace house every Saturday afternoon with the baby sitting on the cross-bar.

Proportions of fathers undertaking various activities in the care of one-year-olds.

	Feed him %	Change nappy %	Play with him %	Bath him %	Get to sleep %	Attend in the night %	Take out alone %
Often	34	20	83	15	31	18	29
Sometimes	44	37	16	24	49	32	39
Never	22	43	1	61	20	50	32

Mr Ross, a highly participant father, was paid this tribute by his wife:

'Oh, he'll do anything for either of them – he always has – bath, change, feed, wash for them. They're all their daddy. There's a scream when he goes and a howl when he comes back in case he's going again. We always have a tantrum when daddy goes. Oh, they delight in their daddy.'

A moderately participant father is one who in general is prepared to help with the children *if he is asked* or in an emergency, but who doesn't do a great deal as a matter of course. Sometimes the father makes a principle of doing certain jobs only if the mother is quite unavailable, and in general he tends to pick and choose as to what he will do and what he won't.

House-painter's wife:

'No, he'll not change a nappy if he can help it. If I'm out he will. But if I ask him, he won't. It isn't his place to change a nappy. He'll give her a bottle though, and fuss her up a bit.'

Mrs Matthew, a non-participant father's wife, found life a continual battle with two high-spirited under-threes to cope with; her husband did not expect, and was not expected, to do anything at all in the house – not even to brush his own shoes.

'He never does anything for either of them – except he might perhaps give Julian a bottle if I was getting his supper ready. That's all he'd do.'

(Would he give Julian his dinner – feed him with a spoon?)

'Oh no – he'd say that was my job – I don't think he'd know how to, anyway.'

(Mr Matthew spends all his time at home lying on the sofa with the paper; his wife does not grumble at this, but thinks it fair and right.)

'He does just look after them on Saturday afternoon – that's when I do my shopping. Well – look after them – he just lies on the sofa and turns away from them, and I think he hopes they won't notice him – anyway, he lets them do whatever they like, just lets them get on with it. I *suppose* he'd stop them falling in the fire. Oh – you should have seen it when I got in last week! They'd got a packet of cornflakes and a packet of sugar out of the cupboard, and they'd emptied them out here all over the mat, and they were digging in it. And he just lay there!'

⌒

Even educated fish do it

From Konrad Lorenz's zoological study,
King Solomon's Ring, 1952

I came, late one evening, into the laboratory. It was already dusk and I wished hurriedly to feed a few fishes which had not received anything to eat that day; amongst them was a pair of jewel fishes who were tending their young. As I approached the container, I saw that most of the young were already in the nesting hollow, over which the mother was hovering. She refused to come for the food when I threw pieces of earthworm into the tank. The father, however, who, in great excitement, was dashing backwards and forwards searching for truants, allowed himself to be diverted from his duty by a nice hind-end of earthworm (for some unknown reason this end is preferred by all worm-eaters to the front one). He swam up and seized the worm, but, owing to its size, was unable to swallow it. As he was in the act of chewing this mouthful, he saw a baby fish swimming by itself across the tank; he started as though stung, raced after the baby and took it into his already filled mouth. It was a thrilling moment. The fish had in its mouth two different things, of which one must go into the stomach and the other into the nest. What would he do? I must confess that, at that moment, I would not have given twopence for the life of that tiny jewel fish. But wonderful what really happened! The fish stood stock still with full cheeks, but did not chew. If ever I have seen a fish think, it was in that moment! What a truly remark-able thing that a fish can find itself in a genuine conflicting situation and, in this case, behave exactly as a human being would; that is to say, it stops, blocked in all directions, and can go neither forward nor backward. For many seconds the father jewel fish stood riveted, and one could almost see how his feelings were working. Then he solved the conflict in a way for which one was bound to feel admiration: he spat out the whole contents of his mouth: the worm fell to the bottom, and the little jewel fish, becoming heavy in the way described above, did the same. Then the father turned resolutely to the worm and ate it up, without haste but all the time with one eye on the child which 'obediently' lay on the bottom beneath him. When he had finished, he inhaled the baby and carried it home to its mother.

Some students, who had witnessed the whole scene, started as one man to applaud.

⌒

Dad's department

Sam Harper, *National Fatherhood Initiative* website, 1999

Last Saturday morning I was about to tap in a birdie putt on the eighteenth green at the Dreamland Country Club, a luxury afforded by the miracle that my kids were also sleeping in, when a series of REM-piercing screams jangled my back-swing. I bolted awake, jumped out of bed, and raced down the hall toward the hubbub.

I found my wife standing on a chair in the kitchen, hyperventilating. Between palpitations she explained that she was flipping pancakes when she heard little paw-steps ticking against linoleum behind her. She turned around. Waddling toward her, following the pancake-scent, was an opossum the size of a cocker spaniel. That's when she screamed. The opossum skritched furiously into the living room and squeezed under a couch. 'Please get that thing out of this house,' she said with an it's-so-icky-I-can't-say-its-name shiver.

Let me point out here that I respect my wife. Deeply. I love her. Deeply. She represents her gender with intelligence, strength, grace and humour. She's a firm, responsible, loving mother and a communicative, thoughtful and giving wife. She can sink back-to-back free throws, carve turns on a snowboard, and where I would simply throw the phone against the wall, she demands to speak to a supervisor. In short, she meets challenges, doesn't shrink from them. So when I saw her standing on the chair, I blinked. It was an odd sight, anachronistic, like a scene from a '60s sitcom; Harriet sees a mouse, squeals, leaps on a chair and is stuck there until Ozzie returns home, summons his faded Boy Scout skills and comically vanquishes the creature.

At the risk of sounding like a chauvinist swine who's making gross generalisations based on sexual stereotypes, I'd like to make some gross generalisations based on sexual stereotypes and suggest that for all the glorious progress men and women have made in achieving parity in the home and workplace, there are still a few domestic chores that are categorised according to gender.

You know what I'm talking about. There's 'Dad's Department' and there's 'Mom's Department'. These departments are era-resistant, defined not by the times, but by an obscure and ageless code of suburban domestic duty that's been handed down from generation to generation. While Mom's Department includes every chore that involves fabric, tableaux and wainscoting, Dad's Department includes the following:

1. Rodents of Unusual Size. When was the last time your wife said, 'Gee, honey, you made the dinner and put the kids to bed last night, why don't I kill that pesky rat today.' Ridding the house of rodents, particularly rodents that resemble dogs, has always been and always will be Dad's department.

2. Noise Patrol. Was that noise a squirrel raiding the bird feeder or a half-dozen crack-crazed, AK-47-toting teenagers ransacking your living room? It doesn't matter. As Dad, you must defend the home, even if you don't have a nasty weapon in your bedside table. So grab your shoehorn and go kick some butt.

3. Zap. Gurgle. BOOM! All problems relating to utilities – electricity, plumbing and gas (also see 'Funky Smells') – are handled out of Dad's department. If you're one of those guys who doesn't know how to operate a hammer, just pretend you know what you're doing. You're good at that.

4. Sharp Things That Move. Jobs that include hedge clippers, lawn mowers, roto-tillers, Bush Hogs or any tool that has a

whirring blade are generally Dad's department. However, as Loraina Bobbit illustrated, there are exceptions.

5. Funky Smells. Gas vapours, septic tank miasma, crawlspace musk, or plain old death in the basement, it's Dad's job to pull that turtleneck collar over his nose and find the source of the offending odour, unless he can convince the dog to do it.

So basically you could say that if the job includes the possibility of bodily injury, it's Dad's department. And there's nothing wrong with that, as far as I'm concerned. I like the idea of being the hero. My wife, after all, is permanently, irrevocably, a hero for having given birth to our children. And if wrestling with an 80-pound rodent will help me achieve parity in the hero department, let's rumble!

So I pulled out my shoehorn and stealthily approached the living-room couch. I lifted the fabric thing that hangs off the bottom of a couch (ask your wife what it's called, that's her department) and looked under. Ooo. It was a big ol' possum. Long snout. Saliva dripping off its sharp teeth.

Did I mention that calling a professional exterminator is a chore that Dad can enjoy, too?

⌒⌒

A classically good father

A portrait of Cato as *pater*, from *Vitae Parallae* by Plutarch (*c.* 46–*c.* 120), translated by Bernadotte Perrin, 1914

He . . . was also a good father, a considerate husband, and a household manager of no mean talent, nor did he give only a fitful attention to this, as a matter of little or no importance. Therefore I think I ought to give suitable instances of his conduct in these relations. He married a wife who was of gentler birth than she was rich, thinking that, although the rich and the high-born may be alike given to pride, still, women of high birth have such a horror of what is disgraceful that they are more obedient to their husbands in all that is honourable. He used to say that the man who struck his wife or child laid violent hands on the holiest of holy things. Also that he thought it more praiseworthy to be a good husband than a great senator, nay, there was nothing else to admire in Socrates of old except that he was always kind and gentle in his intercourse with a shrewish wife and stupid sons. After the birth of his son, no business could be so urgent, unless it had a public character, as to prevent him from being present when his wife bathed and swaddled the babe. For the mother nursed it herself, and often gave suck also to the infants of her slaves, that so they might come to cherish a brotherly affection for her son. As soon as the boy showed signs of understanding, his father took him under his own charge and taught him to read, although he had an accomplished slave, Chilo by name, who was a school-teacher, and taught many boys. Still, Cato thought it not right, as he tells us himself, that his son should be scolded by a slave, or have his ears tweaked when he was slow to learn, still less that he should be indebted to his slave for such a priceless thing as education. He was therefore himself not only the boy's reading-teacher, but his tutor in law, and his athletic trainer, and he taught his son not merely to hurl the javelin and fight in armour and ride the horse, but also to box, to endure heat and cold, and to swim lustily through the eddies and billows of the Tiber. His history of Rome, as he tells us himself, he wrote out with his own hand and in large characters, that his son might have in his own home an aid to acquaintance with his country's ancient traditions. He declares that his son's presence put him on his guard against indecencies of speech as much as that of the so-called Vestal Virgins, and that he never bathed with him.

~~

The father's job

From *Sorrell and Son*, Warwick Deeping, 1925

Sorrell has taken a lowly post as hotel porter to
support his son.

Christopher never asked questions, awkward and embarrassing questions. He accepted his father's job, and he understood the significance of it far more subtly than Sorrell knew. It reacted on the boy, and deepened his sensitive seriousness.

At school he was very careful of his clothes. He did not say much about the school. It was all right. Better than London.

What did he do in the evenings? Oh, – went for walks, mostly. There were woods outside the town, and the river.

Those few minutes were very precious to Sorrell, but they tantalised him. His boy was so apart from him all through the day, and whenever they met he would look eagerly at that frankly radiant face for the shadow of any possible blemish.

He felt so responsible, greedily responsible. The boy's clean eyes made the life at the Angel possible.

On one occasion when he had walked a little way along the footpath with Christopher he became aware of a face at a window. The woman was watching them. He caught her bold, considering eyes fixed on the boy.

He went back rather hurriedly into the passage, and met her there.

'That your kid, Stephen?'

'Yes, madam.'

'He's not a bit like you. The mother's dead, I suppose?'

'I divorced her,' said Sorrell, pale and stiff about the lips.

Usually, it was about eleven at night when he went slowly up the narrow staircase to the top landing where the staff slept. He carried a candle. Sometimes he would hear giggling and chattering in one of the girls' rooms, but he always went straight to his own, shut the door, put the candlestick on the chair, sat down on the bed and turned out his pockets. At this hour he did his precious calculations. His little black notebook was a model of neatness, with credit and debit entries.

July	7:	Wages	£1	10	0	Christopher – Board	£1	0	0
July	7:	Tips		4	6	Tobacco		2	0
July	8:	Tips		3	0	Toothbrush		1	0
July	9:	Tips		0		Christopher – Boots	1	0	0
July	10:	Tips		7	0				
July	11:	Tips		5	6				
July	12:	Tips		1	0				
July	13:	Tips		9	0				

He found that his tips averaged about twenty-five shillings a week. He paid Mrs Barter a pound a week for Christopher's keep. He spent a few odd shillings on himself. He was contriving to save about a pound a week. £52 a year? If his health held out?

Already he had a plan for his boy, an objective that showed like a distant light through the fog of the days' confusion.

'It's my business to do my job thoroughly,' he thought, 'in order to get Kit a better one. I'll save every damned penny.'

My Thoughts

Victor Hugo, written 1837

My thoughts?
Far from the roof
sheltering you, my thoughts
are of you, my children, and the hopes
that lie in you. My summer days
have ripened and the sun
has started its decline. Each year
the shadow of your branches
creeps further up my wall
yet some furled petals still retain
the secret dazzle of your dawn.

I think of the two younger ones
laughing as they cry.
The threshold must be green
where they babble mingling
games with quarrels both with charm –
two flowers occasionally
rub against each other as they sway.

All fathers worry and I think
about the two older ones
already further from the shore
among deeper waves. They lean
their heads to one side now, the boy
all curiosity, the girl all thought.

Alone here, sad, I think these things
while sailors sing beneath the cliff.
The sea at evening
seems to breathe and sigh
when waves advance, recede.
The wind blends salt into the air

that stirs with strange
echoes of land and water.

I think of you, my children, seeing
a table surrounded with laughter,
a fireplace crackling.
all the piety and care
your mother and her father shed
in tenderness.
Here at my feet the clear sea spreads
set with sails and mirroring the stars.
Boatmen casually
glance from the unending
sea to the unending
sky and I think of you, my children,
trying to sound
the depth of love I have for you,
its gentleness, its power –
and in comparison how small the sea!

The tie that binds

Sir Thomas More writes to his children, Margaret,
Elizabeth, Cecilia and John, probably 1517

It is not so strange that I love you with my whole heart, for being
a father is not a tie which can be ignored. Nature in her wisdom
has attached the parent to the child and bound them spiritually
together with a Herculean knot. This tie is the source of my
consideration for your immature minds, a consideration which
causes me to take you often into my arms. This tie is the reason
why I regularly fed you cake and gave you ripe apples and pears.
This tie is the reason why I used to dress you in silken garments
and why I never could endure to hear you cry. You know, for
example, how often I kissed you, how seldom I whipped you.
My whip was invariably a peacock's tail. Even this I wielded hesi-
tantly and gently so that sorry welts might not disfigure your
tender seats. Brutal and unworthy to be called father is he who
does not weep himself at the tears of his child. How other fathers

act I do not know, but you know well how gentle and devoted is my manner towards you, for I have always profoundly loved my own children and I have always been an indulgent parent – as every father ought to be. But at this moment my love has increased so much that it seems to me I used not to love you at all. This feeling of mine is produced by your adult manners, adult despite your tender years; by your instincts, trained in noble principles which must be learned; by your pleasant way of speaking, fashioned for clarity; and by your very careful weighing of every word. These characteristics of yours so strangely tug at my heart, so closely bind me to you, my children, that my being your father (the only reason for many a father's love) is hardly a reason at all for my love of you. Therefore, most dearly beloved children all, continue to endear yourselves to your father and, by those same accomplishments which make me think that I had not loved you before, make me think hereafter (for you can do it) that I do not love you now.

Missing figures

Statistics extracted from *Fathers and Fatherhood in Britain*, The Family Policy Studies Centre, 1997

- One-third of all fathers had their first child before they were 25 years old; of those fathers who had a second child, over two-thirds did so between 25 and 34.
- Fathers were more likely to be married than were men who were not fathers. Nine out of ten children were born to married fathers.
- Fatherhood was less common for young men than motherhood was for young women. Just 1 per cent of teenage men were fathers, while 5 per cent of teenage women were mothers.
- A majority of fathers – six in ten – reached their thirties before having their first child.
- More than eight in ten fathers of dependent children lived with all their own biological children and more than seven in ten were doing so within their first family.

- Of the 84 per cent of fathers of dependent children living with all of their own biological children, 6 per cent were in a relationship subsequent to their first relationships, and 5 per cent were lone fathers.
- One in six fathers lived apart from some or all of his own biological children. But these fathers were no more likely to be living apart from their daughters than their sons.

No striker

From the diary of Reverend Henry Newcombe

22 February 1662

. . . a night of much dreameinge. Esp[ecially] how in ye way a lad had angered mee. & I had stricken him with a little sticke in my hand. But I was after much troubled at it, & yt of ye ap[?] came in upon mee. Ye servant of God must not strive. No striker. I was ashamed much at it, but glad w[he]n in it was but a dreame. But I desire to take warning hereby.

Eppie was reared without punishment

From George Eliot, *Silas Marner*, 1861

By the time Eppie was three years old, she developed a fine capacity for mischief, and for devising ingenious ways of being troublesome, which found much exercise, not only for Silas's patience, but for his watchfulness and penetration. Sorely was poor Silas puzzled on such occasions by the incompatible demands of love. Dolly Winthrop told him punishment was good for Eppie, and that, as for rearing a child without making it tingle a little in soft and safe places now and then, it was not to be done.

'To be sure, there's another thing you might do, Master Marner,' added Dolly, meditatively: 'you might shut her up once i' the coal-hole. That was what I did wi' Aaron; for I was that silly wi' the youngest lad, as I could never bear to smack him. Not as I could find i' my heart to let him stay i' the coal-hole more nor a minute, but it was enough to colly him all over, so as he must be new washed and dressed, and it was as good as a rod to him – that was. But I put it upon your conscience, Master Marner, as there's one of 'em you must choose – ayther smacking or the coal-hole – else she'll get so masterful, there'll be no holding her.'

Silas was impressed with the melancholy truth of this last remark; but his force of mind failed before the only two penal methods open to him, not only because it was painful to him to hurt Eppie, but because he trembled at a moment's contention with her, lest she should love him the less for it. It was clear that Eppie, with her short toddling steps, must lead father Silas a pretty dance on any fine morning when circumstances favoured mischief.

For example. He had wisely chosen a broad strip of linen as a means of fastening her to his loom when he was busy: it made a broad belt round her waist, and was long enough to allow of her reaching the truckle-bed and sitting down on it, but not long enough for her to attempt any dangerous climbing. One bright summer's morning Silas had been more engrossed than usual in 'setting up' a new piece of work, an occasion on which his scissors were in requisition. These scissors, owing to an especial warning of Dolly's, had been kept carefully out of Eppie's reach; but the click of them had had a peculiar attraction for her ear. Silas had seated himself in his loom, and the noise of weaving had begun; but he had left his scissors on a ledge which Eppie's arm was long enough to reach; and now, like a small mouse, watching her opportunity, she stole quietly from her corner, secured the scissors, and toddled to the bed again, setting up her back as a mode of concealing the fact. She had a distinct intention as to the use of the scissors; and having cut the linen strip in a jagged but effectual manner, in two moments she had run out at the open door where the sunshine was inviting her, while poor Silas believed her to be a better child than usual. It was not until he happened to need his scissors that the terrible fact burst upon him: Eppie had run out by herself – had perhaps fallen into the Stone-pit. Silas, shaken by the worst fear that could have befallen him, rushed out, calling 'Eppie!' and ran eagerly about the unenclosed space, exploring the dry cavities into which she might have fallen, and then gazing with questioning dread at the smooth red surface of the water. The cold drops stood on his brow. How long had she been out? There was one hope – that she had crept through the stile and got into the fields where he habitually took her to stroll. The meadow was searched in vain; and he got over the stile into the next field, looking with dying hope towards a small pond which was now reduced to its summer shallowness, so as to leave a wide margin of good adhesive mud. Here, however, sat Eppie, discoursing cheerfully to her own small boot, which she was using as a bucket to convey the water into a deep hoof-mark, while her little naked foot was planted comfortably on a cushion of olive-green mud. A red-headed calf was observing her with alarmed doubt through the opposite hedge.

It was not until he had carried her home, and had begun to think of the necessary washing, that he recollected the need that he should punish Eppie, and 'make her remember'. The idea that she might run away again and come to harm, gave him unusual resolution, and for the first time he determined to try the coal-hole – a small closet near the hearth.

'Naughty, naughty Eppie,' he suddenly began, holding her on his knee, and pointing to her muddy feet and clothes – 'naughty to cut with the scissors, and run away. Eppie must go into the coal-hole for being naughty. Daddy must put her in the coal-hole.'

He half expected that this would be shock enough, and that Eppie would begin to cry. But instead of that, she began to shake herself on his knee, as if the proposition opened a pleasing novelty. Seeing that he must proceed to extremities, he put her into the coal-hole, and held the door closed, with a trembling sense that he was using a strong measure. For a moment there was silence, but then came a little cry, 'Opy, opy!' and Silas let her out again, saying, 'Now Eppie 'ull never be naughty again, else she must go in the coal-hole – a black naughty place.'

The weaving must stand still a long while this morning, for now Eppie must be washed and have clean clothes on; but it was to be hoped that this punishment would have a lasting effect, and save time in future – though, perhaps, it would have been better if Eppie had cried more.

In half an hour she was clean again, and Silas having turned his back to see what he could do with the linen band, threw it down again, with the reflection that Eppie would be good without fastening for the rest of the morning. He turned round again, and was going to place her in her little chair near the loom, when she peeped out at him with black face and hands again, and said, 'Eppie in de toal-hole!'

This total failure of the coal-hole discipline shook Silas's belief in the efficacy of punishment. 'She'd take it all for fun,' he observed to Dolly, 'if I didn't hurt her, and that I can't do, Mrs Winthrop. If she makes me a bit o' trouble, I can bear it. And she's got no tricks but what she'll grow out of.'

'Well, that's partly true, Master Marner,' said Dolly, sympathetically; 'and if you can't bring your mind to frighten her off touching things, you must do what you can to keep 'em out of her way. That's what I do wi' the pups as the lads are allays a-rearing. They *will* worry and gnaw – worry and gnaw they will, if it was one's Sunday cap as hung anywhere so as they could drag it. They know no difference, God help 'em: it's the pushing o' the teeth as sets them on, that's what it is.'

So Eppie was reared without punishment.

⌐⌐

Batter up

From Bill Cosby, *Fatherhood*, 1986

A few days later, I called from Las Vegas and learned from my wife that this law of the house [obeying parental commands] had been broken. I was hardly taken by surprise to learn that the outlaw was my son.

'Why didn't you do what you were told?' I said to him on the phone. 'This is the second time I've had to tell you, and your mother's very upset. The school also says you're not coming in with the work.'

'Well, I just don't feel like doing it,' he said.

'Very well. How does this idea strike you? When I come home on Thursday, I'm going to kick your butt.'

Now I know that many distinguished psychologists feel that

kicking butt is a reversion to the Stone Age. But kids may have paid more attention in the Stone Age. When a father said, 'No shrinking heads this week,' his boy may have listened.

On Thursday, I came home, but I couldn't find the boy. He didn't make an appearance at dinner, and when I awoke the next morning, he still wasn't there. So I assembled my staff and solemnly said, 'Ladies, where is my son?'

'He's around here *somewhere*,' one of my daughters said. They were the French underground hiding one of their heroes from the Nazis.

At last, just before dinner, he entered the house, tired of wandering in the wilderness.

'Young man,' I said, 'I told you that when I came home, I would kick your behind.'

'Yes, Dad,' he replied.

'And you know why, don't you?'

'Yes, Dad.'

'Then let's go over to the barn.'

He may have been slow in his studies, but by now he must have suspected that I wasn't planning a lesson in animal husbandry. When we reached the barn, I said, 'Son, we are now going to have a little talk about breaking the law and lying.'

As the boy watched me roll up my sleeves, his usual cool gave way to fear, even though I was a father with absolutely no batting average: I had never before hit him or any of the other children. Was I making a mistake now? If so, it would just be mistake number nine thousand, seven hundred, and sixty-three.

'Dad, I know I was wrong,' he said, 'and I'm really sorry for what I did. I'll never do it again.'

'I appreciate your saying that,' I said, 'and I love you; but I made a promise to you and you wouldn't respect me if I broke it.'

'Oh, Dad, *I'd* respect you – I'd respect you like crazy!'

'Son, it's too late.'

'It's *never* too late!'

He was reaching heights of legal eloquence, which didn't help him because I've often wanted to hit lawyers, too.

'Just turn around,' I said. 'I want you to know that this is a form of punishment I truly do not believe in.'

'I hate to see you go against your *principles*, Dad.'

'I can make an exception. I also won't say that this will hurt me more than it will hurt you. That would be true only if I turned around and let you hit *me*. This is simply a barbaric form of punishment, but it happens to match your barbaric behaviour.'

And then I hit him. He rose up on his toes in the point position and the tears began.

'Now do you understand my point about never lying again?' I said.

'Oh *yes*, Dad!' he said. 'I've never understood it better.'

'Fine. Now you can go.'

He turned around to leave and I hit him again. When he turned back to me with a look of having been betrayed, I said, 'I'm sorry; I lied. Do you ever want me to lie to you again?'

'No, Dad,' he said.

And to this day, he has not lied again to me or my wife. Moreover, we received a letter from his school taking credit for having done a wonderful job on our son. I'm glad I had been able to supplement this work by the school with my own parent–student conference in the barn.

Could I have done anything else to put him on the road to righteousness? My wife and I spent long hours pondering this question. The problem was that the reservoir was empty: we had tried all the civilised ways to redirect him, but he kept feeling he could wait us out and get away with anything. And we loved him too much to let him go on thinking that.

The week after our trip to the barn, a friend of mine, Dr Eddie Newman, said something that clicked with the boy.

'My boy is having his problems being a serious student,' I told Eddie.

'Well, your studying is very important,' Eddie said, while the boy sat smiling a smile that said: an old person is about to hand out some Wisdom. Could this please be over fast? 'You know, a jet plane burns its greatest energy taking off; but once it reaches its cruising altitude, it burns less fuel. Just like studying. If you're constantly taking off and landing, you're going to burn more fuel as opposed to taking off and staying up there and maintaining that altitude.'

A few days later, I ran into my son in the house. (He was around a lot more now that he knew the designated hitter had retired.)

'How's school?' I said.

Without a word, he raised his arm and laid his palm down and flat like a plane that had levelled off. He suddenly knew it was the only way to fly.

There are many good moments in fathering, but few better than that.

⌒

Distress of sperm donor children

Article in *The Times*, 31 August 2000

Children conceived by anonymous sperm donation often experience deep shock, feelings of abandonment and betrayal when they discover their origins, new research shows.

Their distress is further heightened when they discover they have no rights to find out the identity of their genetic father and must accept that they will never know who he is.

The study, conducted by psychologists at the University of Surrey and published in the scientific journal *Human Reproduction*, raises important questions about how much information should be made available to people born as a result of assisted reproduction techniques.

Until now, the debate on donor-assisted pregnancies has focused largely on the needs of the adults involved, with relatively little attention being given to the interests of the resulting children and their 'right to know' about their origins.

In Britain, more than 10,000 children have been born using donor insemination since 1991.

⌒

Generations

Evan Jones, *Two Centuries of Australian Poetry*,
1988

I go to see my parents
we chew the rag a bit,

I turn the telly on
and sit and look at it . . .

I go to see my son,
I'm like a Santa Claus;
he couldn't like me more;
mad about him, of course.

Still years before he learns
to judge, condemn, dismiss.
I stand against the light
and bleed for both of us.

⟋⟋

The cat's in the cradle

Hit song by Harry and Sandra Chapin, 1974

My child arrived just the other day
He came to the world in the usual way
But there were planes to catch and bills to pay
He learned to walk while I was away
And he was talkin' 'fore I knew it
And as he grew, he'd say.
'I'm gonna be like you, Dad
You know I'm gonna be like you'

And the cat's in the cradle and the silver spoon
Little boy blue and the man in the moon
When you comin' home, Dad?
I don't know when, but we'll get together then
You know we'll have a good time then

My son turned ten just the other day
He said, 'Thanks for the ball, Dad, c'mon, let's play
Can you teach me to throw?' I said, 'Not today
I got a lot to do,' he said, 'That's OK'
And he walked away but his smile never dimmed
It said, 'I'm gonna be like him, yeah
You know I'm gonna be like him'

I've long since retired, my son's moved away
I called him up just the other day
I said, 'I'd like to see you if you don't mind'
He said, 'I'd love to, Dad, if I can find the time
You see, my new job's a hassle and the kids have the flu
But it's sure nice talkin' to you, Dad
It's been sure nice talkin' to you'
And as I hung up the phone, it occurred to me
He'd grown up just like me
My boy was just like me

The big event

From William Saroyan's autobiography, *Here Comes, There Goes, You Know Who*, 1961

My kids came out to California from New York that summer, and mainly we had a lot of fun, but one thing happened that was no fun.

We drove up to San Francisco to spend a couple of weeks at my sister's home, and then we drove back to Malibu, by way of Fresno, and as we were driving around among the vineyards near Malaga my son asked me to stop, so we could pick some grapes. So we could *steal* some, if you like. I stopped, and ran out into the vineyard and began picking the grapes, only to notice that my son was just standing there looking at them. I told him to start picking, but he just went right on looking.

'I don't think they're ripe,' he said.

'Even so,' I said, 'pick a couple of bunches.'

I ran back to the car. He came back, taking his time, but he didn't have a single bunch of grapes with him.

This bothered me.

He had asked me to stop, and I had stopped, and then he hadn't done anything to make the stop worth anything.

I bawled him out about this, and about his boredom all during the drive, and then I bawled out my daughter, too. My sister said something, and I bawled her out too, and then for an hour or more nobody spoke.

By that time I felt foolish, but at the same time I couldn't understand my son, so I asked him if he had had a bowel movement in the morning.

He hadn't. And he'd had a headache all day.

I told him about myself when I had been his age. I had had nothing, but I had always been interested, fascinated even, by everything. On and on.

I knew it at the time, I know it now, and I suppose he knew it too: I was being angry at his mother.

It was stupid, but I couldn't help it, that's all.

I stopped somewhere for an aspirin for him, but he said he believed a Coke would do him more good, so he had a Coke, as everybody did, but whatever had been going on went right on going on.

My past was kicking me around, and with it I was kicking my son around, and every now and then my daughter, a little, too.

I tried to get out of it, to get myself out of being so mad at their mother, and at them, too, but it didn't work, and so I blamed my son.

Why wasn't he livelier, more comic, more alert, so that I would be driven out of the madness?

He didn't know. All he knew, but didn't say, was that he hated me, and I couldn't blame him, but I hated being hated.

I said that my trouble had been that I had loved them too much, had tried to do too much for them, had paid too much attention to every wish they had ever had, and of course they knew I meant their mother hadn't, which I believed to be true. From now on I would be different, I said. I would be like other fathers. I would give them orders. The other fathers were right, I was mistaken. I had looked upon them from the beginning as equals, or even superiors, and now I could see the folly of that.

I talked for hours and miles, and nobody replied, nobody dared, or cared, or needed to.

Now, I must point out that such talking is traditional in my family. It is invariably loud, intense, righteous, and critical of all others.

All families probably have their own procedure for the achievement of psychiatric therapy or the restoration of balance, and the better part of this procedure is based upon talk, although it frequently moves along to shouting and fighting.

Six or seven times during the long recitation I tried to get out of the whole thing by laughing at myself, by making known that I knew I was being a fool, by saying things I believed were both true and amusing, but nobody laughed.

It was a very hot day in July, and from the beginning it had been a bad day.

In the back of the old Cadillac my daughter sat beside my sister, and beside me sat my son, drawn away on the car seat, the old Saroyan scowl all over his face.

At last the car began to climb the hills of Pacific Palisades, and soon we would be home.

I was still going strong when suddenly my son said in a tone of voice that still hurts me, and has twice come to me in my sleep: 'Papa, Papa, will you stop the car, please?'

I stopped the car, he leaped out, and in the very leap began to buckle and vomit, trying to hide behind a tree whose trunk was too narrow for hiding. The sound of his sickness sickened me. Once, twice, three times, four times, five times. Silence. His face was drained of colour and covered with sweat.

Immediately after he had jumped out of the car my daughter jumped out, saying, 'Aram, what's the matter? What's the matter, Aram?'

My sister said in Armenian, 'You've made the poor boy sick. He isn't like you. He's like himself.'

We got home, and I got him into the shower, and then into a robe, and at the table for some hot chocolate and toast and boiled eggs, and then I had them both go to bed, even though it was only beginning to be dark, and their old friends in the neighbourhood were coming to the door to ask them out for games.

That's the thing that bothered me in 1958, and will go right on bothering me the rest of my life.

I only hope it isn't the last thing I remember.

He told me the next day that it hadn't been my hollering at him that had made him sick, it had been other things.

I thanked him, but I didn't believe him, because I couldn't.

And my sister had been right in saying that he wasn't like me, only she'll never know how like him I was, but never vomited, because if I had, I might not be able to stop.

And I was sorry he wasn't like me, in that, because it is better not to get sick, it is better to find out how not to, it is better to insist on it, even, until it's almost impossible to get that sick, because getting sick doesn't get it, doesn't do it, at all.

But he hurt me, he hurt me deeper even than the failure and death of friends, and I loved him more than ever, and despised myself for never having been able to get sick that way, and for having made him sick that way, making him vomit for me forty years ago.

I went home one night from the winter streets of Fresno, possessed. Something had taken possession of me, hushed me, estranged me, put me aside from myself, and I wanted to get rid of it. The house was dark and empty when I got there, and cold, and I didn't know what to do. In the dining room was a bench my mother had made by placing planks over two apple-boxes and putting a coarse woven covering over the planks: red and black checks made out of some kind of sacking, made in Bitlis by somebody in the family. I couldn't sit and I couldn't lie down, so I kneeled on this bench and then put my head down, as Muslims do in praying, and I began to rock back and forth slowly because by doing that the thing that had taken possession of me, the sickness, the uselessness, whatever it was, seemed to go away. I half-slept, I half-prayed, and I thought, What *is* this, for God's sake? What's the matter? Why is my head like a damned rock?

At last I heard somebody at the door and quickly sat in the corner of the room, on the bench. My mother turned on a light, came in, and looked at me. I got up and fetched sawdust from the barn, so she could get the fire going, and in that way she wasn't able to notice that I was possessed, I was sick, I was useless, my head was a rock. Nobody would know.

The big event of 1958 was my son's sickness, known.

⌒

And the son's-eye view

Aram Saroyan on his father, William Saroyan,
quoted in Jon Winokur's *Fathers*, 1994

My father never liked me or my sister, and he never liked our mother either, after an initial infatuation, and in fact, he never liked anyone at all after an hour or two, no, no one except a stooge, someone he could depend on to be a lackey, a nitwit he could make fun of behind his back, someone he could control completely by whatever means he could make work – fear, intimidation, or, because he was a famous and admired man, blind worshipfulness.

And he wanted me and Lucy and my mother to die.

~~

Keeping Mum about Dad

Television review by Joe Joseph, *The Times,*
June 2000

It used to be thought that, in these days of easy promiscuity and high divorce rates, the most that a child could expect is that its father be present at the conception. But it seems that fathers may have been painted more blackly than they deserve. TV scientists now estimate that one in 20 people in this country – and maybe one in ten in America – don't have the father they think they have. Well, that should take some of the shine off this Sunday's Father's Day, unless you're planning to send your pop a DNA-testing kit instead of cufflinks.

But the evidence seems to suggest that it's promiscuous women who are fuelling the paternity crisis. Time and again, in *Family Secrets: Who's Your Father?* (Channel 4), it was blameless men who'd been duped into accepting another man's child as their own.

Women may like to blame Nature for this, and to cite research that shows that because women are biologically programmed to seek the best genes for their children, they are not only more likely to have sex with their lovers during their fertile times than with their regular sexual partners, but that they also retain more semen from their lovers. (Who exactly dreamt of measuring these things in the first place, let alone volunteered to do it?) It has also been found that young women in discos dress more provocatively when they're ovulating.

Imagine how many men would get away with offering biological excuses like that ('Darling, it was out of my control. When that provocatively dressed, ovulating woman at the party dragged me into a bedroom the laws of Nature took over. It was all as erotic as a physics lesson').

Who's Your Father was a documentary which made you wonder about the blessings of modern science. For every mother, or father, or child, that was relieved to have resolved nagging doubts about a child's paternity by means of DNA-testing, there seemed to be dozens more whose lives had shattered, like a dropped glass, on hearing the truth. If a father loves a child, how easy is it to love it in quite the same way once he has found out that it isn't his? As tricky as adoring your Picasso in quite the same way, once it's been identified as a fake?

Each case study in this film seemed to be more tragic than the last: a father finding out that three of his four children bore about as much matching DNA to him as would a cheese sandwich: another divorced father discovering that the daughter he dotes on is not actually his, jeopardising the future of her weekend visits to him on shared-custody agreements with his former wife. And there was Bryan Good who, for 43 years, had carried in his wallet a black-and-white photo of a baby girl. It was sent to him by the girl's mother who had refused to marry him and instead sent 'their daughter' for adoption. When Good finally traced the girl in the snap, both father and daughter were ecstatic until a DNA test proved he was not her father at all. A central pillar of Good's life for 43 years crumpled like a cigarette ash.

As Professor John Burn, head of Human Genetics at Newcastle University, points out to anyone thinking of undergoing DNA-testing: 'If you have a test and discover that you are not the father of a child you thought you were the father of, you can't unlearn that. And that's why it's really critical for people to think before they act.'

⌒

Don't Call Me Mr Mom! Or, what not to say to a Stay-at-home Dad

Buzz McClain, *slowlane.com* web page, 1999

Men who choose to stay at home to raise their children while the mothers commute to work experience things most fathers do not. Not the least of which are the insensitive comments by people who can't comprehend the concept.

It's the price at-home dads pay for being both daring and non-traditional. After all, it's not every day you encounter an at-home dad. Then again, maybe you do, and you just don't realise it. An at-home father looks like an ordinary father, except he has slightly more spit-up on his shoulders. So you can't be blamed for saying the wrong thing, right? Well, we're here to help. Here are a few things that make at-home fathers cringe, according the members of the North Texas At-home Dads Network, who have heard it all.

1. 'What are you going to do when you go back to work in the real world?'

    Oh, how at-home dads hate this. It implies raising children isn't real, and it isn't work. It is lots of both.

2. 'Wouldn't it be better for the kids if the mother stayed at home?'

    No offence, but no. Studies show that working mothers are more involved in their children's lives when the father stays at home than when they are given over to professional day care. And because of the circumstances, the fathers are more involved with the children than dads who see their children only briefly after work and on weekends. The kids get two parents with strong influences.

3. 'What do you do with all your spare time?'

    No matter what the ages and number of kids, this statement is baloney. There is no spare time. Besides seeing to the children's feeding, clothing, bedding, amusement and education, at-home dads typically assume command of household chores – from laundry to kitchen duty to lawn care. And you can't punch a clock after eight hours and go home. You are home.

4. 'Who wears the pants in the family?'

    This implies staying at home with the children makes you less masculine. True, at-home dads are likely to wash more dishes, fold more laundry and go to the tot lot more than the father who commutes. But when mom's home, dads play and watch just as many sports, ogle just as many women and perform just as many testosterone-driven activities as other fathers. And they do it with more gusto because getting out of the house means more to them.

5. 'Oh, so you're a Mr Mom.'

   Don't call us 'Mr Mom'. The kids already have a mother. At-home fathers do not replace mothers; they simply assume duties traditionally performed by them. If you must call at-home dads something, try 'Mr Dad'.

6. 'That's a nice Mommy Wagon you drive.'

   Ahem. It is not a Mommy Wagon. It's a marvellously functional all-purpose utility vehicle that happens to have enough room for more than half the Stingers Little League soccer team.

7. 'What does your wife think about you not working?'

   Ordinarily a fair question, but often asked to see how the woman is handling the pressure of being the primary breadwinner. Get real: the empowerment is a heady sensation, one most women don't get to experience, and they love it. As a bonus, she goes to the office each day knowing her baby is in good hands. Real men deal with the role change very well, thank you.

8. 'How can you stand to change diapers all the time?'

   Usually asked by the 'traditional man', the kind who will overhaul an engine but can't wipe a baby's butt. I know of one such man who, when confronted with a messy diaper, put the baby in the bathtub until the mother came home. Diapers are easy, pal. (Plum-and-sweet potato spit-up is another thing altogether.)

9. 'Do you miss the security of having a job?'

   Maybe at first, but who isn't disillusioned by the general lack of loyalty companies express these days? Mergers, takeovers, lay-offs, forced relocations and a slavish devotion by corporations to the bottom line are enough to rattle anyone's sense of security. An at-home dad has the job of a lifetime – you can't be fired or transferred to a lesser position.

10. 'What do you mean, you didn't get a chance to finish the laundry?'

    Most often asked by frazzled wives coming home from work. Well, honey, things got really fun at the tot lot with the playgroup, and we stayed a few hours longer than we expected.

Mothers ruin

From James Joyce, 'Ivy Day in the Committee
Room', *Dubliners*, 1914

Mr O'Connor tore a strip off the card and, lighting it, lit his cigarette. As he did so the flame lit up a leaf of dark glossy ivy in the lapel of his coat. The old man watched him attentively and then, taking up the piece of cardboard again, began to fan the fire slowly while his companion smoked.

'Ah, yes,' he said, continuing, 'it's hard to know what way to bring up children. Now who'd think he'd turn out like that! I sent him to the Christian Brothers and I done what I could for him, and there he goes boozing about. I tried to make him somewhat decent.'

He replaced the cardboard wearily.

'Only I'm an old man now I'd change his tune for him. I'd take the stick to his back and beat him while I could stand over him – as I done many a time before. The mother you know, she cocks him up with this and that . . .'

'That's what ruins children,' said Mr O'Connor.

'To be sure it is,' said the old man. 'And little thanks you get for it, only impudence. He takes th'upper hand of me whenever he sees I've a sup taken. What's the world coming to when sons speaks that way to their fathers?'

'What age is he?' said Mr O'Connor.

'Nineteen,' said the old man.

'Why don't you put him to something?'

'Sure, amn't I never done at the drunken bowsy ever since he left school? "I won't keep you," I says. "You must get a job for yourself." But, sure it's worse whenever he gets a job; he drinks it all.'

Mr O'Connor shook his head in sympathy, and the old man fell silent, gazing into the fire.

The devil is in the definition

Ambrose Bierce, *The Devil's Dictionary*, 1911

Father, *n.* A quartermaster and commissary of subsistence provided by nature for our maintenance in the period before we have learned to live by prey.

⌒

Tugging at the purse strings

Letter from Robert Louis Stevenson,
aged sixteen, 1866

Respected Paternal Relative,
   I write to make a request of the most moderate nature. Every year I have cost you an enormous – nay, elephantine – sum of money for drugs and physician's fees, and the most expensive time of the twelve months was March.
   But this year the biting Oriental blasts, the howling tempests, and the general ailments of the human race have been successfully braved by yours truly.
   Does not this deserve remuneration?
   I appeal to your charity, I appeal to your generosity, I appeal to your justice, I appeal to your accounts, I appeal, in fine, to your purse.
   My sense of generosity forbids the receipt of more – my sense of justice forbids the receipt of less – than half-a-crown. Greeting from, Sir, your most affectionate and needy son,
   R. Stevenson

⌒

Artful fellow

Dalton Trumbo writes to his son, November 1958

I have at hand your most recent letter addressed, I believe, both to your mother and to me. That portion which I assume was designed to capture my attention has. I refer to your addled account of an exchange between you and Mike [Butler] relative to mensal checks from home. You may be sure I shall give it much thought.

You also inform us you haven't made holiday travel reservations because you haven't the money to pay for them. Artful fellow! Do you truly think me so stupid as to send the fare directly to you, who'd only squander it in high living and end up stranded on Christmas Eve begging poorman's pudding in some snow-swept Bowery breadline?

The procedure is this: go at once to an airline office and make round-trip reservations (not de luxe, not a milk-run either). Do it immediately, for the seasonal rush is already at hand. Notify me of the airline, flight number, date and hour of arrival, and within twenty-four hours a cheque made out to the airline will be delivered into your greedy fist. Take it to the seller and the deal is consummated without laying you open to temptation.

⌒

To the poorhouse with a smile

From Bill Cosby, *Fatherhood*, 1986

It doesn't make any difference how much money a father earns, his name is always Dad-Can-I; and he always wonders whether these little people were born to beg. I bought each of my five children everything up to a Rainbow Brite Jacuzzi and still I kept hearing 'Dad, can I get . . . Dad, can I go . . . Dad, can I buy . . .'

Like all other children, my five have one great talent: they are gifted beggars. Not one of them ever ran into the room, looked up at me, and said, 'I'm really happy that you're my father, and as a tangible token of my appreciation, here's a dollar.' If one of them had ever done this, I would have taken his temperature.

A parent quickly learns that no matter how much money you have, you will never be able to buy your kids everything they want. You can take a second mortgage on your house and buy what you think is the entire Snoopy line: Snoopy pyjamas, Snoopy underpants, Snoopy linen, Snoopy shoelaces, Snoopy cologne and Snoopy soap, but you will never have it all. And if Snoopy doesn't send you to the poorhouse, Calvin Klein will direct the trip. Calvin is the slick operator who sells your kids things for eighty-five dollars that cost seven at Sears. He has created millions of tiny snobs, children who look disdainfully at you and say, 'Nothing from Sears.' However, Dad-Can-I fought back: I got some Calvin Klein labels and sewed them into Sears undershorts for my high fashion junkies.

Sometimes, at three or four in the morning, I open the door to one of the children's bedrooms and watch the light softly fall across their little faces. And then I quietly kneel beside one of the beds and just look at the girl lying there because she is so beautiful. And because she is not begging. Kneeling there, I listen reverently to the sounds of her breathing.

And then she wakes up and says, 'Dad, can I . . .'

The fathering class of the 1950s re-examined

From David Blankenhorn, *Fatherless America*, 1995

In much of our current cultural discourse, of course, the 1950s are portrayed as a paternal wasteland: workaholic commuter Dads in grey flannel suits; violence-prone tyrants who lorded it over women and children; materialists who thought fatherhood meant paying bills; and cold, emotionally remote Old Fathers who wounded their children through distance.

Doubtless there were such fathers in the 1950s. We know they existed in part because so many of their highly educated children have written books saying so. But as a group, the fathers of the 1950s did rather well by their children, at least compared to the fathers who preceded and followed them. They got and stayed married. They earned a lot of money, much of which went to their children. Many of them worked in physically demanding jobs, wearing blue collars and washing their hands with Lava soap. If these fathers sometimes fell asleep after dinner while reading the paper or watching TV, they did so partly because their work made them tired.

They spent more time with their children than their own fathers had with them, and also more than their sons, living in a divorce culture, would later spend with *their* children. They coached Little League, installed Sears swing sets in the backyard, took countless photos of the kids, attended games, practices, and school plays, interviewed boys who wanted to date their daughters, washed the car, pottered in the yard, took the garbage out, came home every night for dinner. They stayed around.

⌒

They don't make them like that any more

From Tony Parsons, *Man and Boy*, 1999

'Hello, Harry. Happy birthday, son. Have you met our guests?'

At his feet were two youths, belly down on the carpet with their hands tied behind their backs.

At first I thought I recognised them – they had exactly the same washed-out menace that I had seen on the face of Sally's boyfriend over at Glenn's place, although they didn't look quite so menacing now – but I only recognised the type. Expensive trainers, designer denim, hair so slick with gel that it looked as sticky and brittle as the skin of a toffee apple. My dad had trussed them up with the pair of silk ties I had bought him last Christmas.

'Saw them out on the street a bit earlier. Skylarking around, they were. But it turned out to be a bit more than skylarking.'

Sometimes it felt like my old man was the curator of the English language. As well as his love for outmoded hipster jive, another peculiarity of his speech was his use of expressions from his youth that everyone else had thrown out with their ration books.

He was always using words like skylarking – his arcane expression for mischief, fooling around and generally just mucking about – words that had gone out of fashion around the same time as the British Empire.

'They came in through the French windows, bold as brass. Thought nobody was home. Your mother was doing the shopping for your birthday – she's got a lovely roast – and I was upstairs getting spruced up.'

Getting spruced up. That was another one he was preserving for the archives.

'They were trying to unplug the video when I walked in. One of them had the cheek to come at me.' He lightly prodded the thinnest, meanest looking youth with a carpet slipper. 'Didn't you, old chum?'

'My fucking brother's going to fucking kill you,' the boy muttered, his voice as harsh in this room where I had been a child as a fart in church. There was a yellow and purple bruise coming up on one of his pimply cheekbones. 'He'll kill you, old man. He's a gangster.'

My dad chuckled with genuine amusement.

'Had to stick one on him.' My father threw a beefy right hook into the air. 'Caught him good. Went out like a bloody light. The other one tried to make a run for it, but I just got him by the scruff of the neck.'

The muscles on my father's tattooed arms rippled under his short-sleeved shirt as he demonstrated his technique for getting a teenage burglar by the throat. He had my mother's name in a heart inscribed on one arm, the winged dagger of the Commandos on the other. Both tattoos were blurred with the ages.

'Got him on the floor. Lucky I was deciding which tie to wear when they appeared. Came in handy, those ties you gave me.'

'Jesus Christ, Dad, they could have had knives!' I exploded. 'The papers are full of have-a-go heroes who get killed for tackling criminals. Why didn't you just call the law?'

My dad laughed good-naturedly. This wasn't going to be one of our arguments. He was enjoying himself too much for that.

'No time, Harry. Came downstairs and there they were. Large as life, in my home. That's a bit naughty, that is.'

I was angry with him for taking on the two little goons, although I knew he was more than capable of handling them. I also felt the furious relief that comes when you finally find a child who has gone missing. But there was also something else. I was jealous.

What would I have done if I had found these two yobs – or any of the million like them – in my home? Would I have had the sheer guts and the bloody-minded stupidity to take them on? Or would I have run a mile?

Whatever I would have done, I knew I wouldn't have done it with the manly certainty of my father. I couldn't have protected my home and my family in quite the same way that he had protected his home and family. I wasn't like him. But with all my heart, I wanted to be.

⌒

Teacher man

Seventeenth-century English proverb

One father is worth more than a hundred schoolmasters.

⌒

Paternity and posterity

From Sir Francis Bacon, *Essayes or Counsels*, 1601

The joys of parents are secret: and so are their griefs and fears. They cannot utter the one, nor they will not utter the other. Children sweeten labours, but they make misfortunes more bitter. They increase the cares of life, but they mitigate the remembrance of death. The perpetuity by generation is common to beasts, but memory, merit, and noble works are proper to men. And surely a man shall see the noblest works and foundations have proceeded from childless men, which have sought to express the images of their minds, where those of their bodies have failed. So the care of posterity is most in them that have no posterity. They that are the first raisers of their houses are most indulgent towards their children, beholding them as the continuance not only of their kind but of their work; and so both children and creatures.

⌒

Power and paternity

From *The Father*, August Strindberg, 1887

LAURA.	You can't be sure that you are Bertha's father.
CAPTAIN.	I – can't be sure – !
LAURA.	No. No one can be sure, so you can't.

CAPTAIN.	Are you trying to be funny?
LAURA.	I'm only repeating what you've taught me. Anyway, how do you know I haven't been unfaithful to you?
CAPTAIN.	I could believe almost anything of you, but not that. Besides, if it were true you wouldn't talk about it.
LAURA.	Suppose I were prepared for anything – anything – to be driven out, despised, anything – rather than lose my child? Suppose I am telling you the truth now, when I say to you: 'Bertha is my child, but not yours!' Suppose—!
CAPTAIN.	Stop!
LAURA.	Just suppose. Your power over her would be ended.
CAPTAIN.	If you could prove I was not the father.
LAURA.	That wouldn't be difficult. Would you like me to?
CAPTAIN.	Stop it! At once!
LAURA.	I'd only need to name the true father, and tell you the time and place. For instance – when was Bertha born? Three years after our marriage—
CAPTAIN.	Stop it, or—!
LAURA.	Or what? All right, I'll stop. But think carefully before you take any decision. And, above all, don't make yourself ridiculous.
CAPTAIN.	God – I could almost weep – !
LAURA.	Then you *will* be ridiculous.
CAPTAIN.	But not you!
LAURA.	No. Things have been arranged more wisely for us.
CAPTAIN.	That is why one cannot fight with you.
LAURA.	Why try to fight with an enemy who is so much stronger?
CAPTAIN.	Stronger?
LAURA.	Yes. It's strange, but I've never been able to look at a man without feeling that I am stronger than him.

CAPTAIN.	Well, for once you're going to meet your match
	And I'll see you never forget it.
LAURA.	That'll be interesting.
NURSE (*enters*).	Dinner's ready. Will you come and eat?
LAURA.	Thank you.

Paternal ballast

From Jean-Paul Sartre, *The Words*, 1964, translated
by Bernard Frechtman

A father would have weighted me with a certain stable obstinacy. Making his moods my principles, his ignorance my knowledge, his disappointments my pride, his quirks my law, he would have inhabited me. That respectable tenant would have given me self-respect, and on that respect I would have based my right to live. My begetter would have determined my future. As a born graduate of the Ecole Polytechnique, I would have felt reassured for ever. But if Jean-Baptiste Sartre had ever known my destination, he had taken the secret with him. My mother remembered only his saying, 'My son won't go into the Navy.' For want of more precise information, nobody, beginning with me, knew why the hell I had been born. Had he left me property, my childhood would have been changed. I would not be writing, since I would be someone else. House and field reflect back to the young heir a stable image of himself. He touches himself on *his* gravel, on the diamond-shaped panes of *his* veranda, and makes of their inertia the deathless substance of his soul. A few days ago, in a restaurant, the owner's son, a little seven-year-old, cried out to the cashier, 'When my father's not here, *I'm* the boss!' There's a man for you! At his age, I was nobody's master and nothing belonged to me. In my rare moments of lavishness, my mother would whisper to me, 'Be careful! We're not in our own home!' We were never in our own home, neither on the Rue le Goff nor later, when my mother remarried. This caused me no suffering since everything was loaned to me, but I remained abstract. Worldly possessions reflect to their owner what he is; they taught me what I was not. *I was not* substantial or permanent, *I was not* the future continuer of my father's work, *I was not* necessary to the production of steel. In short, I had no soul.

~

My father thought it bloody queer

Simon Armitage, 1963–

My father thought it bloody queer,
the day I rolled home with a ring of silver in my ear
half hidden by a mop of hair. 'You've lost your head.
If that's how easily you're led
you should've had it through your nose instead.'

And even then I hadn't had the nerve to numb
the lobe with ice, then drive a needle through the skin,
then wear a safety-pin. It took a jeweller's gun
to pierce the flesh, and then a friend
to thread a sleeper in, and where it slept
the hole became a sore, became a wound, and wept.

At twenty-nine, it comes as no surprise to hear
my own voice breaking like a tear, released like water,
cried from way back in the spiral of the ear. *If I were you,*
I'd take it out and leave it out next year.

~

Disgusted of Albemarle Street

The Marquess of Queensberry writes to his son,
Alfred Douglas, concerning the latter's homosexual
relationship with Oscar Wilde

Carter's Hotel,
Albemarle Street,
1 April 1894

Alfred,
    It is extremely painful for me to have to write to you in the strain I must; but please understand that I decline to receive any

answers from you in writing in return. After your recent hysterical impertinent ones I refuse to be annoyed with such, and I decline to read any more letters. If you have anything to say do come here and say it in person. Firstly, am I to understand that, having left Oxford as you did, with discredit to yourself, the reasons of which were fully explained to me by your tutor, you now intend to leaf and loll about and do nothing. All the time you were wasting at Oxford I was put off with the assurance that you were eventually to go into the Civil Service or to the Foreign Office, and then I was put off with an assurance that you were going to the Bar. It appears to me that you intend to do nothing. I utterly decline, however, to just supply you with sufficient funds to enable you to leaf about. You are preparing a wretched future for yourself, and it would be most cruel and wrong for me to encourage you in this. Secondly, I come to the more painful part of this letter – your intimacy with this man Wilde. It must either cease or I will disown you and stop all money supplies. I am not going to try and analyse this intimacy, and I make no charge; but to my mind to pose as a thing is as bad as to be it. With my own eyes I saw you both in the most loathsome and disgusting relationship as expressed by your manner and expression. Never in my experience have I ever seen such a sight as that in your horrible features. No wonder people are talking as they are. Also I now hear on good authority, but this may be false, that his wife is petitioning to divorce him for sodomy and other crimes. Is this true, or do you know of it? If I thought the actual thing was true, and it became public property, I should be quite justified in shooting him at sight. These Christian English cowards and men, as they call themselves, want waking up.

Your disgusted so-called father,
Queensberry

The children are revolting

Phil Hogan, *The Observer* magazine, 18 June 2000

I can't quite work it out, but there has to be some reason why our fun-loving eleven-year-old turns into a monosyllabic

sociopath the minute I collect him from school. Hay fever?
Lack of essential vitamins and minerals? Bad day's Pokémon
trading?

'Good day today?' I ask.

'Nnnn.'

'Excellent. Better tie those laces, you'll be tripping over them.'

He ignores me.

'Laces, please.'

'Dad, don't bother, OK?'

Don't bother. What does that mean?

'Look,' I say, 'either you fasten those shoelaces or you don't
get in the car.'

He shrugs. 'I don't care.'

I lean towards him. 'You *will* care in a minute,' I hiss, which
is his cue to recoil dramatically, as if I'm about to beat him with
a golf club, a ploy he has picked up from *Grange Hill* as the one
best calculated to trigger a show of synchronised turning heads
from teachers and other parents.

I manage an indulgent smile while he takes all day tucking his
laces in.

'So. Where's your lunchbox?' I ask briskly, chivvying in tone
but not without warmth, cleverly changing the subject with a
question he might be able to answer without spitting at me. He
sighs. 'Duh, how about . . . in my *bag*?' he says, adopting his
bug-eyed home lobotomy kit expression.

I ignore him now. 'So – everyone else all right?' I say, turning
to the neglected other two, who of course don't care what mood
their big brother is in so long as he's not giving them grief about
breathing too loud when he's trying to watch *Buffy the Vampire
Slayer*, or why they insist on having such sad hair when they
could have it glued down with an upturned skateboard run at
the front like any normal kids who know the first thing about
being fashionable.

I march Mr Impossible to the car. 'In the car,' I bark. 'Hurry
up.' Soon we are roaring away on two wheels as if there's a helicopter gunship from the battlestar Unintuitive Parent Minor on
our tail as we make our escape from the powerful forcefield of
what his schoolmates think of him.

'Can we have the tape on, Dad?' he says with sudden brightness, clearly having decided to miraculously change back into

Doctor Jekyll for the purposes of getting home with musical accompaniment.

I drive on, tight-lipped.

'Daaad?'

The thing is, am I now supposed to lighten up and pretend nothing has happened or does the punishment of my own now uncommunicative, sullen bearing fit the crime of his? Do two wrongs make a right? Am I being Edwardian? I tut heavily and switch it on.

'Love you, Dad!' he says, as though we have spent the last fifteen minutes healthily bonding. What is his problem?

'Love you,' I say, even though my memory is longer than his.

When we get back, my wife is busy pressing karate outfits. 'He's probably just embarrassed at being picked up from school,' she says. 'It's probably hormones.'

Maybe she's right. He has been spending a lot of time in the bathroom recently spraying himself indiscriminately with Lynx body spray specially formulated for 18–30 holidays. And, come to think of it, what was it I heard on Radio 4 recently about scientists discovering that pubescent children start growing more brain cells than they know what to do with, causing untold consternation in the prefrontal cortex as they are confronted by a bewilderment of moral choices before the survival of the most sensible synaptic connections prevails in a frenzy of neural Darwinism, by which time the erstwhile deviants have settled safely into careers as civil engineers and assume habits no more objectionable than a spot of karaoke?

'He's growing up,' my wife says.

He dashes breathless into the house wearing only mud and a pair of Day-Glo shorts, beside himself with excitement because our three-year-old has urinated into a cup and thrown the contents all over him. Perhaps they have a future as performance artists.

'Er . . . have you thought about washing your hands,' I say.

'Don't bother, Dad,' he says, standing at the fridge door guzzling a pint of milk before charging out again. OK, I won't.

Did I really break my daughter's tooth?

From Hugo Williams, 'What Shall We Do Now That
We Have Done Everything?', 1992

When I think about fatherhood, a single memorable day comes
back to haunt me, cutting me off for ever from any comfortable
feelings I might have on the subject.

My daughter (fourteen) and I (thirty-seven) were drawing up
our troops on the battlefield of the lunch table. There followed
an explosion and an exit. I ran after her and, with a solicitude
that was really anger, asked what was the matter. She flew at me
with fists flying and I slapped her round the top of her head. I
wore my watch on my right wrist in those days and as I lashed
out the bracelet expanded and the watch hit her in the mouth.
Blood began to flow. Moments of horror followed as I realised
it was not just her lip that was broken: I had chipped one of her
precious front teeth. It occurred to me that one ought to be able
to decide against anything so grotesque, in the way that one
decides not to poke a pen in one's eye. But no. There it was in
my hand, a piece of my daughter's body that would not grow
back again.

The horror increased as the three of us sat in a taxi on our
way to University College Hospital. There was a bus strike that
day and like the blood in our veins the traffic was frozen solid.
For one terrible hour we sat murmuring and bleeding into hand-
kerchiefs in the back of that taxi, which seemed to be transporting us gradually to hell.

Does one grow up suddenly at such times, or down? I remember
wanting to turn away into the darkness, yet knowing that I had
to fumble forward, pretending there was light up ahead,
pretending I was still me.

Looking back, the wilderness of our joint adolescence stretches
as far as the eye can see, while behind it, obscured by it, the
much longer period of childhood seems to have concertinaed
inexplicably with only one or two ecstatic moments sticking up
from the gathered folds. My daughter's head hovering just behind
my own as she perches on my back, head and shoulders above
the world, reaching out to touch people's hair at some gallery
opening. Her tangled blond hair flowing in the wind as she races

down Parliament Hill on one of her birthday party picnics, ice-cream all over her face.

For a brief period, she spoke poetry. Quickly grasping the new game, she would stand beside my desk, dictating them as fast as I could write. If I look up now, I'll see her outside on the pavement, standing on a chair, selling them to passers-by for 10p each. If I listen, I can hear her on her walkie-talkie, playing 'Star Trek to the Planet of the Apes', which is in the attic with the dressing-up clothes. One person has to stay on base, while the other moves around the house saying, 'Beam me up, Scotty.' I remember having to rush back home from somewhere to find the LSD which I'd left lying around, visions of our little darling pinned to the wall by dinosaurs, never again to recognise her dad, who'd be in prison anyway.

All sense of time passing is lost in the glow of those golden days that I didn't know were golden. Did she have growing pains once, or many times? Did I rub her legs for her, or did I give her an aspirin and tell her to go back to sleep? I know what I'd do now, of course, but it is too late. All that is gone and doesn't bear thinking of.

Why do I feel such a helter-skelter of joy and remorse looking back on my family life? When I look at photographs of us then, photo-booth snaps on the way to Paris, off to Brighton, going back to school, I feel a split second of shame at some mysterious deficiency lurking almost visibly in my expression, before pride wells up to mask it. I look again and it is gone. Surely I can't have been faking it all those years?

Fatherhood is a mirror in which we catch glimpses of ourselves as we really are. It seems to me now that I skimped on my daughter's childhood in order to have my own life. You can do that if you only have one child: the parents outnumber it two to one, so the child has to grow up fast and join their gang. Better than no gang at all, I suppose, but it isn't the same as running wild in the country.

If children provide a glimmer of self-knowledge for their parents, does this knowledge include a true perception of their children? What a joke! That clarity is reserved for their perception of us – from their infantile fascination with our absurd noses, to their teenage contempt for our absurd values. Ashamed of my cheapskate life on the dole and grant, my daughter told her friends

I was manager of the Waterman's pen factory. I felt no qualms about letting her sleep with her boyfriend in the house, but perhaps she wished I had.

I remember so well opening the front door on her first short sticking-up bleached blond hairdo, the look of interested defiance on her face as I travelled the million miles from dismay to acceptance, from father to friend.

– What do you think?
– I like it.
– Really?
– Yeah.

And I did like it. I loved it. Or rather I liked something about it, its dandified contempt for what was given. Even as I smothered my sadness for the chestnut mane that had gone, I loved its mad bravado, its air of taking on the world. I looked at her with shocked, admiring eyes, and yet I experienced a sinking feeling, as if a great ship were getting under way, its thousands of streamers lifting and breaking finally as it pulled away from the quay.

Writing about fatherhood I have the impression I am cutting up sentimentality into smaller and smaller parcels in order to disguise its true nature: the dangerous illusion of flesh and blood, that it is part of us. When I saw her new hair, I found myself wanting to say, 'You're just so brilliant you can do anything,' as if I were talking to myself. I had to stop myself, having no way of proving it. In the past, my wishful compliments and reassurances have sometimes overshot the world's opinions and been returned to me with a disappointed look, as if she would rather have found out for herself that she couldn't draw very well, or play darts.

The fact remains that from the moment I first saw her, lying quietly in her first clothes, having a nap after her ordeal, I was convinced of her superior beauty and intelligence. I presume this is the mechanism which tries to persuade us to put our children's needs before our own, which tortures us if we fail to do so, and which finally persuades the child to agree with us and leave home.

Our daughter is grown up now, with a past of her own – as I write she is somewhere in Asia – while we two imagine we are still young, with a future ahead of us. What shall we do next, I wonder, now that we have done everything? I would like to look forward, but it is hard, with the weight of such experience dragging one back. Did these things really happen? Did I really once break my own daughter's front tooth?

I'm afraid so, but there's a happy ending to the story. At the end of a seemingly endless journey across London, the traffic would part, the taxi we were huddled in would reach University College Hospital and a man would stick a little false piece on to my daughter's tooth. Colour would seep back into the world, words would be tried out like very thin ice, we would buy a teddy bear and a duvet in the Reject Shop and by some twist of irony my daughter would thank me. I remember we went to see some terrifying film about violence in a post-holocaust wilderness. Magically, she enjoyed herself. A smile was attempted. A mirror was looked in without undue horror. Tea was made.

～

Detained by the boss

From 'Forty-five a Month' R. K. Narayan, 1906–

Venkat Rao, Shanta's father, was about to start for his office that morning when a *jutka* passed along the street distributing cinema handbills. Shanta dashed to the street and picked up a handbill. She held it up and asked, 'Father, will you take me to the cinema today?' He felt unhappy at the question. Here was the child growing up without having any of the amenities and the simple pleasures of life. He had hardly taken her twice to the cinema. He had no time for the child. While children of her age in other houses had all the dolls, dresses and outings that they wanted, this child was growing up all alone and like a barbarian more or less. He felt furious with his office. For forty rupees a month they seemed to have purchased him outright.

He reproached himself for neglecting his wife and child – even the wife could have her own circle of friends and so on: she was after all a grown-up, but what about the child? What a drab, colourless existence was hers! Every day they kept him at the office till seven or eight in the evening, and when he came home the child was asleep. Even on Sundays they wanted him at the office. Why did they think he had no personal life, a life of his own? They gave him hardly any time to take the child to the park or the pictures. He was going to show them that they weren't to toy with him. Yes, he was prepared even to quarrel with his manager if necessary.

He said with resolve, 'I will take you to the cinema this evening. Be ready at five.'

'Really! Mother!' Shanta shouted. Mother came out of the kitchen.

'Father is taking me to a cinema in the evening.'

Shanta's mother smiled cynically. 'Don't make false promises to the child –' Venkat Rao glared at her. 'Don't talk nonsense. You think you are the only person who keeps promises –'

He told Shanta, 'Be ready at five, and I will come and take you positively. If you are not ready, I will be very angry with you.'

He walked to his office full of resolve. He would do his normal work and get out at five. If they started any old tricks of theirs, he was going to tell the boss, 'Here is my resignation. My child's happiness is more important to me than these horrible papers of yours.'

All day the usual stream of papers flowed onto his table and off it. He scrutinised, signed and drafted. He was corrected, admonished and insulted. He had a break of only five minutes in the afternoon for his coffee.

When the office clock struck five and the other clerks were leaving, he went to the manager and said, 'May I go, sir?' The manager looked up from his paper. 'You!' It was unthinkable that the cash and account section should be closing at five. 'How can you go?'

'I have some urgent private business, sir,' he said, smothering the lines he had been rehearsing since the morning. 'Herewith my resignation.' He visualised Shanta standing at the door, dressed and palpitating with eagerness.

'There shouldn't be anything more urgent than the office work; go back to your seat. You know how many hours I work?' asked the manager. The manager came to the office three hours before opening time and stayed nearly three hours after closing, even on Sundays. The clerks commented among themselves, 'His wife must be whipping him whenever he is seen at home; that is why the old owl seems so fond of his office.'

'Did you trace the source of that ten–eight difference?' asked the manager.

'I shall have to examine two hundred vouchers. I thought we might do it tomorrow.'

'No, no, this won't do. You must rectify it immediately.'

Venkat Rao mumbled, 'Yes, sir,' and slunk back to his seat.

The clock showed 5:30. Now it meant two hours of excruciating search among vouchers. All the rest of the office had gone. Only he and another clerk in his section were working, and of course, the manager was there. Venkat Rao was furious. His mind was made up. He wasn't a slave who had sold himself for forty rupees outright. He could make that money easily; and if he couldn't, it would be more honourable to die of starvation.

He took a sheet of paper and wrote: 'Herewith my resignation. If you people think you have bought me body and soul for forty rupees, you are mistaken. I think it would be far better for me and my family to die of starvation than slave for this petty forty rupees on which you have kept me for years and years. I suppose you have not the slightest notion of giving me an increment. You give yourselves heavy slices frequently, and I don't see why you shouldn't think of us occasionally. In any case it doesn't interest me now, since this is my resignation. If I and my family perish of starvation, may our ghosts come and haunt you all your life –' He folded the letter, put it in an envelope, sealed the flap and addressed it to the manager. He left his seat and stood before the manager. The manager mechanically received the letter and put it on his pad.

'Venkat Rao,' said the manager, 'I'm sure you will be glad to hear this news. Our officer discussed the question of increments today, and I've recommended you for an increment of five rupees. Orders are not yet passed, so keep this to yourself for the present.' Venkat Rao put out his hand, snatched the envelope from the pad and hastily slipped it in his pocket.

'What is that letter?'

'I have applied for a little casual leave, sir, but I think . . .'

'You can't get any leave for at least a fortnight to come.'

'Yes, sir. I realise that. That is why I am withdrawing my application, sir.'

'Very well. Have you traced that mistake?'

'I'm scrutinising the vouchers, sir. I will find it out within an hour . . .'

It was nine o'clock when he went home. Shanta was already asleep. Her mother said, 'She wouldn't even change her frock, thinking that any moment you might be coming and taking her out. She hardly ate any food; and wouldn't lie down for fear of crumpling her dress . . .'

Venkat Rao's heart bled when he saw his child sleeping in her pink frock, hair combed and face powdered, dressed and ready to be taken out. 'Why should I not take her to the night show?' He shook her gently and called, 'Shanta, Shanta.' Shanta kicked her legs and cried, irritated at being disturbed. Mother whispered, 'Don't wake her,' and patted her back to sleep.

Venkat Rao watched the child for a moment. 'I don't know if it is going to be possible for me to take her out at all – you see, they are giving me an increment –' he wailed.

Tips for working fathers

From James A. Levine and Todd L. Pittinsky,
*Working Fathers: New Strategies for Balancing
Work and Family*, 1997

- Turn down extra work by showing why it would not be good for the business, or propose an alternative such as: 'I'll be able to take on this assignment if I give up some of the other stuff on my plate.'
- Take control of your working hours by creating your own flexible schedule. Let people know when you will be working and how to reach you. Report your progress regularly and be prepared to change your schedule in order to meet an emergency business need.
- Make a weekly date with your wife, *without* your children or other couples. If you don't have much money, go window shopping, take a walk or go to a coffee shop.
- Take your kids to work with you one day to help them to understand why you are not always available for them.
- Spend some time with each child individually. Rather than thinking of your weekend household chores as time away from your kids, get them to help you.
- Set aside time devoted exclusively to worrying, lasting anything from fifteen minutes to an hour. By focusing

your worries in a concentrated way you increase the likelihood of finding a solution.

- Block out half an hour to an hour for yourself each day or every other day for some physical exercise, an evening walk or a hobby.
- Instead of using your journey to work to read office memos, read something for fun. If you drive, switch off news and play some music.
- Make sure you share the childcare fairly with your spouse.
- If your job requires you to travel, explain this to your children in terms they can understand. Fax drawings to your children and leave special notes to be put into their lunch box or under their pillow.

⌐⌐

Daddy matters

From *Raising Cain*, Dan Kindlon and
Michael Thompson, 1999

Two important developments reflecting this new wave of father research were an October 1996 conference on father involvement sponsored by the American National Institutes of Health and the publication in May 1998 of a special issue of the journal *Demography* that was devoted to new research on fathers' influence on the lives of their children. These new research findings are compelling and show clearly that having a father in the picture, especially an involved one, is good for kids: they tend to be smarter, have better psychological health, do better in school, and get better jobs. When presenting their findings, some of these researchers even depart from the normally arid language of science to use words such as *remarkable* and *astonishing* to describe the powerful influence they found fathers to have on their children's development.

⌐⌐

Dad

Berlie Doherty, *Another First Poetry Book*, 1987

Dad is the dancing-man
The laughing-bear, the prickle-chin,
The tickle-fingers, jungle-roars,
Bucking bronco, rocking-horse,
The helicopter roundabout
The beat-the-wind at swing-and-shout
Goal-post, scarey-ghost,
Climbing-jack, humpty-back.

But sometimes he's
A go-away-please!
A snorey-snarl, a sprawly slump
A yawny mouth, a sleepy lump,

And I'm a kite without a string
Waiting for Dad to dance again.

At least the big brown squiggle lives at home

Tom Kemp, *Daily Telegraph*, 26 June 1999

The first I knew that last Sunday was Father's Day was when my five-year-old shook me awake soon after dawn, shouted 'Happy Father's Day' and thrust a home-made card into my hand. School-made, I should say, because his teacher had set aside a lesson for all the children in his class to make Father's Day cards.

At the top of mine, on the front, was a thick stripe drawn in blue felt-tip. Beneath it, enclosed in square brackets, were two ant-like squiggles in brown, one bigger than the other, with a black dot between them. At the bottom was another thick stripe of felt-tip, this one green.

Inside the card, my son had written 'Happy Father's Day, with love', and I found myself wondering unpleasantly what the many children in his class with absentee fathers had written in theirs: 'Happy Male Carer's Day', perhaps. (I once had a letter from his

school that began, and I swear that this is true: 'Dear Male Carer
. . .' But that is by the way.)

It is always an awkward moment for me when the five-year-
old shows me one of his drawings. I have lost count of the times
when I have said, 'Gosh, what a lovely dinosaur', only to be told
with a hurt look: 'But it's a *spaceship*, Daddy.'

This time I was taking no chances. 'It's . . . it's *beautiful*,' I
said. 'Tell me what it is, exactly.'

'Can't you *see*?'

It was too early in the morning, and I didn't feel bright enough
to hazard a guess. 'I give up. You tell me.'

'It's you and me playing football, silly!'

Of course it was. The thick stripes, blue and green, were the
sky and the grass. The square brackets were the goals. The big
brown squiggle was me, the small one him, and the black dot
was the ball.

'I *see* now,' I said. 'It's brilliant. What an idiot I am.'

'Idiot, idiot,' he chanted and skipped out of the room.

I shouted after him: 'Oi! I'm allowed to call myself an idiot.
You're not.' He popped his head round the door, repeated 'Idiot,
idiot' and ran away. Happy Father's Day, indeed. The big brown
squiggle turned over and tried to get back to sleep. Five o'clock
. . . six o'clock . . . seven o'clock . . . Still no luck.

Of my three other sons, only the twelve-year-old, the nice one,
bothered to mark Father's Day. When I got up, he was already
out of the house and on his way to the newsagent to buy me
two bars of chocolate with his own pocket money. One of them
had a picture of Homer Simpson on its wrapper, slobbing on a
sofa with a can of beer on his stomach. The boy was obviously
worried that I might be offended by the joke, thinking it too
close to home. So he bought me a bar of Cadbury's Cappuccino
as well. He and I share a passion for cappuccino: the coffee, I
mean – I am not so sure about the chocolate. But I mustn't be
ungrateful. I admit that I was touched.

On the whole, however, I do not approve of Father's Day. I
do not know whether it is true that it was dreamt up by an
American greetings card company, as everybody says. But I do
know that we never marked Father's Day when I was a boy and
I suspect that my own father would have thrown up if we had.

I disapprove of it not only because the idea of Father's Day smacks of Disney sentimentality but because every year when it comes round, I find myself dwelling on my own shortcomings as a father. I hardly ever see my sons, except at weekends. They are on their way to school by the time I get up in the mornings, and they are usually fast asleep when I get home at night. I no longer do a stroke of housework, leaving everything to my wife.

I am exactly like those fathers in last week's survey, who said that they had given up the struggle to balance the demands of their jobs and their families. Nowadays, I concentrate entirely on the breadwinning, telling myself that I am doing it for my wife and the boys as much as for myself, yet at the same time feeling very bad about neglecting them.

But I am sick of feeling guilty. I may not be at home very often, but at least I live there. And it must be better, surely, for a child to have a benign male presence in the house from time to time than to have nobody to call an idiot at five o'clock in the morning on Father's Day.

⌒

True wealth

From Craig Raine, *Rich*, 1984

When I was eleven, I won a scholarship to a local public school where Robin, another rich cousin, a Mulholland, was already a pupil. His father, my uncle John, had made his money by selling birds' eggs. The scholarship paid my tuition fees and half my board. The remainder was paid for partly by the country education authority, partly by my mother's long stints at the sewing machine. The RAF Benevolent Fund made an initial contribution towards my clothes, and Mr Grice, their representative, would come round after work and help my mother fill in the forms. My father's way of showing his gratitude was to collect money for the Fund on Wings Day, which commemorates the Battle of Britain. He was busy trying to break all records in the charity business. No one was allowed to pass without a contribution: he knew everyone and covered the clubs, the pubs, the chip shops, the football ground. Each day he'd return with ten cans heavy with coins, five to a hand, the strings cutting his fingers. He broke all records, but it was my mother who filled in the forms.

I was bought a large trunk and Uncle Charlie came round one Saturday morning and sign-wrote my name on both ends, with my house number. On my last afternoon at home, surrounded by grey shirts and socks, I looked from the window and saw Bobby Bowen in his best suit with the extra-wide trousers walking quickly down the hill, whistling beautifully as he always did, with lots of grace notes. And I remembered how my father had once interfered when Bobby's wife Ena had lost her temper with one of her sons. The boy was cowering outside. She stood, fat, filling the doorway, holding a full-size plastic rifle, shouting, 'In. In. *In.*' Finally, the boy tried to squirm past her like a silverfish but she had him by the hair and was breaking the rifle over his head and shoulders when my father stopped her. He was, as he could be, abusive: he called her a 'fat sadist'. It was the first time I had come across the word. He came back and used another word I knew of course but had never heard my father, or any adult, say before. My mother dashed in from the kitchen, 'Norman, there's *no excuse for that.*' It was enough. We got on with our game of chess and, as usual, I exploded with anger when he cheated. 'Are you sure you want to move your queen there?' I'd say. 'When you take your finger off, you can't change it, you know. All right, you've taken your finger off. Are you sure? This is your last chance. OK?' But it wasn't OK and when I reached for my bishop, he'd wave his arms over the board like a referee who's just counted somebody out – and change his move.

I thought that by going away to school I would be leaving nothing behind. Bobby would still whistle in his brown double-breasted suit. My Rudd Cup football medal would nestle in its cotton wool till I got back in the holidays. In fact, I was leaving my father behind. I was completely proud of him and he was proud of me. He was the only father who ever came to our primary school football matches. He would race up and down the touchline, shouting advice and encouragement. At half-time, he'd come on to the pitch and give the whole team extra-strong mints, rearrange the tactics, change our positions, tell us we were playing downhill in the second half, tell us that a six-goal deficit was nothing. Mr Newby, the teacher nominally in charge, would

suck a mint and listen like the rest of us. We won every game.
He willed us to do it.

At my boarding school, I learned to be ashamed of him. It was
a complicated process. I was very much his son and it was six or
seven weeks before I learned that the self-confidence he'd given
me, genetically and by example, to other people was mere boasting.
Modesty wasn't something he'd taught me. I knew when I had
played the best game on the rugby field. I remembered my father's
story of how he'd played in a game 'against the pick, the *pick*,
of Catterick Camp' and won it single-handed by tackling again
and again a big winger from the Scots Guards. I had been brought
up to be a hero. Gradually, I was made to feel unpopular and I
applied these new standards to him. In the first few days, too, I
was made to realise my relative poverty. My father had taught
me to do a proper somersault. I would bounce on a bed till I was
high enough, then I'd do the turn, backwards and forwards. I was
showing this off in my first week – wishing I could walk on my
hands too, like my father – when I broke the bed's cast-iron frame.
The school bursar, to whom I had to report the damage, was stern
but not unkind. 'You must realise, Raine 3,' he said, 'that you are
different from the other boys. Your parents can't afford to pay
for a new bed. The school won't charge you this time, but you
must cut your coat according to your cloth.' I broke no more beds
and when Humphreys, whose father was a market gardener, asked
me what my father did, I said he was a football manager. I told
Manders he was a brain surgeon.

I was at school for seven years. It wasn't until my second year
that I told anything like the truth about my father. I had been
taken out to lunch by Wakefield's grandparents one Sunday. 'What
does your father do?' the old man asked, a trickle of fat in the
cleft of his chin. 'He's war disabled,' I replied. I couldn't lie to
an adult. 'So you're on a scholarship, then?' 'Yes,' I said. It wasn't
so bad, after all.

Yet I must have conveyed some uneasiness to my parents.
Perhaps my father couldn't be bothered, perhaps he was worried
about his unpredictable epilepsy (I was), but he never came to
see the school. My mother would visit on Speech Day and Sports
Day, wearing a Jaeger-style home-made camel coat and a pillbox
hat, or her green velvet coat that made her look, I thought, like
the Queen. If she was uneasy, she disguised it well. I was sixteen

before I took any of my school friends home. They adored my father. He told them dirty jokes, irrepressible as ever.

And I felt rich again.

Not even kissed by self-contempt.

∼⌒

Human bondage

Fathers and slavery in the ante-bellum South, recounted by Robert Griswold, *Fatherhood in America*, 1993

The bonds between slave fathers and children, of course, went well beyond teaching survival skills. In a brutal and exploitative world, they gave meaning to men's lives, a point made by fathers forced to cope with the sale of their children. Georgia slave Abream Scriven poignantly revealed his sentiments in a letter to his wife in 1858: 'Give my love to my father & mother and tell them good Bye for me. And if we Shall not meet in this world I hope to meet in heaven. My Dear wife for you and my Children my pen cannot Express the griffe I feel to be parted from you all.'"" 'Other men simply wept, while one expressed his sentiments more brutally: to prevent forced separation from his son, he chopped off his left hand with a hatchet.

∼⌒

Access denied

An article in *The Times*, 25 July 2000

When Paul Lander's marriage ended, his wife took their son, aged three, to live with her parents. Divorce proceedings and questions of custody and access followed.

Paul's high-pressure media job and lack of home help made it untenable for him to seek custody, and it was decided that he could see his son every two weeks. The legal fight was tough, and Paul believes it cost him his job. 'I was worn to jelly: something had to give,' he says.

Such stories have prompted a study at London's Birkbeck College into relations between fathers and their children after separation. Dr Helen Barrett, the research officer, points out that while much is known about the way women fare at such times, far less research has assessed the situations of fathers. As part of the project, funded by the Wellcome Trust, Dr Barrett hopes that 500 fathers will answer a questionnaire about contacts with their children, and that some will be interviewed.

'Many fathers are distressed by the difficulties of maintaining relationships with their children. I have been asked by some people how often suicide is connected with this issue,' she says.

When Tom, an unemployed father of eight-year-old twins, parted from their mother five years ago she took the children from the family home in Manchester to live in Dover. At first Tom was allowed to take them home at weekends, but after a year their mother stipulated that he could see them, in Dover, only for a week during school holidays. After a court hearing, Tom's access was reinstated, but there have been months when he didn't see them.

Inevitably, children suffer in such circumstances. Many agree that one of the key issues is not only fathers' rights to see their children, but the rights of children to have access to both parents. As Lander says: 'Agreements made between parents at the time of divorce to protect children's interests are often ignored by the custodial parent, harming the interests of the children. The court gives access to the parent, but what about the child's right of access to both parents? That should be top of the agenda.'

Some names have been changed.

FATHERS: LINKS
www.depressionalliance.org
Depression Alliance: 020–76330557

www.fnf.org.uk
Families Need Fathers: 020–76135060

Life is half made up of partings

Charles Dickens to his eldest son, on the latter's
emigration to Australia in 1868

I need not tell you that I love you dearly, and am very, very sorry
in my heart to part with you. But this life is half made up of
partings, and these pains must be borne. It is my comfort and
my sincere conviction that you are going to try the life for which
you are best fitted. I think its freedom and wildness more suited
to you than any experiment in a study or office would ever have
been, and without that training, you could have followed no
other occupation. . . .

Never take a mean advantage of anyone in any transaction,
and never be hard upon people who are in your power. Try to
do to others, as you would have them do for you, and do not
be discouraged if they fail sometimes. It is much better for you
that they should fail in obeying the greatest rule laid down by
our Saviour, than that you should. . . .

Only one more thing on this head. The more we are in earnest
as to feeling it, the less we are disposed to hold forth about it.
Never abandon the wholesome practice of saying your own
private prayers, night and morning. I have never abandoned it
myself, and I know the comfort of it.

I hope you will always be able to say in life, that you had a
kind father.

⌒

'Even if I Cannot See You'

Isaac Austin Brooks, a Union soldier in the
US Civil War, writes home

Camp Caldwell
13 October 1861

My Dear Children,

As there are so many of you in the nest at home, I cannot
write to each one, and therefore send this to you all. I think you
will be glad to hear from me, in a letter to you all, as well as to

hear of me through Mothers letters, for I never forget you, even if I do not write to you. Mothers accounts of you are very gratifying to me, for I think you are all trying to be good children, to give Mother as little trouble as you can, & to improve yourselves. My life here, is not very pleasant, but I submit to it because I think it is for the best and it is the duty of us all, to do what we can for our country and to preserve its integrity even to the sacrifice of our lives, if that is necessary. It is a glorious country, and *must* be preserved to our children. It was given to *us entire*, and *we* must give it to you, entire and *you* must give it as you receive it, to those who come after you. Remember your *country* is next to your God, in love, and never see it injured, or disgraced, if you have a hand, or a mind, to put forth in its defence. I hope to return to you in due time, safe and well, and find *you* are well and happy, but should it be so ordered that we do not meet again on earth, remember to love, and serve your country in whatever way it may be your lot to do so. To do this, many things are needed, which you will all learn in due time, but one of the *foundations* will be, to be sober, honest, and industrious.

So be good children all of you, & remember I *think* of you all, *daily*, even if I can not see you.

Your Affectionate Father

⌐⌐

'Each night I sing out my love'

Letter from Corporal Samuel Furash, a US soldier, to his infant daughter at home in America

Somewhere in England
3 February 1944

My dearest Toby:
Probably by the time you receive this, you will have reached your first birthday; and by the time you will be able to read and understand it, we will be together as father and daughter, living through the days being missed now. Then again, there is always the possibility that never shall we know the relationship which is so deserving of us, but that possibility is quite remote. However, whatever the future holds in store for us, now is the

time for us to get acquainted. As difficult as it may be, your mother's words to me through letters are descriptive enough to offer a realisation of your habits, characteristics, personality, and other traits of you in different stages of your young life, the scene still remains incomplete, of course, because we are still strangers to each other. However, Toby darling, I'm speaking to you now, because the words I say are my sincere beliefs and always will be, and some day you, too, shall share these thoughts with your mother and me.

You were born into a world which was experiencing the second stage of the 'dark ages', a world filled with turmoil, suffering and grief, and a civilisation on the verge of destruction and total chaos. By this statement you might easily assume that the responsibility for all this lies upon the shoulders of all mankind; and you would be right! I do not mean by this, that man is evil; to the contrary, man is good, *but* he has been lax and smug and because of this has allowed his basic principle of life, freedom, to be snatched from his hands by the long, murderous talons of fascistic tyranny through the rule of a small group of individuals. At this moment, this group of men have not succeeded in their attempts in this nation and a few others, but even though the people of these nations are in an all-out war against fascists and the principles of fascism, these men are still in important positions in our own set-up of government. And that is where you come in Toby, dear. You see, though we are fighting a war now, which we will undoubtedly win, the victory alone will not bring about the complete and happy change in our way of life. No! The struggle will then only begin and you and your generation will be the spearhead and main body of our fighting forces. We have begun the drive; you will finish it! Our victory will destroy tyranny; yours will establish freedom, freedom in every sense of the word; and that job constitutes the renovation of our whole system of society. Your mother and I are the fighters of the present; *you* are the builders of the future.

You are lucky, Toby, because your life will be full of love. It can be no other way; you see, you were born out of love. Never has there been a more perfect relationship than your mother's and mine, for when we are together, we are united as one individual, laughing as one, crying as one, thinking as one. We are melody, harmony and rhythm, together with courage, forming the most stirring symphony of love. Your mother is the 'zenith' of kindness and understanding, and as you originated within her, and will learn from her now, you will be the same. You are under the watchful and loving eyes of four grandparents who cherish you as their own child; and you have a father, who as yet has offered you nothing materially, only a little help in the assurance of your free future.

You shall benefit by your parents' tutelage, and soon will be aiding us in the education of your younger brothers and sisters, for there will be more, and we shall be more than a family for we have a foundation which is stronger than the very earth that holds us, the belief in truth, righteousness, and the right of all men to live and work happily in a society of social and economic equality, and to receive all the fruits of his labours. You shall live to see this, for you shall believe as strongly as we, and shall fight to achieve such a glorious goal.

The things I am trying to say are difficult, but you will understand later for you will read the works of the great poets and authors, listen to the music of great composers, and their words and melodies shall fill your heart and mind with the understanding and spirit to carry on in the battle for freedom.

Though my body be miles away, my heart is with you and I remain forever, your father, whose heart is filled with love for you and your mother. You are the nearest stars in my heaven and each night I sing out my love and best wishes.

⌒

Walking Away
(For Sean)

Cecil Day Lewis, *The Complete Poems*, 1992

It is eighteen years ago, almost to the day –
A sunny day with the leaves just turning,
The touch-lines new-ruled – since I watched you play
Your first game of football, then, like a satellite
Wrenched from its orbit, go drifting away

Behind a scatter of boys. I can see
You walking away from me towards the school

With the pathos of a half-fledged thing set free
Into a wilderness, the gait of one
Who finds no path where the path should be.

That hesitant figure, eddying away
Like a winged seed loosened from its parent stem,
Has something I never quite grasp to convey
About nature's give-and-take – the small, the scorching
Ordeals which fire one's irresolute clay.

I have had worse partings, but none that so
Gnaws at my mind still. Perhaps it is roughly
Saying what God alone could perfectly show –
How selfhood begins with a walking away,
And love is proved in the letting go.

⟋⟍

Growing up and away

James Agee to Father Flye, 1950

Mia had to take Teresa to town yesterday, to start 'school' this morning. Another reason I feel the year, and all of existence so far as I'm concerned, is taking a deep turn under. She's been a lovely and happy child so far; and I've felt, however foolishly, always within my sight and reach. I know that from now on will be just as before, the usual mixture of good and terrible things and of utterly undiscernible things: but all I can feel is, God help her now. I begin to get just a faint sense of what heartbreak there must be in it even at the best, to see a child keep growing up.

⟋⟍

When Willie Wet the Bed

Eugene Fields, 1850–95

When Willie was a little boy,
Not more than five or six,
Right constantly did he annoy

His mother with his tricks.
Yet not a picayune cared I
For what he did or said,
Unless, as happened frequently,
The rascal wet the bed.

Closely he cuddled up to me,
And put his hand in mine,
Till all at once I seemed to be
Afloat in seas of brine.
Sabean odours clogged the air
And filled my soul with dread,
Yet I could only grin and bear
When Willie wet the bed.

'Tis many times that rascal has
Soaked all the bedclothes through,
Whereat I'd feebly light the gas
And wonder what to do.
Yet there he lay so peaceful-like,
God bless his curly head!
I quite forgave the little tyke
For wetting of the bed.

Ah, me! Those happy days have flown,
My boy's a father, too,
And little Willies of his own
Do what he used to do.
And I, ah! all that's left for me
Are dreams of pleasures fled,
My life's not what it used to be
When Willie wet the bed!

The road not taken

From Carl Sandburg, *Always the Young Strangers*,
1952

I remember walking on Christmas morning with my hand in my
father's. I had been reading in the books about stars and I had
this early morning been taking a look now and then up at a sky

of clear stars. I turned my face up toward my father's and said, pointing with the loose hand, 'You know, some of those stars are millions of miles away.' And my father, without looking down toward me, gave a sniff, as though I were a funny little fellow, and said, 'We won't bodder about dat now . . .' For several blocks neither of us said a word and I felt, while still holding his hand, that there were millions of empty miles between us.

'I may have been mistaken'

From Jean-Jacques Rousseau, *The Confessions,*
1782–9

Never, for a single moment in his life, could Jean-Jacques have been a man without feeling, without compassion, or an unnatural father. I may have been mistaken, never hardened. If I were to state my reasons, I should say too much. Since they were strong enough to mislead me, they might mislead many others, and I do not desire to expose young people, who may read my works, to the danger of allowing themselves to be misled by the same error. I will content myself with observing, that my error was such that, in handing over my children to the State to educate, for want of means to bring them up myself, in deciding to fit them for becoming workmen and peasants rather than adventurers and fortune-hunters, I thought that I was behaving like a citizen and a father, and considered myself a member of Plato's Republic. More than once since then, the regrets of my heart have told me that I was wrong; but, far from my reason having given me the same information, I have often blessed Heaven for having preserved them from their father's lot, and from the lot which threatened them as soon as I should have been obliged to abandon them. If I had left them with Madame d'Epinay or Madame de Luxembourg, who, from friendship, generosity, or some other motive, expressed themselves willing to take charge of them, would they have been happier, would they have been brought up at least as honest men? I do not know; but I do know that they would have been brought up to hate, perhaps to betray, their parents; it is a hundred times better that they have never known them.

My third child was accordingly taken to the Foundling Hospital, like the other two. The two next were disposed of in the same manner, for I had five altogether. This arrangement appeared to me so admirable, so rational, and so legitimate, that, if I did not openly boast of it, this was solely out of regard for the mother; but I told all who were acquainted with our relations. I told Grimm and Diderot. I afterwards informed Madame d'Epinay, and, later, Madame de Luxembourg, freely and voluntarily, without being in any way obliged to do so, and when I might easily have kept it a secret from everybody; for Gouin was an honourable woman, very discreet, and a person upon whom I could implicitly rely. The only one of my friends to whom I had any interest in unbosoming myself was M. Thierry, the physician who attended my poor 'aunt' in a dangerous confinement. In a word, I made no mystery of what I did, not only because I have never known how to keep a secret from my friends, but because I really saw no harm in it. All things considered, I chose for my children what was best, or, at least, what I believed to be best for them. I could have wished, and still wish, that I had been reared and brought up as they have been.

~

In Chalkwell Park

John Fowles, 1992

the staring-green October green
the common grass intent on thriving
out of step
when all else dies this is the season

we walk
this tired municipal park
and Sunday sky
we walk the grass
my slow father and I

and the sun is tepidly warm
the sky a non-committal blue
with a few clouds dying

the death of leaves
mourning chrysanthemums
Li Po
we inspect the Michaelmas daisies
a new dwarf stock
a milky blue

and death

I cannot say
swift passage
I cannot say

most natural thing
and cannot say
cannot say

he mumbles on
'I thought it would be fine,
the glass was high'

cannot say
do not die
my father my father do not die

Do not go gentle into that good night

Dylan Thomas, *The Poems*, 1974

Do not go gentle into that good night,
Old age should burn and rave at close of day;
Rage, rage against the dying of the light.

Though wise men at their end know dark is right,
Because their words had forked no lighting they
Do not go gentle into that good night.

Good men, the last wave by, crying how bright
Their frail deeds might have danced in a green bay,
Rage, rage against the dying of the light.

Wild men who caught and sang the sun in flight,
And learn, too late, they grieved it on its way,
Do not go gentle into that good night.

Grave men, near death, who see with blinding sight
Blind eyes could blaze like meteors and be gay,
Rage, rage against the dying of the light.

And you, my father, there on the sad height,
Curse, bless, me now with your fierce tears, I pray.
Do not go gentle into that good night.
Rage, rage against the dying of the light.

✃

Dad

Elaine Feinstein, *Some Unease and Angels*, 1977

Your old hat hurts me, and those black
fat raisins you liked to press into
my palm from your soft heavy hand:
I see you staggering back up the path
with sacks of potatoes from some local farm,
fresh eggs, flowers. Every day I grieve

for your great heart broken and you gone.
You loved to watch the trees. This year
you did not see their Spring.
The sky was freezing over the fen
as on that somewhere secretly appointed day
you beached: cold, white-faced, shivering.

What happened, old bull, my loyal
hoarse-voiced warrior? The hammer
blow that stopped you in your track
and brought you to a hospital monitor
could not destroy your courage
to the end you were
uncowed and unconcerned with pleasing anyone.

I think of you now as once again safely
at my mother's side, the earth as

chosen as a bed, and feel most sorrow for
all that was gentle in
my childhood buried there
already forfeit, now forever lost.

～

To My Dead Father

Frank O'Hara, 1926–66

Don't call to me father
Wherever you are I'm
still your little son
running through the dark

I couldn't do what you
say even if I could hear
your roses no longer grow
my heart's black as their

bed their dainty thorns
have become my face's
troublesome stubble you
must not think of flowers

And do not frighten my
blue eyes with hazel flecks
or thicken my lips when
I face my mirror don't ask

that I be other than your
strange son understanding
minor miracles not death
father I am alive! father

forgive the roses and me

～

Lonely

From *Clinging to the Wreckage*, the autobiography of John Mortimer, 1982

After my father died I had slept for two days without interruption. I wrote, at the end of a play: 'I'd been told of all the things you're meant to feel. Sudden freedom, growing up, the end of dependence, the step into the sunlight when no one is taller than you and you're in no one's shadow. I know what I felt. Lonely.'

~~

His father's grave

Albert Camus, *The First Man*, 1994

The caretaker opened a large book bound in wrapping paper and with his dirty finger went down a list of names. His finger came to a stop. 'Cormery Henri,' he said, 'fatally wounded at the Battle of the Marne, died at Saint-Brieuc 11 October 1914.'

'That's it,' said the traveller.

The caretaker closed the book. 'Come,' he said. And he led the way to the first row of gravestones, some of them simple, others ugly and pretentious, all covered with that bead and marble bric-à-brac that would disgrace any place on earth. 'Was he related to you?' he asked absently.

'He was my father.'

'That's rough,' the other man said.

'No, it isn't. I was less than a year old when he died. So, you see.'

'Yes,' said the caretaker, 'but even so. Too many died.'

Jacques Cormery did not answer. Surely, too many had died, but, as to his father, he could not muster a filial devotion he did not feel. For all these years he had been living in France, he had promised himself to do what his mother, who stayed in Algeria, what she [sic] for such a long time had been asking him to do: visit the grave of his father that she herself had never seen. He thought this visit made no sense, first of all for himself, who had never known his father, who knew next to nothing of what he had been, and who loathed conventional gestures and behaviour; and then for his mother, who never spoke of the dead man and could picture nothing of what he was going to see. But since his old mentor had retired to Saint-Brieuc and so he would have an opportunity to see him again, Cormery had made up his mind to go and visit this dead stranger, and had even insisted on doing it before joining his old friend so that afterwards he would feel completely free.

'It's here,' said the caretaker. They had arrived at a square-shaped area, enclosed by small markers of grey stone connected with a heavy chain that had been painted black. The gravestones – and they were many – were all alike: plain inscribed rectangles set at equal intervals row on row. Each grave was decorated with a small bouquet of fresh flowers. 'For forty years the French Remembrance has been responsible for the upkeep. Look, here he is.' He indicated a stone in the first row. Jacques Cormery stopped at some distance from the grave. 'I'll leave you,' the caretaker said.

Cormery approached the stone and gazed vacantly at it. Yes, that was indeed his name. He looked up. Small white and grey clouds were passing slowly across the sky, which was paler now, and from it fell a light that was alternately bright and overcast. Around him, in the vast field of the dead, silence reigned. Nothing but a muffled murmur from the town came over the high walls. Occasionally a black silhouette would pass among the distant graves. Jacques Cormery, gazing up at the slow navigation of the clouds across the sky, was trying to discern, beyond the odour of damp flowers, the salty smell just then coming from the distant motionless sea when the clink of a bucket against the marble of a tombstone drew him from his reverie. At that moment he read on the tomb the date of his father's birth, which he now discovered he had not known. Then he read the two dates. '1885–1914', and automatically did the arithmetic: twenty-nine years. Suddenly he was struck by an idea that shook his very body. He was forty years old. The man buried under that slab, who had been his father, was younger than he.

And the wave of tenderness and pity that at once filled his heart was not the stirring of the soul that leads the son to the memory of the vanished father, but the overwhelming compassion that a grown man feels for an unjustly murdered child – something here was not in the natural order and, in truth, there was no order but only madness and chaos when the son was older than the father. The course of time itself was shattering around him while he remained motionless among those tombs he now no longer saw, and the years no longer kept to their places in the great river that flows to its end. They were no more than waves and surf and eddies where Jacques Cormery was now struggling in the grip of anguish and pity. He looked at the other inscriptions in that section and realised from the dates that this soil was strewn with children who had been the fathers of greying men who thought they were living in this present time. For he too believed he was living, he alone had created himself, he knew his own strength, his vigour, he could cope and he had himself well in hand. But, in the strange dizziness of that moment, the statue every man eventually erects and that hardens in the fire of the years, into which he then creeps and there awaits its final crumbling – that statue was rapidly cracking, it was already collapsing. All that was left was this anguished heart, eager to live, rebelling against the deadly order of the world that had been with him for forty years, and still struggling against the wall that separated him from the secret of all life, wanting to go farther, to go beyond, and to discover, discover before dying, discover at last in order to be, just once to be, for a single second, but for ever.

He looked back on his life, a life that had been foolish, coura-geous, cowardly, wilful, and always straining towards that goal which he knew nothing about, and actually that life had all gone by without his having tried to imagine who this man was who had given him that life and then immediately had gone off to die in a strange land on the other side of the seas. At twenty-nine, had he himself not been frail, been ailing, tense, stubborn, sensual, dreamy, cynical and brave? Yes, he had been all that and much else besides; he had been alive, in short had been a man, and yet he had never thought of the man who slept there as a living being, but as a stranger who passed by on the land where he himself was born, of whom his mother said that he looked like him and that he died on the field of battle. Yet the secret he had eagerly sought to learn through books and people now seemed to him to be intimately linked with this dead man, this younger father, with what he had been and what he had become, and it seemed that he himself had gone far afield in search of what was close to him in time and in blood. To tell the truth, he had received no help. In a family where they spoke little, where no one read or wrote, with an unhappy and listless mother, who would have informed him about this young and pitiable father? No one had known him but his mother and she had forgotten him. Of that he was sure. And he had died unknown on this earth where he had fleetingly passed, like a stranger. No doubt it was up to him to ask, to inform himself. But for someone like him, who has nothing and wants the world entire, all his energy is not enough to create himself and to conquer or to understand that world. After all, it was not too late; he could still search, he could learn who this man had been who now seemed closer to him than any other being on this earth. He could . . .

Now the afternoon was coming to its end. The rustle of a skirt, a black shadow, brought him back to the landscape of tombs and sky that surrounded him. He had to leave: there was nothing more for him to do here. But he could not turn away from this name, those dates. Under that slab were left only ashes and dust. But, for him, his father was again alive, a strange silent life, and it seemed to him that again he was going to forsake him, to leave his father to haunt yet another night the endless solitude he had been hurled into and then deserted. The empty sky resounded with a sudden loud explosion: an invisible aeroplane had crossed the sound barrier. Turning his back on the grave, Jacques Cormery abandoned his father.

⌒

Farewell words

Letter from Captain John Coull, of the
Royal Fusiliers, to his son

Coull was killed in September 1918, six weeks before
the end of the First World War.

France 2.4.17 1 pm

My dear boy Fred,

This is a letter you will never see unless your daddy falls in the field. It is his farewell words to you in case anything happens. My boy I love you dearly and would have greatly liked to get

leave for a few days to kiss you and shake hands again, after a
few months separation, but as this seems at the present moment
unlikely, I drop you this few lines to say 'God bless you' and
keep you in the true brave manly upright course which I would
like to see you follow.

You will understand better as you get older that your daddy
came out to France for your sakes and for our Empire's sake. If
he died it was in a good cause and all I would ask of you dear
boy, is that you will keep this note in memory of me, and
throughout your life may all that is good attend you and influence you. May you be strong to withstand the temptations of life
and when you come to the evening of your days may you be able
to say with St Paul 'I have fought the good fight'.

Goodbye dear boy and if it is that we are not to meet again
in this life, may it be certain that we shall meet in another life
to come, which faith I trust you will hold on to and live up to.

I remain ever
Your loving Daddy
J. F. Coull

Broken heart

From Roald Dahl's autobiography, *Boy*, 1982

In 1920, when I was still only three, my mother's eldest child, my
own sister Astri, died from appendicitis. She was seven years old
when she died, which was also the age of my own eldest daughter,
Olivia, when she died from measles forty-two years later.

Astri was far and away my father's favourite. He adored her
beyond measure and her sudden death left him literally speech-
less for days afterwards. He was so overwhelmed with grief that
when he himself went down with pneumonia a month or so afterwards, he did not much care whether he lived or died.

If they had had penicillin in those days, neither appendicitis
nor pneumonia would have been so much of a threat, but with
no penicillin or any other magical antibiotic cures, pneumonia in
particular was a very dangerous illness indeed. The pneumonia
patient, on about the fourth or fifth day, would invariably reach

what was known as 'the crisis'. The temperature soared and the pulse became rapid. The patient had to fight to survive. My father refused to fight. He was thinking, I am quite sure, of his beloved daughter, and he was wanting to join her in heaven. So he died. He was fifty-seven years old.

⌒

Nothing compared to her

Plutarch, (*c*. 46–*c*. 120) writes to his wife about the death of their two-year-old daughter, Timoxena

. . . besides that natural fatherly affection which commonly men have toward little babes, there was one particular property that gave an edge thereto, and caused me to love her above the rest; and that was a special grace that she had, to make joy and pleasure, and the same without any mixture at all of curstnesse or frowardnesse, and nothing given to whining and complaint; for she was of a wonderful kind and gentle nature, loving she was again to those that loved her, and marvellous desirous to gratifie and pleasure others; in which regards, she both delighted me, and also yielded no small testimony of rare debonairity that nature had endued her withal, for she would make prety meanes to her nurse, and seem (as it were) to entreat her to give the brest or pap, not onely to other infants, like her selfe, her play feeres, but also to little babies and puppets, and such like gawds as little ones take joy in, and wherewith they use to play; as if upon a singular courtesie and humanity she could find in her heart to communicate and distribute from her own table, even the best things she had, among them that did her any pleasure. But I see no reason (sweet wife) why these lovely qualities and such like, wherein we took contentment and joy in her lifetime, should disquiet and trouble us now, after her death, when we either think or make relation of them: and I fear againe, lest by our dolour and grief we abandon and put clean away all the remembrance thereof, like as *Clymene* desired to do, when she said

> *I hate the bow so light of cornel tree:*
> *All exercise abroad, farewell for me;*

as avoiding alwayes and trembling at the remembrance and commemoration of her son, which did no other good but renew her grief and dolour; for naturally we seek to flee all that troubleth and offendeth us. We ought, therefore, so to demean ourselves that as whiles she lived, we had nothing in the world more sweet to embrace, more pleasant to see, or delectable to hear than our daughter; so the cogitation of her may still abide and live with us all our life time, having by many degrees our joy multiplyed more than our heavinesse augmented.

⌒

My Boy Jack

Rudyard Kipling's only son, Jack, was posted missing in action during the Battle of Loos on the Western Front in 1915; his body was never recovered.

'Have you news of my boy Jack?'
Not this tide.
'When d'you think that he'll come back?'
Not with this wind blowing, and this tide.

'Has any one else had word of him?'
Not this tide.
For what is sunk will hardly swim,
Not with this wind blowing, and this tide.

'Oh, dear, what comfort can I find?'
None this tide,
Nor any tide,
Except he did not shame his kind –
Not even with that wind blowing, and that tide.

Then hold your head up all the more,
This tide,
And every tide;
Because he was the son you bore,
And gave to that wind blowing and that tide!

⌒

Such a child I never saw

From the diary of John Evelyn, 1620–1706

27 January [1658]:
After six fits of a quartan ague with which it pleased God to
visite him, died my deare son Richard, to our inexpressible griefe
and affliction, 5 yeares and 3 days old onely, but at that tender
age a prodigy for witt and understanding; for beauty of body a
very angel; for endowment of mind of incredible and rare hopes.
To give onely a little taste of some of them, and thereby glory
to God, who out of the mouths of babes and infants does sometimes perfect his praises: at 2 yeares and halfe old he could
perfectly reade any of the English, Latine, French, or Gottic letters,
pronouncing the three first languages exactly. He had before the
5th yeare, or in that yeare, not onely skill to reade most written
hands, but to decline all the nouns, conjugate the verbs regular,
and most of the irregular; learn'd out Puerilis, got by heart almost
the entire vocabularie of Latine and French primitives and words,
could make congruous syntax, turne English into Latine, and *vice
versa*, construe and prove what he read, and did the government
and use of relatives, verbs, substantives, elipses, and many figures
and tropes, and made a considerable progress in Comenius's
Janua; began himselfe to write legibly, and had a stronge passion
for Greeke. The number of verses he could recite was prodigious,
and what he remember'd of the parts of playes; which he would
also act; and when seeing a Plautus in one's hand, he ask'd what
booke it was, and being told it was comedy, and too difficult for
him, he wept for sorrow. Strange was his apt and ingenious application of fables and morals, for he had read Aesop; he had a
wonderful disposition to mathematics, having by heart divers
propositions of Euclid that were read to him in play, and he
would make lines and demonstrate them. As to his piety, astonishing were his applications of Scripture upon occasion, and his
sense of God; he had learn'd all his Catechisme early, and understood the historical part of the Bible and New Testament to a
wonder, how Christ came to redeeme mankind, and how, compre-
hending these necessarys himselfe, his godfathers were discharg'd
of their promise. These and the like illuminations far exceeded
his age and experience, considering the prettinesse of his addresse

and behaviour, cannot but leave impressions in me at the memory
of him. When one told him how many dayes a Quaker had fasted,
he replied that was no wonder, for Christ had said man should
not live by bread alone, but by the Word of God. He would of
himselfe select the most pathetic psalms, and chapters out of Job,
to reade to his mayde during his sicknesse, telling her when she
pitied him that all God's children must suffer affliction. He
declaim'd against the vanities of the world before he had seene
any. Often he would desire those who came to see him to pray
by him, and a yeare before he fell sick, to kneel and pray with
him alone in some corner. How thankfully would he receive admo-
nition, how soon be reconciled! how indifferent, yet continually
chererful! He would give grave advice to his brother John, beare
with his impertinencies, and say he was but a child. If he had
heard of or saw any new thing, he was unquiet till he was told
how it was made; he brought to us all such difficulties as he
found in books, to be expounded. He had learn'd by heart divers
sentences in Latin and Greeke, which on occasion he would
produce even to wonder. He was all life, all prettinesse, far from
morose, sullen, or childish in any thing he said or did. The last
time he had ben at church (which was at Greenwich), I ask'd
him, according to costome, what he remembered of the sermon;
two good things, father, said he, *bonum gratiae* and *bonum
gloriae*, with a just account of what the preacher said. The day
before he died he cal'd to me, and in a more serious manner
than usual told me that for all I loved him so dearly I should
give my house, land, and all my fine things, to his brother Jack,
he should have none of them; the next morning, when he found
himself ill, and that I persuaded him to keepe his hands in bed,
he demanded whether he might pray to God with his hands
unjoyn'd; and a little after, whilst in greate agonie, whether he
should not offend God by using his holy name so often calling
for ease. What shall I say of his frequent pathetical ejaculations
utter'd of himselfe; Sweete Jesus save me, deliver me, pardon my
sinns, let thine angels receive me! So early knowledge, so much
piety and perfection! But thus God having dress'd up a Saint fit
for himselfe, would not longer permit him with us, unworthy
of the future fruites of this incomparable hopefull blossome.
Such a child I never saw: for such a child I blesse God in whose
bosome he is! May I and mine become as this little child, who

now follows the child Jesus that Lamb of God in a white robe
whithersoever he goes; Even so, Lord Jesus, *fiat voluntas tua!*
Thou gavest him to us, Thou hast taken him from us, blessed
be the name of the Lord! That I had any thing acceptable to
Thee was from thy grace alone, since from me he had nothing
but sin, but that Thou hast pardon'd! blessed be my God for
ever, amen!

⌒

Would you like to see the baby?

From Vernon Scannell, *The Tiger and
the Rose*, 1971

At half-past nine I borrowed my father-in-law's car and drove to
the hospital. I was a little early but the doctor saw me straight
away. He was a dark, tired-looking man, mercifully unfussy and
practical.

He said, 'I am afraid this is a very unpleasant shock for you.
As you know, one of the babies seems to be perfectly normal. A
normal delivery, quite an easy one. The second wasn't so easy.
He's suffering from what is called a meningocele, that's a hernia
of the meninges, the membranes over the brain and spinal cord.
He's got a big swelling on the back of his head and this will have
to be removed. I think the chances of his surviving this are pretty
good but how much brain damage he's likely to suffer I couldn't
possibly say. I'm not a specialist on this, you see. But I know
enough about it to say that the damage might be very considerable indeed. Encephalitis is common with these cases and you
can be certain that the child will never be able to lead a normal
life. I'd go as far as to say that it's very doubtful that he'd be
able to walk or talk, though – as I've said – you must wait for
specialist opinion before you decide what you're going to do.

I must have looked blank. 'Do?'

He said, 'I mean whether you would look after the child yourselves or leave him in the hospital he'd be sent to for the operation. That's St Mary's at Carshalton. They look after a lot of
similar cases there.'

I said, 'I see.' But I did not see or feel much at all. A sense of unreality was settling over me, cushioning me against the sharper edges of what was happening.

'What about Jo?' I said. 'My wife. Does she know about this?'

'She's been told only that the second twin is weak and has a spinal injury. We thought it might be better if you told her the facts.'

'Yes, I suppose so.'

He said, 'Would you like to see the baby? I must warn you that he's not – that the growth is large and unsightly. You might prefer not to . . . for the present, anyway . . .'

'Yes, I'd like to see him.'

I was not so sure that I did want to see him, but I felt I could not tell Jo about his condition unless I knew what he looked like.

'Very well.'

I followed the doctor along some corridors and we stopped outside a door.

'You sure you wouldn't like to leave it till a bit later?' he said.

I felt a flutter at the heart, a blurring of vision and a weakness in the legs. Panic. Was the baby so hideous? Would I make a fool of myself, be sick on the spot or collapse in a dead faint?

'No. I want to see him now.' I was mildly surprised that my voice sounded quite calm and firm.

We went into the room. There were a dozen or so incubators in it, each one like a glass box with a doll inside.

The doctor said, 'Here we are, this is the one.'

I realised that my fists were tightly clenched and I was digging the fingernails into the palms of my hands. I looked and, for a second, I was utterly bewildered and, wildly, I wondered if I could be the victim of a lunatic hoax. Then I felt a surge of relief that was instantly followed by a drench of pure joy and wonder at the beauty of the child. I had never seen anything so beautiful. He lay on one side with his eyes closed, and the tiny features looked at once exquisitely carved yet tenderly human like the head of one of those babies you see in fifteenth-century Flemish paintings, an idealisation of the infant. I could see one tiny hand, perfectly formed, the minute fingers curved near his cheek. The swelling at the back of the head seemed irrelevant; it ballooned out, a dark congested purple, a little like the bulb on an old-fashioned motor horn, about the size of the head itself. It could have been something left there by mistake, touching the little skull but not really connected to it. I looked closer and saw that the meningocele was indeed a malignant appendage attached to the back of the little head but I could feel no horror, only wonder that a child so handicapped could be so beautiful.

The doctor said, 'All right, Mr Scannell?'

I said, 'He's marvellous.'

I felt his hand on my arm. I think he was afraid that I might behave in some unpredictable and embarrassing manner.

I said, 'All right, thank you,' and he took me out of the room and directed me to the ward where Jo lay, a cot beside her bed with the other twin in it.

She was awake and she looked pale but quite composed.

She said, 'Have you seen Benjamin?'

I nodded. 'That's his name, is it?'

'Yes. He's been baptised already. They said he was weak. They baptise them at once if they think . . . have you seen him? Yes, you just said you had. What's he like? Is he all right?'

'He's fine. He's beautiful. But there's something wrong with him. He's going to be okay, I think. I mean he's going to survive. But he'll be handicapped.' I knew that she would not wish me to tell her anything but the truth as I knew it so I repeated to her all that the doctor had told me.

I held her hand. 'Don't worry,' I said. 'Everything's going to be all right. He's going to be fine. Believe me. He's the nicest baby I've ever seen.'

I thought she was going to cry but she did not. She said, 'We'll keep him at home, won't we? Whatever he's like? Whatever happens?'

'Of course.'

'Good. I thought you'd say that.'

We sat for a while, not saying much. Then Jo said, 'You haven't looked at Toby.'

'Toby?'

'Tobias. Your other son.'

I looked into the cot at the bedside. It contained a baby, an ordinary baby.

Jo said, 'Isn't he lovely?'

'Yes, he's lovely.'

But all I could think of was the tiny creature in the glass box, his grave sleeping face, the little head resting against the swollen bulb of dark flesh.

Presently a nurse came along and told me that I must leave. I said goodbye to Jo and promised to return that evening. I went out of the hospital. Outside, the sun was still shining and the air was sweet after the hospital smell. I got into the car and drove back to Edenbridge.

We brought Benjamin home from Carshalton towards the end of May. The woman specialist I had spoken to at St Mary's gave us cautious encouragement but was careful not to raise false hopes.

'It is impossible to predict what progress he may make,' she had said. 'But you must realise that he will never be a normal human being. There is absolutely no question of that. At the same time, there's no doubt that a child like this responds far better to the love and care of parents and brothers and sisters in its own home than ever he could to the necessarily more impersonal attention he would get here.'

At nights it was my responsibility to feed Benjamin while Jo was attending to Toby's needs. Benjamin was very frail and, on the rare occasions when he cried, his voice was paper-thin, fluttering on silence like the wings of a dying moth. I still found his face beautiful though I had to admit that it showed none of the expression that Toby's was beginning to display. He would lie, almost weightlessly, in the crook of my arm, so small and so fragile that it seemed impossible that he could be a living human, and after he had taken the little nourishment that he could swallow, I would very softly pat and massage his back until he expelled a tiny gust of wind. I would nurse him for a while, looking into his face for some sign of animation, but it always remained quite expressionless, the eyes either closed or apparently unseeing, a small breathing statue. There was a little lump on the back of his head where the meningocele had been removed. Otherwise, apart from his smallness and impassivity, he looked like any baby except that, to me, his minuscule features were more delicately shaped than any I had seen or could imagine. . . .

Jo and I did not, I am sure, hide from the realities of the situation. We both knew that Benjamin, as he grew older, would become a restraint on our freedom. We both faced the fact that he might never even reach the stage of development that Mary attained, might never perhaps recognise or be able to communicate with us at all, and, as we sternly reminded each other, he would not remain a baby for long; he would grow big and, perhaps, monstrous. It did not matter. We would have to face the fresh problems as they arose. Here and now we were grateful for Benjamin; we, too, felt blessed.

We watched his progress with microscopic care, worrying when he would not take his milk, rejoicing when he seemed hungry, and at nights, however deep our sleep, we would be instantly awakened by his wispy cries. We noticed that there were times when he seemed to find difficulty in breathing and you could hear the faint rasping in the frail cage of his chest and the rate of his breathing seemed too fast. When we took him to our doctor we were told that there was some bronchial congestion but it would probably clear itself up.

One night in late August, or rather in the early hours of the morning, after I had fed Benjamin and seen him back into his cot, I was slipping back into sleep when I was jerked awake by a faint noise. I sat up and listened. Again I heard the sound; it was not his usual dry fluttering cry, but a noise I had never before heard him make, a brief and very soft chirrup and twitter like birds settling in their nests for the night but heard from a considerable distance. I slipped out of bed and went to his side. A night light burned on the chest-of-drawers and shadows made obeisances on the walls. I looked down and saw that Benjamin's eyes were not closed. I bent close and he seemed to be looking back at me.

I waited to see if he would make the sound again but all I could hear was the slight wheezing of his rapid breathing. The little head looked unbearably vulnerable. His eyes were still open. I wished that he would make his new sound again but he just lay there and seemed to return my scrutiny with incurious serenity. Then, just as I was about to go back to bed, the miracle occurred. Benjamin smiled. For the first time the small, almost mask-like face was illumined from within and it became, instead of an idealisation or caricature of infancy, wonderfully and unequivocally human, and the opening of the lips, the upwards curve of each corner of the mouth and the narrowing of eyes, disturbing the perfection of the features in repose, thrilled me with their sweet and mortal imperfection. The smile lasted for perhaps two or three seconds. Then his eyes closed, the little mask of gravity was resumed, and he slept. I have since been told that all I saw was a trick of the flickering candlelight playing over his face or a spasm of indigestion contorting his features, but I am not convinced. I am sure that he smiled.

The next afternoon I had to go to London. I stayed longer than I had intended and I had to hurry to catch the 7.10 from Victoria. It was a fine evening. I walked the mile or so from the station to the village and I reached home soon after eight o'clock. I went into the house and found no one downstairs. I looked in the garden but Jo was not there so I started to go upstairs just as she appeared from our bedroom. I waited for her to come down.

I saw immediately that something was wrong. She looked pale; her eyes had a fixed brightness and her mouth was hard and twisted as if she were biting on something that tasted very bitter.

My heart began to thump with a sudden alarm. I said, 'What's the matter?'

She shook her head with a single flick as if deflecting the question I had thrown at her.

I let her pass me and then I followed her into the kitchen at the back of the house. She sat down at the table. Then her mouth went loose, her face twisted as if she had felt a quick thrust of pain and tears began to stream down her cheeks.

She said, 'Benjamin's dead.'

I sat down. I could taste beer, sour and rebellious in the stomach and throat. I felt parched and sick and I began to tremble.

I said, 'Benjamin?' as if I could not believe what she had said, but it seemed that I had known before she had spoken.

Jo began to speak very quickly and all the time the tears were streaming down her face. 'It wasn't my fault. It was about two o'clock. He started to breathe fast and he couldn't – he didn't seem able to get enough air. Then his face went blue. He couldn't breathe. I picked him up and put him in the car and drove as fast as I could to the hospital. They took him away and I waited. I waited. It wasn't my fault. They said there was nothing I could have done. He just died.'

I sat opposite Jo and watched her cry. I knew I ought to do

something to comfort her but I did nothing. I saw that each of us was alone now. There was nothing, for the moment, that we could do to help one another. Later, perhaps, but not now. I got up and went into the garden. I thought, 'He's gone. There wasn't much of him and now there's nothing.' I did not feel angry – not then – but there was a wedge of pain, dry and abrasive, like a growth in my throat. I thought if I could cry it might help. It might flush the quinsy of grief. But I could not cry. I had not cried for longer than I could remember and, in any case, it would be absurd for a man of my age to be standing in his garden on a summer evening bawling his eyes out. Grown men did not cry. They knew it served no purpose. It was something that women and children did, something you outgrew; its impossibility defined the adult male. It might have helped though, had it been possible. It might, if only for the moment, ease the immediate pain. Then I noticed the hot prickle and itch on my face and I found that I had been crying all the time, but it did not help very much. The pain of loss was not to be washed away by a few drops of salty water. I would have to get accustomed to it; it would become familiar and therefore bearable, but it would stay with me for ever.

Yielded up his soul to God

A letter from William Wordsworth,
2 December 1812

Wednesday Evening
My dear Friend,
 Symptoms of the measles appeared upon my Son Thomas last Thursday; he was most favourable held till tuesday, between ten and eleven at that hour was particularly lightsome and comfortable; without any assignable cause a sudden change took place, an inflammation had commenced on the lungs which it was impossible to check and the sweet Innocent yielded up his soul to God before six in the evening. He did not appear to suffer much in body, but I fear something in mind as he was of an age to have thought much upon death a subject to which

his mind was daily led by the grave of his Sister. My Wife bears the loss of her Child with striking fortitude. My Sister was not at home but is returned to day, I met her at Threlkeld. Miss Hutchinson also supports her sorrow as ought to be done. For myself dear Southey I dare not say in what state of mind I am; I loved the Boy with the utmost love of which my soul is capable, and he is taken from me – yet in the agony of my spirit in surrendering such a treasure I feel a thousand times richer than if I had never possessed it. God comfort and save you and all our friends and us all from a repetition of such trials – O Southey feel for me! If you are not afraid of the complaint, I ought to have said if you have had it come over to us! Best love from everybody – you will impart this sad news to your Wife and Mrs Coleridge and Mrs Lovel and to Miss Barker and Mrs Wilson. Poor woman! she was most good to him – Heaven reward her.

Heaven bless you
Your sincere Friend
W. Wordsworth

Will Mrs Coleridge please to walk up to the Calverts and mention these afflictive news with the particulars. I should have written but my sorrow over-powers me.

Remembrance of my deare Mary

From the diary of the Reverend Ralph Josselin

27 [May 1650]: This day a quarter past two in the afternoone my Mary fell asleepe in the Lord, her soule past into that rest where the body of Jesus, and the soules of the saints are, shee was: 8 yeares and 45 dayes old when shee dyed, my soule had aboundant cause to blesse god for her, who was our first fruites, and those god would have offered to him, and this I freely resigned up to him(,) it was a pretious child, a bundle of myrrhe, a bundle of sweetnes, shee was a child of ten thousand, full of wisedome, woman-like gravity, knowledge, sweet expre[*ssions of god, apt in her learning,*] tender hearted and loving, an [*obed*]ient child

[*to us.*] it was free from [*the rudenesse of*] litle children, it was to us as a boxe of sweet ointment, which now its broken smells more deliciously then it did before, Lord I rejoyce I had such a present for thee, it was patient in the sicknesse, thankefull to admiracion; it lived desired and dyed lamented, thy memory is and will bee sweete unto mee,

28: This day my deare Mary was buried in Earles Colne church by the 2 uppermost seats, shee was accompanyed thither with most of the towne; Mrs Margarett Harlakenden, and Mrs Mabel Elliston layd her in grave, those two and Mrs Jane Clench and my sister carryed her in their hands to the grave, I kist her lips last, and carefully laid up that body the soule being with Jesus it rests there till the resurrection.

16 [June]: God was in many outward mercies exceeding good to mee and mine, my deare wife somewhat faint and weakely but cheerfull, god helpes us under our great losses I am sometimes ready to bee overwhelmed in remembrance of my deare Mary . . .

⌣

The Distress'd Father or, the Author's Tears over his Dear Darling Rachel

Henry Carey, c. 1687–1743

Oh! lead me where my Darling lies,
Cold as the Marble Stone;
I will recall her with my Cries,
And wake her with my Moan.

Come from thy Bed of Clay, my dear!
See! where thy Father stands;
His Soul he sheds out Tear by Tear,
And wrings his wretched Hands.

But ah! alas! thou canst not rise,
Alas! thou canst not hear,
Or, at thy tender Father's Cries,
Thou surely wouldst appear.

Since then my Love! my Soul's delight!
Thou canst not come to me,
Rather than want thy pleasing sight,
I'll dig my way to thee.

✑

On My First Son

Ben Jonson, 1572–1637

Farewell, thou child of my right hand, and joy;
My sin was too much hope of thee, loved boy:
Seven years thou wert lent to me, and I thee pay,
Exacted by thy fate, on the just day.
O could I lose all father now! for why
Will man lament the state he should envy,
To have so soon 'scaped world's and flesh's rage,
And, if no other misery, yet age?
Rest in soft peace, and asked, say, 'Here doth lie
Ben Jonson his best piece of poetry.'
For whose sake henceforth all his vows be such
As what he loves may never like too much.

✑

Three Years She Grew

William Wordsworth, 1770–1850

Three years she grew in sun and shower,
Then Nature said, 'A lovelier flower
On earth was never sown;
This Child I to myself will take;
She shall be mine, and I will make
A Lady of my own.

'Myself will to my darling be
Both law and impulse: and with me
The Girl, in rock and plain,
In earth and heaven, in glade and bower,
Shall feel an overseeing power
To kindle or restrain.

'She shall be sportive as the fawn
That wild with glee across the lawn
Or up the mountain springs;
And hers shall be the breathing balm,
And hers the silence and the calm
Of mute insensate things.

'The floating clouds their state shall lend
To her; for her the willow bend;
Nor shall she fail to see
Even in the motions of the Storm
Grace that shall mould the Maiden's form
By silent sympathy.

'The stars of midnight shall be dear
To her; and she shall lean her ear
In many a secret place
Where rivulets dance their wayward round,
And beauty born of murmuring sound
Shall pass into her face.

'And vital feelings of delight,
Shall rear her form to stately height,
Her virgin bosom swell;
Such thoughts to Lucy I will give
While she and I together live
Here in this happy dell.'

Thus Nature spake – the work was done –
How soon my Lucy's race was run!
She died, and left to me
This health, this calm, and quiet scene;
The memory of what has been,
And never more will be.

The Death of Jean

Mark Twain, 1911

Stormfield, Christmas Eve, *11 a.m., 1909. – Jean is dead!*

Has any one ever tried to put upon paper all the little happenings connected with a dear one – happenings of the twenty-four hours preceding the sudden and unexpected death of that dear one? Would a book contain them? would two books contain them? I think not. They pour into the mind in a flood. They are little things that have been always happening every day, and were always so unimportant and easily forgettable before – but now! Now, how different! how precious they are, how dear, how unforgettable, how pathetic, how sacred, how clothed with dignity!

Last night Jean, all flushed with splendid health, and I the same, from the wholesome effects of my Bermuda holiday, strolled hand in hand from the dinner table and sat down in the library and chatted, and planned, and discussed, cheerily and happily (and how unsuspectingly!) until nine – which is late for us – then went upstairs, Jean's friendly German dog following. At my door Jean said, 'I can't kiss you good night, father: I have a cold, and you could cath it.' I bent and kissed her hand. She was moved – saw it in her eyes – and she impulsively kissed my hand in return. Then with the usual gay 'Sleep well, dear!' from both, we parted.

At half past seven this morning I woke, and heard voices outside my door. I said to myself, 'Jean is starting on her usual horseback flight to the station for the mail.' Then Katy entered, stood quaking and gasping at my bedside a moment, then found her tongue:

'Miss Jean is dead!'

Possibly I know now what the soldier feels when a bullet crashes through his heart.

In her bath-room there she lay, the fair young creature, stretched upon the floor and covered with a sheet. And looking so placid, so natural, and as if asleep. We knew what had happened. She was an epileptic: she had been seized with a convulsion and heart failure in her bath. The doctor had to come several miles. His efforts, like our previous ones, failed to bring her back to life.

It is noon, now. How lovable she looks, how sweet and how tranquil! It is a noble face, and full of dignity; and that was a good heart that lies there so still . . .

There was never a kinder heart than Jean's. From her childhood up she always spent the most of her allowance on charities of one kind and another. After she became secretary and had her income doubled she spent her money upon these things with a free hand. Mine too, I am glad and grateful to say.

She was a loyal friend to all animals, and she loved them all, birds, beasts, and everything – even snakes – an inheritance from me. She knew all the birds: she was high up in that lore. She became a member of various humane socieites when she was still a little girl – both here and abroad – and she remained an active member to the last. She founded two or three societies for the protection of animals, here and in Europe.

She was an embarrassing secretary, for she fished my correspondence out of the waste-basket and answered the letters. She thought all letters deserved the courtesy of an answer. Her mother brought her up in that kindly error.

She could write a good letter, and was swift with her pen. She had but an indifferent ear for music, but her tongue took to languages with an easy facility. She never allowed her Italian, French and German to get rusty through neglect.

The telegrams of sympathy are flowing in, from far and wide, now, just as they did in Italy five years and a half ago, when this child's mother laid down her blameless life. They cannot heal the hurt, but they take away some of the pain. When Jean and I kissed hands and parted at my door last, how little did we imagine that in twenty-two hours the telegraph would be bringing words like these:

'From the bottom of our hearts we send our sympathy, dearest of friends.'

For many and many a day to come, wherever I go in this house, rememberancers of Jean will mutely speak to me of her. Who can count the number of them?

She was in exile two years with the hope of healing her malady – epilepsy. There are no words to express how grateful I am that she did not meet her fate in the hands of strangers, but in the loving shelter of her own home.

'Miss Jean is dead!'

It is true. Jean is dead.

A month ago I was writing bubbling and hilarious articles for magazines yet to appear, and now I am writing – this.

6

Patrimony

Echoing down the ages

Jean-Paul Richter, 1763–1825

The words a father speaks to his children in the privacy of the home are not heard at the time, but, as in whispering galleries, they will be clearly heard at the end and by posterity.

Heracles' last words to his son

From *Sophocles: Women of Trachis*, translated by Ezra Pound, 1956

HERAKLES: Listen first, and show what you're made of,
my stock. My father told me long ago
that no living man should kill me,
but that someone from hell would, and
that brute of a Centaur has done it.
The dead beast kills the living me.
And that fits another odd forecast
breathed out at the Selloi's oak –
Those fellows rough it,
sleep on the ground, up in the hills there.
I heard it and wrote it down
under my Father's tree.
Time lives, and it's going on now.
I am released from trouble.

I thought it meant life in comfort.
It doesn't. It means that I die.
For amid the dead there is no work in service.
Come at it that way, my boy, what

SPLENDOUR,
IT ALL COHERES.

His father's voice

From Tony Parsons, *Man and Boy*, 1999

It was a brochure like any other – tastefully shot, beautifully presented – and the undertaker gently led me through it, starting with the cheapest, simplest pine numbers, going right up to the top of the range model, a large hardwood coffin lined with red satiny material and adorned with big brass handles.

My first instinct was to go for the most expensive one – let's push the boat out, nothing's too good for my old man. But my second instinct was that the top of the range coffin was just a touch too elaborate for my dad to sleep in for all eternity.

I hesitated, and told the undertaker that we would go for the second most expensive coffin. And when Uncle Jack and I were back on the street, I was pleased with my choice.

'Your old man would have had a fit at that posh coffin,' my Uncle Jack grinned.

'The most expensive one?' I smiled. 'Yeah, I thought that was a bit much.'

'Gold handles and a red velvet lining!' chuckled Uncle Jack. 'It looked more like a French knocking shop than a coffin!'

'Talk about turning in your grave,' I laughed. 'I know what he would have said if we'd gone for that one – "*Who do you think I am? Bloody Napoleon?*"'

I could hear his voice.

I would never hear his voice again.

I would always hear him.

◠

To *thine own self be true*

Polonius to his son, Laertes, from Shakespeare's *Hamlet*, Act I, Scene 3, written *c.* 1599

POLONIUS: Look thou character. Give thy thoughts no tongue,
Nor any unproportion'd thought his act.
Be thou familiar, but by no means vulgar.
Those friends thou hast, and their adoption tried,

Grapple them to thy soul with hoops of steel.
But do not dull thy palm with entertainment
Of each new-hatch'd, unfledg'd courage. Beware
Of entrance to a quarrel. But, being in,
Bear't that th' opposed may beware of thee.
Give every man thine ear, but few thy voice.
Take each man's censure, but reserve thy judgment.
Costly thy habit as thy purse can buy,
But not express'd in fancy; rich, not gaudy;
For the apparel oft proclaims the man,
And they in France of the best rank and station
Are of a most select and generous chief in that.
Neither a borrower nor a lender be,
For loan oft loses both itself and friend,
And borrowing dulls the edge of husbandry.
This above all: to thine own self be true,
And it must follow, as the night the day,
Thou canst not then be false to any man.

Blessing

The exiled Walter de la Pole, Duke of Suffolk, writes
to his son, April 1450

Dear and only well-beloved Son,
I beseech our Lord in Heaven, the Maker of all the World, to
bless you, and to send you ever grace to love him, and to dread
him, to the which, as far as a Father may charge his child, I both
charge you, and pray you to set all your spirits and wits to do,
and to know his Holy Laws and Commandments, by the which
ye shall, with his great mercy, pass all the great tempests and
troubles of this wretched world.

And that, also weetingly, ye do nothing for love nor dread of
any earthly creature that should displease him. And there as any
Frailty maketh you to fall, beseech his mercy soon to call you to
him again with repentance, satisfaction, and contrition of your
heart, never more in will to offend him.

Secondly, next him above all earthly things, to be true Liege man in heart, in will, in thought, in deed, unto the King our alder-most high and dread Sovereign Lord, to whom both ye and I be much bound to; charging you, as Father can and may, rather to die than to be contrary, or to know any thing that were against the welfare or prosperity of his most Royal Person, but that as far as your body and life may stretch, ye live and die to defend it, and to let his Highness have knowledge thereof in all the haste ye can.

Thirdly, in the same wise, I charge you, my dear Son, alway as ye be bounden by the Commandment of God to do, to love, to worship, your Lady and Mother; and also that ye obey always her commandments, and to believe her counsels and advices in all your works, the which dread not but shall be best and truest to you.

And if any other body would steer you to the contrary, to flee the counsel in any wise, for ye shall find it nought and evil.

Furthermore, as far as Father may and can, I charge you in any wise to flee the company and counsel of proud men, of covetous men, and of flattering men, the more especially and mightily to withstand them, and not to draw nor to meddle with them, with all your might and power; and to draw to you and to your company good and virtuous men, and such as be of good conversation, and of truth, and by them shall ye never be deceived nor repent you of.

Moreover, never follow your own wit in no wise; but in all your works, of such folks as I write of above, ask your advice and counsel, and doing thus, with the mercy of God, ye shall do right well, and live in right much worship, and great heart's rest and ease.

And I will be to you as good Lord and Father as my heart can think.

And last of all, as heartily and as lovingly as ever Father blessed his child in earth I give you the Blessing of Our Lord and of me, which of his infinite mercy increase you in all virtue and good living; and that your Blood may by his grace from kindred to kindred multiply in this earth to his service, in such wise as after the departing from this wretched world here, ye and they may glorify him eternally amongst his Angels in heaven.

Written of mine hand,
The day of my departing from this Land,
Your true and loving Father,
Suffolk

The ABC of goodness

Samuel Taylor Coleridge to his son Derwent,
aged seven

Ashby de la Zouch, Coleorton,
Saturday night, 7 Feb. 1807.

My dear Derwent,

It will be many times the number of years, you have already lived, before you can know and feel thoroughly, how very much your dear Father wishes and longs to have you on his knees, and in his arms. Your Brother, Hartley, too whirls about, and wrings his hands at the thought of meeting you again: he counts the days and hours, and makes sums of arithmetic of the time, when he is again to play with you, and your sweet squirrel of a Sister. He dreams of you, and has more than once hugged me between waking and sleeping, fancying it to be you or Sara: and he talks of you before his eyes are fully open in the morning, and while he is closing them at night. And this is very right: for nothing can be more pleasing to God Almighty and to all good people, than that Brothers and Sisters should love each other, and try to make each other happy; but it is impossible to be happy without being good, and the beginning and the ABC of goodness is to be dutiful and affectionate to their Parents; to be obedient to them, when they are present, and to pray for them [and to write] frequent letters from a thankful and loving heart when both or either of them chance to be absent. For you are a big Thought, and take up a great deal of room in your Father's Heart: and his eyes are often full of tears thro' his Love of you, and his Forehead wrinkled from the labour of his Brain, planning to make you good, and wise and happy. And your *Mother* has fed and cloathed and taught you, day after day, all your life; and has passed many sleepless nights, watching and lulling you, when you were sick and helpless, and she gave *you* nourishment out of her own Breasts for so long a time, that the moon was at its least and its greatest sixteen times before you lived entirely on any other food, than what came out of her body, and she brought you into the world with shocking Pains, which she suffered for you, and before you were born for eight months together every drop of blood in your body, first beat in *her* Pulses and throbbed in *her* Heart. So it must needs be a horribly wicked thing ever to forget, or wilfully to vex a Father or a Mother, especially a Mother. God is above all: and only good and dutiful children can say their Lord's Prayer, and say to God, '*our Father*,' without being wicked even in their Prayers. But after God's name, the name of Mother is the sweetest and most holy. The next good thing and that without which you cannot either honour any person, or be esteemed by anyone, is *always to tell the truth*. For God gave you a tongue to tell the Truth, and to tell a Lie with it is as silly, as to try to walk on your Head instead of your Feet; besides it is such a base, hateful, and wicked thing, that when good men describe all wickedness put together in one wicked mind, they call it the Devil, which is Greek for *malicious Liar*: and the Bible names him a *Liar* from the beginning, and the Father of *Lies*. Never, never, tell a Lie – even tho' you should escape a whipping by it; for the pain of a whipping does not last above a few minutes, and the Thought of having told a Lie would make you miserable for days – unless, indeed, you are hardened in wickedness and then you must be miserable for ever –

But you are a dear Boy, and will scorn such a vile thing: and whenever you happen to do anything amiss, which *will* happen now and then, you will say to yourself 'Well whatever comes of it, I will *tell the Truth*, both for its own sake, and because my dear Father [spoke] and wrote so to me about it.'

I am greatly delighted that you are desirous to go on with your Greek; and shall finish this letter with a short Lesson of Greek. But more cannot be done till we meet, when we will begin anew, and, I trust, not to leave off, till you are a good scholar. And now go, and give a loving kiss to your little sister and tell her, that Papa sent it to her: and will give hundreds in a little time: for I am, my dear Child,

Your affectionate Father
S. T. Coleridge

P. S. I find that I cannot write in this space what I wished – therefore I will send you, dear child! a whole sheet of Greek Lessons in a few days.

One in ten

Report in *The Daily Telegraph*, November 1996

A new British Social Attitudes survey . . . shows that lack of contact with fathers is relatively high in adult life.

The survey, of more than 2,000 people, reveals that around one adult in 10 never sees his or her father. This compares with one in 33 who had no contact with his or her mother.

~

It makes you blind

Letter from John Evelyn to his son, November 1679,
on the eve of the latter's marriage

. . . Take heed of those filthy lusts even with your own wife, nor delight to feed and satisfy your eyes or incite your fancy with nakedness, or unnatural figures & usages of yourselves, for they will breed impudence, loathing and contempt. . . . be none of those who brag how frequently they can be brutes in one night, for that intemperance will exhaust you, & possibly create importunate expectations when your inclinations are not so fierce. Such excesses do oft times dispose to . . . inconveniences through the straining of nature . . . which are sometimes incurable. . . .

It is likewise experimentally found that carnal caresses upon a full stomach, or in the daytime, or in the excessive heat and cold of weather are very pernicious, & too much frequency of embraces dulls the sight, decays the memory, induces the gout, palsies, enervates and renders effeminate the whole body & shortens life.

There should therefore repose succeed upon those wasting exercises, & therefore physicians permit it after the first concoction is made, namely the first sleep; but rarely in the morning, never totally fasting, as indisposing the body the whole day after.

These particulars I only touch, knowing that young married people will hardly be reasoned into that temperance, & perhaps they are to be indulged some liberties for a time, especially at first, But it is profitable to know these things once, and much better to use moderation. . . . I do not by these abridge you therefore any decent satisfaction; a man may eat . . . not only to satisfy hunger, but to cheer him, & if there were not some gratification of the inferior sense accompanying this & other natural action, the world would cease.

~

A *declaration for dependence*

Letter from Thomas Jefferson to his daughter
Martha, 28 November 1783

The acquirements which I hope you will make under the tutors I have provided for you will render you more worthy of my love, and if they cannot increase it they will prevent its diminution. Consider the good lady who has taken you under her roof, who has undertaken to see that you perform all your exercises, and to admonish you in all those wanderings from what is right or what is clever to which your inexperience would expose you, consider her I say as your mother, as the only person to whom, since the loss with which heaven has been pleased to afflict you, you can now look up; and that her displeasure or disapprobation on any occasion will be an immense misfortune which should you be so unhappy as to incur by any unguarded act, think no concession too much to regain her good will. With respect to the distribution of your time the following is what I should approve.

from 8. to 10 o'clock practise music.

from 10. to 1. dance one day and draw another

from 1. to 2. draw on the day you dance, and write a letter the next day.

from 3. to 4. read French.

from 4. to 5. exercise yourself in music.

from 5. till bedtime read English, write &c.

Strive to be good under every situation and to all living creatures, and to acquire those accomplishments which I have put in your power, and which will go far towards ensuring you the warmest love of your affectionate father.

P. S. Keep my letters and read them at times that you may

always have present in your mind those things which will endear you to me.

⌐⌐

Advice to a son about to depart America

Benjamin and Julia Rush to Jonathan Rush

Directions and advice to Jno. Rush from his father and mother composed the evening before he sailed for Calcutta, May 18th, 1796.

We shall divide these directions into four heads, as they relate to *morals, knowledge, health* and *business.*

I. MORALS

1. Be punctual in committing your soul and body to the protection of your Creator every morning and evening. Implore at the same time his mercy in the name of his Son, our Lord and Saviour Jesus Christ.
2. Read in your Bible frequently, more especially on Sundays.
3. Avoid swearing and even an irreverent use of your Creator's name. *Flee* youthful lusts.
4. Be courteous and gentle in your behaviour to your fellow passengers, and respectful and obedient to the captain of the vessel.
5. Attend public worship regularly every Sunday when you arrive at Calcutta.

II. KNOWLEDGE

1. Begin by studying Guthrie's *Geography.*
2. Read your other books *through* carefully, and converse daily upon the subjects of your reading.
3. Keep a diary of every day's studies, conversations, and transactions at sea and on shore. Let it be composed in a fair, legible hand. Insert in it an account of the population, manners, climate, diseases, &c., of the places you visit.
4. Preserve an account of every person's name and disease whom you attend.

III. HEALTH

1. Be temperate in eating, more especially of animal food. Never *taste* distilled spirits of any kind, and drink fermented liquors very sparingly.

2. Avoid the night air in sickly situations. Let your dress be rather warmer than the weather would seem to require. Carefully avoid fatigue from all causes both of body and mind.

IV. BUSINESS

1. Take no step in laying out your money without the advice and consent of the captain or supercargo.

2. Keep an exact account of all your expenditures. Preserve as vouchers of them all your bills.

3. Take care of all your instruments, books, clothes, &c.

Be sober and vigilant. Remember at all times that while you are seeing the world, the world will see you. Recollect further that you are always under the eye of the Supreme Being. One more consideration shall close this parting testimony of our affection. Whenever you are tempted to do an improper thing, fancy that you see your father and mother kneeling before you and imploring you with tears in their eyes to refrain yielding to the temptation, and assuring you at the same time that your yielding to it will be the means of hurrying them to a premature grave.

~~

Make yourself a delight to all eyes that behold you

Jack London to his daughter, 16 September 1915

Glen Ellen, California

Dear Joan,

First of all, I had Aunt Eliza send you the cheque for $7.00 so that you might buy the two pairs of boots for yourself and Bess.

Second of all, I promised to reply to your letter.

Third of all, and very important, please remember that your Daddy is a very busy man. When you write to society people, or to young people, who have plenty of time, write on your fine stationery and write on both sides of the paper. But, please, when you write to Daddy, take any kind of paper, the cheapest paper for that matter, and write on one side only. This makes it ever so much easier for Daddy to read. A two-sheet letter, such as yours that I am now looking at, written on both sides, is like a Chinese puzzle to a busy man. I take more time trying to find my way from one of the four portions into which your two-sided sheet is divided than I do in reading the letter itself.

Some day I should like to see your French heeled slippers. Joan, you are on the right track. Never hesitate at making yourself a dainty, delightful girl and woman. There is a girl's pride and a woman's pride in this, and it is indeed a fine pride. On the one hand, of course, never over-dress. On the other hand, never be a frump. No matter how wonderful are the thoughts that burn in your brain, always, physically, and in dress, make yourself a delight to all eyes that behold you.

I have met a number of philosophers. They were real philosophers. Their minds were wonderful minds. But they did not take baths, and they did not change their socks and it almost turned one's stomach to sit at table with them.

Our bodies are as glorious as our minds, and, just as one cannot maintain a high mind in a filthy body, by the same token one cannot keep a high mind and high pride when said body is not dressed beautifully, delightfully, charmingly. Nothing would your Daddy ask better of you in this world than that you have a high mind, a high pride, a fine body, and, just as all the rest, a beautifully dressed body.

⌐⌐

The good news

Extracted from Thomas Fuller,
Scripture Observations, 1645

Rehoboam begat Abiam: a bad father begat a bad son. Abiam begat Asa: a bad father a good son. Asa begat Jehoshaphat: a good father a good son. Jehoshaphat begat Joram: a good father a bad son. I see, Lord, from hence, that my father's piety cannot be entailed; that is bad news for me. But I see also that actual impiety is not always hereditary; that is good news for my son.

⌒

Advice to a son

Ernest Hemingway, Berlin, 1931

Never trust a white man,
Never kill a Jew,
Never sign a contract,
Never rent a pew.
Don't enlist in armies;
Nor marry many wives;
Never write for magazines;
Never scratch your hives.
Always put paper on the seat,
Don't believe in wars,
Keep yourself both clean and neat,
Never marry whores.
Never pay a blackmailer,
Never go to law,
Never trust a publisher,
Or you'll sleep on straw.
All your friends will leave you
All your friends will die
So lead a clean and wholesome life
And join them in the sky.

⌒

Paternity and ambition

From Bertrand Russell, *Marriage and Morals*, 1929

As soon as the physiological fact of paternity is recognised, a quite new element enters into paternal feeling, an element which has led almost everywhere to the creation of patriarchal societies. As soon as a father recognises that the child is, as the Bible says, his 'seed', his sentiment towards the child is reinforced by two factors, the love of power and the des survive death. The achievements of a man's descendants are in a sense his achievements, and their life is a continuation of his life. Ambition no longer finds its termination at the grave, but can be indefinitely extended through the careers of descendants. Consider, for example, the satisfaction of Abraham when he is informed that his seed shall possess the land of Canaan. In a matrilineal society, family ambition would have to be confined to women, and as women do not do the fighting, such family ambition as they may have has less effect than that of men. One must suppose, therefore, that the discovery of fatherhood would make human society more competitive, more energetic, more dynamic and hustling than it had been in the matrilineal stage.

Shit

From Philip Roth, *Patrimony*, 1991

We were drinking our coffee when it occurred to me that he was still gone. I quietly left the table and, while the others were talking, slipped into the house, certain that he was dead.

He wasn't, though he might well have been wishing that he were.

I smelled the shit halfway up the stairs to the second floor. When I got to his bathroom, the door was ajar, and on the floor of the corridor outside the bathroom were his dungarees and his undershorts. Standing inside the bathroom door was my father, completely naked, just out of the shower and dripping wet. The smell was overwhelming.

At the sight of me he came close to bursting into tears. In a voice as forlorn as any I had ever heard, from him or anyone, he told me what it hadn't been difficult to surmise. 'I beshat myself,' he said.

The shit was everywhere, smeared underfoot on the bathmat, running over the toilet bowl edge and, at the foot of the bowl, in a pile on the floor. It was splattered across the glass of the shower stall from which he'd just emerged, and the clothes discarded in the hallway were clotted with it. It was on the corner of the towel he had started to dry himself with. In this smallish bathroom, which was ordinarily mine, he had done his best to extricate himself from his mess alone, but as he was nearly blind and just up out of a hospital bed, in undressing himself and getting into the shower he had managed to spread the shit over everything. I saw that it was even on the tips of the bristles of my toothbrush hanging in the holder over the sink.

'It's okay,' I said, 'it's okay, everything is going to be okay.'

I reached into the shower stall and turned the water back on and fiddled with the taps until it was the right temperature. Taking the towel out of his hand, I helped him back under the shower.

'Take the soap and start from scratch,' I said, and while he obediently began again to soap his body all over, I gathered his clothes and the towels and the bathmat together in a heap and went down the hall to the linen closet and got a pillowcase to dump them in. I also found a fresh bath towel for him. Then I got him out of the shower and took him straight into the hallway where the floor was still clean, and wrapped him up in the towel and began to dry him. 'You made a valiant effort,' I said, 'but I'm afraid it was a no-win situation.'

'I beshat myself,' he said, and this time he dissolved in tears.

I got him into his bedroom, where he sat on the edge of the bed and continued to towel himself while I went off and got a terry-cloth robe of mine. When he was dry I helped him into the robe and then pulled back the top sheet of the bed and told him to get in and take a nap.

'Don't tell the children,' he said, looking up at me from the bed with his one sighted eye.

'I won't tell anyone,' I said. 'I'll say you're taking a rest.'

'Don't tell Claire.'

'Nobody,' I said. 'Don't worry about it. It could have happened to anyone. Just forget about it and get a good rest.'

I lowered the shades to darken the room and closed the door behind me.

The bathroom looked as though some spiteful thug had left his calling card after having robbed the house. As my father was tended to and he was what counted, I would just as soon have nailed the door shut and forgotten that bathroom for ever. 'It's like writing a book,' I thought – 'I have no idea where to begin.' But I stepped gingerly across the floor and reached out and threw

open the window, which was a start. Then I went down the back
stairway to the kitchen, and keeping out of sight of Seth and
Ruth and Claire, who were still in the summer room talking, I
got a bucket, a brush, and a box of Spic and Span from the
cabinet under the sink and two rolls of paper towels and came
back upstairs to the bathroom.

Where his shit lay in front of the toilet bowl in what was more
or less a contiguous mass, it was easiest to get rid of. Just scoop
it up and flush it away. And the shower door and the windowsill
and the sink and the soap dish and the light fixtures and the
towel bars were no problem. Lots of paper towels and lots of
soap. But where it had lodged in the narrow, uneven crevices of
the floor, between the wide old chestnut planks, I had my work
cut out for me. The scrub brush seemed only to make things
worse, and eventually I took down my toothbrush and, dipping
it in and out of the bucket of hot sudsy water, proceeded inch
by inch, from wall to wall, one crevice at a time, until the floor
was as clean as I could get it. After some fifteen minutes on my
knees, I decided that flecks and particles down so deep that I still
couldn't reach them we would simply all live with. I removed
the curtain from the window, even though it looked to be clean,
and shoved it in the pillowcase with all the other soiled things,
and then I went into Claire's bathroom and got some eau de
cologne, which I sprinkled freely over the swabbed and scoured
room, flicking it off my fingertips like holy water. I set up a small
summer fan in one corner and got it going, and I went back to
Claire's bathroom and washed my arms and my hands and my
face. There was a little shit in my hair, so I washed that out, too.

I tiptoed back into the bedroom where he was asleep, still
breathing, still living, still with me – yet another setback outlasted
by this man whom I had known unendingly as my father. I felt
awful about his heroic, hapless struggle to cleanse himself before
I had got up to the bathroom and about the shame of it, the
disgrace he felt himself to be, and yet now that it was over and
he was so deep in sleep, I thought I couldn't have asked anything
more for myself before he died – this, too, was right and as it
should be. You clean up your father's shit because it has to be
cleaned up, but in the aftermath of cleaning it up, everything
that's there to feel is felt as it never was before. It wasn't the first
time that I'd understood this either: once you sidestep disgust

and ignore nausea and plunge past those phobias that are forti-
fied like taboos, there's an awful lot of life to cherish.

Though maybe once is enough, I added, addressing myself
mentally to the sleeping brain squeezed in by the cartilaginous
tumour; if I have to do this every day, I may not wind up feeling
quite so thrilled.

I carried the stinking pillowcase downstairs and put it into a
black garbage bag which I tied shut, and I carried the bag out
to the car and dumped it in the trunk to take to the laundry.
And *why* this was right and as it should be couldn't have been
plainer to me, now that the job was done. So *that* was the patrimony. And not because cleaning it up was symbolic of something
else but because it wasn't, because it was nothing less or more
than the lived reality that it was.

There was my patrimony: not the money, not the tefillin, not
the shaving mug, but the shit.

The four commandments

G. I. Gurdjieff, *Meetings with Remarkable Men*,
1963

My father had a very simple, clear, and quite definite view on
the aim of human life. He told me many times in my youth that
the fundamental striving of every man should be to create for
himself an inner freedom toward life and to prepare for himself
a happy old age. He considered that the indispensability and
imperative necessity of this aim in life was so obvious that it
ought to be understandable to everyone without any wiseacring.
But a man could attain this aim only if, from childhood up to
the age of eighteen, he had acquired data for the unwavering
fulfilment of the following four commandments:

First – To love one's parents.
Second – To remain chaste.
Third – To be outwardly courteous to all without distinction,
whether they be rich or poor, friends or enemies, power-possessors
or slaves, and to whatever religion they may belong, but inwardly

to remain free and never to put much trust in anyone or anything.

Fourth – To love work for work's sake and not for its gain.

My father, who loved me particularly as his first-born, had a great influence on me.

My personal relationship to him was not as toward a father, but as toward an elder brother; and he, by his constant conversations with me and his extraordinary stories, greatly assisted the arising in me of poetic images and high ideals.

~~

Aristocratic advice

Lord Chesterfield to his son, 15 July 1751

My dear Friend,

As this is the last, or the last letter but one, that I think I shall write before I have the pleasure of seeing you here, it may not be amiss to prepare you a little for our interview, and for the time we shall pass together. Before kings and princes meet, ministers on each side adjust the important points of precedence, arm-chairs, right hand and left, etc., so that they know previously what they are to expect, what they have to trust to: and it is right they should; for they commonly envy or hate, but most certainly distrust each other. We shall meet upon very different terms; we want no such preliminaries: you know my tenderness, I know your affection. My only object, therefore, is to make your short stay with me as useful as I can to you; and yours, I hope, is to co-operate with me. Whether, by making it wholesome, I shall make it pleasant to you, I am not sure. Emetics and cathartics I shall not administer, because I am sure you do not want them; but for alteratives you must expect a great many; and I can tell you, that I have a number of *nostrums*, which I shall communicate to nobody but yourself. To speak without a metaphor, I shall endeavour to assist your youth with all the experience that I have purchased at the price of seven and fifty years. In order to this, frequent reproofs, corrections, and admonitions will be necessary; but then, I promise you, that they shall be in a gentle, friendly, and secret manner; they shall not put you

out of countenance in company, nor out of humour when we are
alone. I do not expect that at nineteen, you should have that
knowledge of the world, those manners, that dexterity, which
few people have at nine and twenty. But I will endeavour to give
them you; and I am sure you will endeavour to learn them, as
far as your youth, my experience, and the time we shall pass
together, will allow. You may have many inaccuracies (and to be
sure you have, for who has not at your age?) which few people
will tell you of, and some nobody can tell you of but myself.
You may possibly have others, too, which eyes less interested,
and less vigilant than mine, do not discover: all those you shall
hear of from one whose tenderness for you will excite his curiosity
and sharpen his penetration. The smallest inattention, or error
in manners, the minutest inelegancy of diction, the least awkward-
ness in your dress and carriage, will not escape my observation,
nor pass without amicable correction . . .

As fathers commonly go, it is seldom a misfortune to be fatherless; and considering the general run of sons, as seldom a misfortune to be childless. You and I form, I believe, an exception to
that rule; for I am persuaded that we would neither of us change
our relation, were it in our power. You will, I both hope and
believe, be not only the comfort, but the pride of my age; and I
am sure I will be the support, the friend, the guide of your youth.
Trust me without reserve; I will advise you without private
interest, or secret envy. Mr Harte will do so too; but still there
may be some little things proper for you to know, and necessary
for you to correct, which even his friendship would not let him
tell you of so freely as I should; and some of which he may
possibly not be so good a judge of as I am, not having lived so
much in the great world.

One principal topic of our conversation will be, not only the
purity but the elegancy of the English language; in both which
you are very deficient. Another will be the constitution of this
country, of which, I believe, you know less of than of most other
countries in Europe. Manners, attentions and address, will also
be the frequent subjects of our lectures; and whatever I know of
that important and necessary art, the art of pleasing, I will unre-
servedly communicate to you. Dress too (which, as things are, I
can logically prove, requires some attention) will not always
escape our notice. Thus, my lectures will be more various, and

in some respects more useful, than Professor Mascow's; and therefore, I can tell you, that I expect to be paid for them; but, as
possibly you would not care to part with your ready money, and
as I do not think that it would be quite handsome in me to accept
it, I will compound for the payment, and take it in attention and
practice.

Pray remember to part with all your friends, acquaintances,
and mistresses, if you have any, at Paris, in such a manner as
may make them not only willing but impatient to see you there
again. Assure them of your desire of returning to them; and do
it in a manner that they may think you in earnest, that is *avec
onction et une espèce d'attendrissement* All people say pretty
nearly the same things upon those occasions; it is the manner
only that makes the difference; and that difference is great.

Don't bet on it

Charles Kingsley to one of his sons away at boarding
school, *c.* 1860

My dearest Boy,
There is a matter which gave me great uneasiness when you
mentioned it. You said you had put into some lottery for the
Derby and had hedged to make it safe.

Now all this is bad, bad, nothing but bad. Of all the habits
gambling is the one I hate most and have avoided most. Of all
habits it grows most on eager minds. Success and loss alike make
it grow. Of all habits, however much civilised man may give way
to it, it is one of the most intrinsically *savage*. Historically it has
been the peace excitement of the lowest brutes in human form
for ages past. Morally it is unchivalrous and unchristian.

1. It gains money by the lowest and most unjust means, for
   it takes money out of your neighbour's pocket without
   giving him anything in return.
2. It tempts you to use what you fancy your superior knowledge of a horse's merits – or anything else – to your neighbour's harm.

If you know better than your neighbour, you are bound to give him your advice. Instead, you conceal your knowledge to win from his ignorance; hence come all sorts of concealments, dodges, deceits – I say the Devil is the only father of it. I'm sure, moreover, that B. would object seriously to anything like a lottery, betting, or gambling.

I hope you have not won. I should not be sorry for you to lose. If you have won I should not congratulate you. If you wish to please me, you will give back to its lawful owners the money you have won. If you are a loser in gross thereby, I will gladly reimburse your losses this time. As you had put in you could not in honour draw back till after the event. Now you can give back your money, saying you understand that Mr B. and your father disapprove of such things, and so gain a very great moral influence.

Recollect always that the stock argument is worthless. It is this: 'My friend would win from me if he could, *therefore* I have an equal right to win from him.' Nonsense. The same argument would prove that I have a right to maim or kill a man if only I give him leave to maim or kill me if he can and will.

I have spoken my mind once and for all on a matter on which I have held the same views for more than twenty years, and trust in God you will not forget my words in after life. I have seen many a good fellow ruined by finding himself one day short of money, and trying to get a little by playing or betting – and then the Lord have mercy on his simple soul for simple it will not remain long.

Mind, I am not in the least *angry* with you. Betting is the way of the world. So are all the seven deadly sins under certain rules and pretty names, but to the Devil they lead if indulged in, in spite of the wise world and its ways.

Your loving,
Pater

ᴄ

The Marxist theory of seduction

Letter from Groucho Marx to his son, Summer, 1940

Dear Arthur,

Glad to hear from you and to know that you are recovering. I am also pleased to learn that you have a rich dame who wants to put you up while you are recuperating. How does she have her money? – Is it in jewels or securities, or just plain gold? Some night, when you are grappling with her in the moonlight, you might find out. Do it discreetly, for God's sake. Don't come out bluntly and say, 'How much dough have you got?' That wouldn't be the Marxian way. Use finesse. Well, I will leave the whole thing to you.

Love,
Padre

Three little sentences that will get you through life

Advice from the supposedly dying Homer Simpson to son Bart in *The Simpsons*, episode 'One Fish, Two Fish, Blowfish, Blue Fish', 1991

Homer to Bart: '. . . Three little sentences that will get your through life . . . Number 1: (whispers) Cover for me. Number 2: Oh, good idea, Boss! Number 3: It was like that when I got here.'

In your dreams

From Sigmund Freud, *The Interpretation of Dreams*, 1913

The fact that dreams of a dead father were the first to furnish us with examples of absurdity in dreams is by no means accidental. The conditions for the creation of absurd dreams are here grouped together in a typical fashion. The authority proper to the father has at an early age evoked the criticism of the child, and the strict demands which he has made have caused the child, in self-defence, to pay particularly close attention to every weakness of his father's; but the piety with which the father's personality is surrounded in our thoughts, especially after his death, intensifies the censorship which prevents the expression of this criticism from becoming conscious.

Starlight memory

Samuel Taylor Coleridge, aged eight in 1780

My father was fond of me, & used to take me on his knee, and hold long conversations with me. I remember, that at eight years old I walked with him one winter evening from a farmer's house, a mile from Ottery – & he told me the names of the stars – and how Jupiter was a thousand times larger than our world – and that the other twinkling stars were Suns that had worlds rolling round them – & when I came home, he showed me how they rolled round . . . I heard him with a profound delight & admiration.

⌒

Awakening

From James Dodson, *Final Rounds*, 1997

Eventually, when I calmed down and grew up, golf became much more than a game between my old man and me. It acted as my personal entry hatch to my father's morally advanced cosmos – a means of seeing who this funky, funny, oddball philosopher really *was*, and who I needed to become. I know no other game that would have permitted us the opportunity to compete so thoroughly, so joyfully, for so long. The golf course – any golf course, anywhere – became our playground and refuge, the place where we sorted things out or escaped them altogether, debated without rancor, found common ground, discovered joy, suspended grief, competed like crazy, and took each other's pocket change.

We played the day Neil Armstrong walked on the moon, and the day Martin Luther King was gunned down in Memphis. We played the day before I got married, and the day after my son Jack was born. We played through rain, wind, heat, birth, death. We played on holidays, birthdays, to celebrate nothing and everything, so many rounds in so many places, I couldn't possibly remember them all. We played some of the best courses in America, and some of the worst cow pastures and goat tracks, too. We discovered that in good company there is no such thing as a bad golf course.

We preferred to play late in the day, following our shadows in the last of the light, the fairway ahead of us robed in hues of red and gold and very often deserted. You could see the contours of the earth so well then, feel the coolness of approaching night, perhaps witness a sliver of moon rising over the creek poplars. Our routine almost never varied. My father would leave work early, I would ride my bike to the club, with my bag swaying on my back. After the round, he would put my bike in the trunk of his car. Sometimes we would grab dinner at the Boar and Castle on the way home, sit eating our Castle steaks in the rustling grapevine arbour while eavesdropping on the murmurous voices of teenage lovers in the musky foliage around us, or sit in the glowing foxfire of the Buick's radio, listening to the evening news report. There were race riots going on in Memphis and Miami one summer. A full-blown war was raging in Southeast Asia. Poor people marched on Washington, Bobby Kennedy was shot. A tidal wave of so much news – and yet so *far away* from us. A couple times, we stayed out on the golf course to look at stars. My father knew the constellations. He showed me Venus, the evening star, Aries the ram, how to find the North Star if I was ever lost in the woods. I never got lost in the woods, but I loved those times and never even knew it. It's as if I were sleepwalking and he was inviting me to awaken.

꒜

A model father

As remembered by George Bernard Shaw, 1856–1950

I cannot remember having ever heard a single sentence uttered by my mother in the nature of moral or religious instruction. My father made an effort or two. When he caught me imitating him by pretending to smoke a toy pipe he advised me very earnestly never to follow his example in any way; and his sincerity so impressed me that to this day I have never smoked, never shaved, and never used alcoholic stimulants. He taught me to regard him as an unsuccessful man with many undesirable habits, as a warning and not as a model. In fact, he did himself some injustice lest I should grow up like him; and I now see that this anxiety on his part was admirable and lovable; and that he was really just what he so carefully strove not to be: that is, a model father.

᭰

Smile

From Angela Carter, 'Sugar Daddy', 1983

Himself, he is a rich source of anecdote. He has partitioned off a little room in the attic of his house, constructed the walls out of cardboard boxes, and there he lies, on a camp-bed, listening to the World Service on a portable radio with his cap on. When he lived in London, he used to wear a trilby to bed but, a formal man, he exchanged it for a cap as soon as he moved. There are two perfectly good bedrooms in his house, with electric blankets and everything, as I well know, but these bedrooms always used to belong to his siblings, now deceased. He moves downstairs into one of these when the temperature in the attic drops too low for even his iron constitution, but he always shifts back up again, to his own place, when the ice melts. He has a ferocious enthusiasm for his own private space. My mother attributed this to a youth spent in the trenches, where no privacy was to be had. His war was the War to end Wars. He was too old for conscription in the one after that.

When he leaves this house for any length of time, he fixes up a whole lot of burglar traps, basins of water balanced on the tops of doors, tripwires, bags of flour suspended by strings, so that we worry in case he forgets where he's left what and ends up hoist with his own petard.

He has a special relationship with cats. He talks to them in a soft chirruping language they find irresistible. When we all lived in London and he worked on the night news desk of a press agency, he would come home on the last tube and walk, chirruping, down the street, accompanied by an ever-increasing procession of cats, to whom he would say good night at the front door. On those rare occasions, in my late teens, when I'd managed to persuade a man to walk me home, the arrival of my father and his cats always caused consternation, not least because my father was immensely tall and strong.

He is the stuff of which sitcoms are made.

His everyday discourse, which is conducted in the stately prose of a thirties *Times* leader, is enlivened with a number of stock phrases of a slightly eccentric, period quality. For example. On a wild night: 'Pity the troops on a night like this.' On a cold day:

> *Cold, bleak, gloomy and glum,*
> *Cold as the hairs on a polar bear's—*

The last word of the couplet is supposed to be drowned by the cries of outrage. My mother always turned up trumps on this one, interposing: 'Father!' on an ascending scale.

At random: 'Thank God for the Navy, who guard our shores.' On entering a room: 'Enter the fairy, singing and dancing.' Sometimes, in a particularly cheerful mood, he'll add to this formula: 'Enter the fairy, singing and dancing and waving her wooden leg.'

Infinitely endearing, infinitely irritating, irascible, comic, tough, sentimental, ribald old man, with his face of a borderline eagle and his bearing of a Scots Guard, who, in my imagination as when I was a child, drips chocolates from his pockets as, a cat dancing in front of him, he strides down the road bowed down with gifts, crying: 'Here comes the Marquess of Carrabas!' The very words, 'my father', always make me smile.

~~

Daddytrack

From Robert L. Griswold, *Fatherhood in America*, 1993

A variety of other surveys introduced as evidence supported James A. Levine's findings. Forty-eight per cent of fathers in metropolitan Washington. DC, for example, claimed they reduced their working hours to spend more time with their children, and 23 percent reported they had passed up a promotion for the same reason. In a 1990 poll by the *Los Angeles Times*,

39 per cent of the fathers said they would quit their jobs if they could in order to spend more time with their children, and 28 per cent felt their parental obligations hurt their careers. *Time* magazine reported that 48 per cent of men between the ages of eighteen and twenty-four expressed an interest in staying home with their children. Another survey found that '74 per cent of men said they would rather have a "daddy track" job than a "fast track" job', and a *Washington Post*/ABC News poll found that 43 per cent of the fathers had actually cut back on their working hours to be with their children. *Fortune* magazine reported similar results, including the startling finding that more fathers than mothers thought companies should do more to help parents work out career and family responsibilities. Perhaps Peter Lynch, one of the most successful mutual fund managers in the country, can speak for millions of American men in describing why he left his position to spend more time with his family: 'Children are a great investment. They beat the hell out of stocks.'

Nothing good gets away

Letter from John Steinbeck to his son, aged fourteen

10 November 1958

Dear Thom,

We had your letter this morning. I will answer it from my point of view and of course Elaine will from hers.

First – if you are in love – that's a good thing – that's about the best thing that can happen to anyone. Don't let anyone make it small or light to you.

Second – There are several kinds of love. One is a selfish, mean, grasping, egotistical thing which uses love for self-importance. This is the ugly and crippling kind. The other is an outpouring of everything good in you – of kindness, and consideration and respect – not only the social respect of manners but the greater respect which is recognition of another person as unique and valuable. The first kind can make you sick and small and weak but the second can release in you strength, and courage and goodness and even wisdom you didn't know you had.

You say this is not puppy love. If you feel so deeply – of course it isn't puppy love.

But I don't think you were asking me what you feel. You know that better than anyone. What you wanted me to help you with is what to do about it – and that I can tell you.

Glory in it for one thing and be very glad and grateful for it.

The object of love is the best and most beautiful. Try to live up to it.

If you love someone – there is no possible harm in saying so – only you must remember that some people are very shy and sometimes the saying must take that shyness into consideration.

Girls have a way of knowing or feeling what you feel, but they usually like to hear it also.

It sometimes happens that what you feel is not returned for one reason or another – but that does not make your feeling less valuable and good.

Lastly, I know your feeling because I have it and I am glad you have it.

We will be glad to meet Susan. She will be very welcome. But Elaine will make all such arrangements because that is her province and she will be very glad to. She knows about love too and maybe she can give you more help than I can.

And don't worry about losing. If it is right, it happens – The main thing is not to hurry. Nothing good gets away.

Love

Fa

⌒⌒

In heaven, as it is on earth

From the diary of Reverend Ralph Josselin

13 [July 1661]: My son Thomas came down from London to see us, so I saw my six children togither on earth, blessed bee god, and lett us all bee togither in heaven

⌒⌒

A son departs

Extracted from *The Vicar of Wakefield*,
Oliver Goldsmith, 1776

As my eldest son was bred a scholar, I determined to send him to town, where his abilities might contribute to our support and his own. The separation of friends and families is, perhaps, one of the most distressful circumstances attendant on penury. The day soon arrived on which we were to disperse for the first time. My son, after taking leave of his mother and the rest, who mingled their tears with their kisses, came to ask a blessing from me. This I gave him from my heart, and which, added to five guineas, was all the patrimony I had now to bestow. 'You are going, my boy,' cried I, 'to London on foot, in the manner Hooker, your great ancestor, travelled there before you. Take from me the same horse that was given him by the good bishop Jewel, this staff, and take this book too, it will be your comfort on the way: these two lines in it are worth a million, *I have been young, and now am old; yet never saw I the righteous man forsaken, or his seed begging their bread*. Let this be your consolation as you travel on. Go, my boy, whatever be thy fortune, let me see thee once a-year; still keep a good heart, and farewell.' As he was possessed of integrity and honour, I was under no apprehensions from throwing him naked into the amphitheatre of life; for I knew he would act a good part whether vanquished or victorious.

The crown and the glory

Proverbs, 17: 6

Children's children are the crown of old men;
And the glory of children are their fathers.

Love Anyhow

F. Scott Fitzgerald's epistolic advice to his daughter

8 August 1933

Dear Pie,

I feel very strongly about you doing [your] duty. Would you give me a little more documentation about your reading in French? I am glad you are happy – but I never believe much in happiness. I never believe in misery either. Those are things you see on the stage or the screen or the printed page, they never really happen to you in life.

All I believe in in life is the rewards for virtue (according to your talents) and the *punishments* for not fulfilling your duties, which are doubly costly. If there is such a volume in the camp library, will you ask Mrs Tyson to let you look up a sonnet of Shakespeare's in which the line occurs '*lilies that fester smell far worse than weeds.*'

Have had no thoughts today, life seems composed of getting up a *Saturday Evening Post* story. I think of you, and always pleasantly; but if you call me 'Pappy' again I am going to take the White Cat out and beat his bottom *hard, six times for every time you are impertinent.* Do you react to that?

I will arrange the camp bill.

Halfwit, I will conclude.

Things to worry about:
    Worry about courage
    Worry about cleanliness
    Worry about efficiency
    Worry about horsemanship
    Worry about . . .
Things not to worry about:
    Don't worry about popular opinion
    Don't worry about dolls
    Don't worry about the past
    Don't worry about the future
    Don't worry about growing up
    Don't worry about anybody getting ahead of you
    Don't worry about triumph

Don't worry about failure unless it comes through your own fault
Don't worry about mosquitoes
Don't worry about flies
Don't worry about insects in general
Don't worry about parents
Don't worry about boys
Don't worry about disappointments
Don't worry about pleasures
Don't worry about satisfactions
Things to think about:
What am I really aiming at?
How good am I really in comparison to my contemporaries in regard to:
(a) Scholarship
(b) Do I really understand about people and am I able to get along with them?
(c) Am I trying to make my body a useful instrument or am I neglecting it?

With dearest love,

[Daddy]

P. S. My come-back to your calling me Pappy is christening you by the word Egg, which implies that you belong to a very rudimentary state of life and that I could break you up and crack you open at my will and I think it would be a word that would hang on if I ever told it to your contemporaries. 'Egg Fitzgerald'. How would you like that to go through life with – 'Eggie Fitzgerald' or 'Bad Egg Fitzgerald' or any form that might occur to fertile minds? Try it once more and I swear to God I will hang it on you and it will be up to you to shake it off. Why borrow trouble?

Love anyhow.

Acknowledgements

My greatest thanks are due to my wife, Penny, and children, Tristram and Freda, for simply being there.

The editor has made every effort to locate all persons having any rights in the selections appearing in this anthology and to secure permission from the holders of such rights. Queries regarding the use of material should be addressed to the editor c/o the publishers. If any errors have inadvertently been made, corrections will, of course, be made in future additions.

Agee, James
Extract from *Letters of James Agee to Father Flye*, George Braziller Inc. Copyright © James Harold Flye and the James Agee Trust 1962.

Anderson, Sherwood
Extract from *Sherwood Anderson: A Critical Edition*, ed. Ray Lewis White, University of North Carolina Press, 1969. Copyright © Eleanor Anderson 1942, 1969. Reprinted by permission of Harold Ober Associates.

Armitage, Simon
'My Father Thought it Bloody Queer', from *Book of Matches* by Simon Armitage, copyright © the author 1993. Reprinted by permission of Faber & Faber.

Balzac, Honoré de
Selections from *Old Goriot* by Honoré de Balzac, translation copyright © Margaret Ayrton Crawford 1951. Reprinted by permission of Penguin UK.

Beauvoir, Simone de
Extract from *The Second Sex* (*Le Deuxième Sex*), Knopf, 1953. Translation copyright © 1953 Jonathan Cape. Reprinted by permission of The Random House Group Ltd.

Berlin, Irving
'Mary Be Good' by Irving Berlin, copyright © Irving Berlin 1933.

Blankenhorn, David
Extracts from *Fatherless America* by David Blankenhorn, copyright © Institute for American Values 1995. Reprinted by permission of Perseus Books Group.

Bly, Robert
Extract from *The Sibling Society* by Robert Bly, Addison-Wesley, 1996. Copyright © Robert Bly 1996.
   Extract from *Iron John* by Robert Bly, Addison-Wesley, 1990. Copyright © Robert Bly 1993.

Booth, Philip
'First Lesson' from *Relations*, copyright © Philip Booth 1957. Reprinted by permission of Penguin Group (USA) Inc.

Bradshaw, Jonathan, Stimson, Carol, Skinner, Christine, and Williams, Julie
Extract from *Absent Fathers* by Jonathan Bradshaw, Carol Stimson, Christine Skinner, and Julie Williams, copyright © the authors 1999. Reprinted by permission of ITPS on behalf of Routledge.

Burgess, Adrienne
Extract from *Fatherhood Reclaimed* by Adrienne Burgess, copyright © Adrienne Burgess 1997. Reprinted by permission of The Random House Group Ltd.

Camus, Albert
Extract from *The First Man* by Albert Camus, Knopf, 1995. Translation copyright © David Hapgood 1994. Reprinted by permission of Penguin UK.

Carter, Angela
Selections from 'Sugar Daddy' by Angela Carter, copyright ©
Angela Carter 1983. First published in *Fathers*, 1983. Reprinted
by permission of Rogers, Coleridge and White.

Carver, Raymond
'On an old photograph of my son' from *All of Us: The Collected
Poems* by Raymond Carver. Knopf, 1996. Copyright © Tess
Gallagher 1996. Reprinted by permission of Alfred A. Knopf, a
division of Random House, Inc.

Cash, Johnny
'A Boy Named Sue'. Lyrics by Shel Silverstein, copyright © TRO
Essex Music Ltd.

Cellini, Benvenuto
Extract from *The Autobiography of Benvenuto Cellini*, translation copyright © George Bull 1956. Reprinted by permission
of Penguin UK.

Chapin, Harry and Sandra
'The Cat's in the Cradle' by Harry and Sandra Chapin, copyright
© Story Songs 1974.

Citino, David
'The Father and the Son' from *The House of Memory* by David
Citino, copyright © the author 1990. Reprinted by permission
of Ohio University Press and the author.

Coleridge, Samuel Taylor
Extract from *The Collected Letters of Samuel Taylor Coleridge*,
6 vols, edited by E. L. Griggs (Oxford, 1965–71), copyright ©
Oxford University Press 1965. Reprinted by permission of Oxford
University Press.

Cosby, Bill
Selections from *Fatherhood* by Bill Cosby, Dolphin Doubleday,
1996. Copyright © William H. Cosby Jr 1986.

Dahl, Roald
Extract from *Boy* by Roald Dahl, published by Jonathan Cape/Penguin Books. Copyright © Roald Dahl 1984. Reprinted by permission of David Higham Associates.

The Daily Telegraph
Articles from *The Daily Telegraph* © *The Daily Telegraph* 1999 and 2000. Reprinted by permission of *The Daily Telegraph*.

Deeping, Warwick
Extract from *Sorrell and Son* by Warwick Deeping, copyright © 1925.

De la Mare, Walter
'The Birthnight' from *The Complete Poems of Walter De La Mare*, copyright © Walter de la Mare 1969. Reprinted by permission of the Society of Authors.

Dodson, James
Extract from *Final Rounds* by James Dodson, Bantam, 1997. Copyright © James Dodson 1997. Reprinted by permission of Random House, Inc.

Doherty, Berlie
'Dad' from *Another First Poetry Book*, copyright © B. Doherty 1987.

Douglas, Kirk
Extracts from *The Ragman's Son* by Kirk Douglas, Simon & Schuster, 1988. Copyright © Kirk Douglas 1988. Reprinted by permission of Simon & Schuster.

Durcan, Paul
'Study of a figure in a landscape' from *Daddy, Daddy* by Paul Durcan, copyright © the author 1990. Reprinted by permission of The Blackstaff Press.

Dylan, Bob
'Forever Young', copyright © Ram's Horn Music 1973. First performed on the album *Planet Waves*, 1974. Reprinted by permission of the Bob Dylan Music Group.

Elman, Richard M.
Selection from *Fredi, Shirl & the Kids: The Autobiography in Fable of Richard M. Elman*, Charles Scribner's Sons, 1972. Copyright © Richard M. Elman 1972.

Esquire magazine
'Things a Man Should Know About Fatherhood', copyright © *Esquire* (USA) 1999. Reprinted by permission of the publisher.

Faulkner, William
Extract from *Absalom, Absalom!* by William Faulkner, copyright © William Faulkner 1936.

Feinstein, Elaine
'Dad' by Elaine Feinstein, copyright © Elaine Feinstein 1977. Reprinted by permission of Rogers, Coleridge and White.

Fitzgerald, F. Scott
Selection from *The Letters of F. Scott Fitzgerald*, edited by Andrew Turnbull. Copyright © Frances Scott Lanahan 1962. Reprinted by permission of Harold Ober Associates.

Fowles, John
'In Chalkwell Park' by John Fowles, from *Fathers and Sons*, edited by J. Hoyland 1992, copyright © John Fowles 1992. Reprinted by permission of Sheil Land Associates.

Freud, Sigmund
Extract from *The Letters of Sigmund Freud*, Hogarth Press, edited by Ernest L. Freud. Copyright © The Estate of Sigmund Freud 1961. Reprinted by permission of Random House Archive and Library.
Extract from *The Interpretation of Dreams* copyright © Sigmund Freud 1913. Reprinted by permission of ITPS on behalf of Routledge.

Geoffrey of Monmouth
'The Grief of Lear', quoted in *Anthology of English Prose*, 1914.

Gilmore, Mikal
Extract from *Shot in the Heart: One Family's History of Murder* by Mikal Gilmore, Doubleday, 1994. Copyright © Mikal Gilmore 1994.

Graham, Harry
'Thoughtlessness' by Harry Graham, from *When Grandma Fell off the Boat*, copyright © V. Thesiger 1986. 'The Stern Parent' from *Ruthless Rhymes*, 1899.

Green, Maureen
Extract from *Goodbye Father* by Maureen Green, copyright © Maureen Green 1976. Reprinted by permission of ITPS Ltd on behalf of Routledge.

Griswold, Robert L.
Extracts from *Fatherhood in America* by Robert L. Griswold, copyright © Basic Books 1993. Reprinted by permission of the publisher.

Gurdjieff, G. I.
Extract from *Meetings with Remarkable Men* by G. I. Gurdjieff, copyright © Editions Janus 1963.

Hall, Donald
'My Son, My Executioner' from *One Day: Poems 1947–1990* by Donald Hall, Carcanet Press, copyright © Donald Hall 1988. Reprinted by permission of the publisher.

Harper, Sam
'Dad's Department' by Sam Harper, copyright © Sam Harper 1999. Reprinted by permission of the author.

Harrison, Fraser
Extracts from *A Father's Diary* by Fraser Harrison, copyright © Fraser Harrison 1985. Reprinted by permission of the author.

Hearn, Lafcadio
Extract from *The Life and Letters of Lafcadio Hearn*, Houghton Mifflin, 1906. Copyright © L. Hearn 1906.

Hemingway, Ernest
'Advice to a Son' by Ernest Hemingway, copyright © the Ernest Hemingway Foundation and Nicholas Georgiannis 1979. Reprinted by permission of Harcourt Inc.

Hewlett, Barry
Extract from *Intimate Fathers* by Barry Hewlett, copyright © Barry Hewlett 1991. Reprinted by permission of the University of Michigan Press.

Hogan, Phil
'The Children Are Revolting' by Phil Hogan, *The Observer*, 18 June 2000. Reprinted by permission of Guardian Newspapers Ltd.

Horn, Dr Wade F.
Selections from *The Washington Times* by Dr Wade F. Horn, copyright © Wade F. Horn 1999. Reprinted by permission of Wade F. Horn, PhD, and *The Washington Times*.

Jennings, Charles
Extracts from *Father's Race* by Charles Jennings, copyright © Charles Jennings 1999. Reprinted by permission of Little, Brown & Company (UK) and the author's agent, Sara Menguc.

Jones, Evan
'Generations' by Evan Jones, from *Two Centuries of Australian Poetry*, edited by Mark O'Connor. Copyright © Evan Jones 1988. Reprinted by permission of Oxford University Press (Australia).

Joyce, James
Extracts from *Dubliners*, copyright © James Joyce 1914.
  Extracts from *Ulysses*, copyright © James Joyce 1917–18. Reprinted from 1922 edition courtesy of Oxford University Press.

Kafka, Franz
Extract from 'The Judgement' reprinted from *Fathers and Sons*, edited by Alberto Manguel, Chronicle 1998.

Keane, Fergal
Extract from *Letter to Daniel: Dispatches from the Heart* by Fergal Keane, copyright © Fergal Keane 1996. Reprinted by permission of Penguin UK.

Kindlon, Dan, and Thompson, Michael
Extract from *Raising Cain* by Dan Kindlon and Michael Thompson, copyright © the authors 1999. Reprinted by permission of Penguin UK (Michael Joseph).

LaRossa, Ralph
Extract from *The Modernisation of Fatherhood* by Ralph LaRossa, copyright © the University of Chicago Press 1997. Reprinted by permission of the publishers.

Lawrence, D. H.
Extracts from *The Rainbow*, 1915.

Lee, Laurie
Extracts from *The Firstborn* by Laurie Lee, William Morrow, 1984. Copyright © Laurie Lee 1959. Reprinted by permission of Random House UK and PFD.
    Extract from *Two Women*, copyright © Laurie Lee 1983. Reprinted by permission of Andre Deutsch Ltd and PFD.

Leonard, Marjorie
Extract from 'Fathers and Daughters' by Marjorie Leonard, copyright © Marjorie Leonard 1981. First published in the *International Journal of Psychoanalysis*.

Levine, James A., and Pittinsky, Todd L.
Extract from *Working Fathers: New Strategies for Balancing Work and Family* by James A. Levine and Todd L. Pittinsky, copyright © James A. Levine and Todd L. Pittinsky 1997.

Lewis, Cecil Day
'Walking Away' by Cecil Day Lewis, copyright © the estate of © Cecil Day Lewis 1992. Reprinted by permission of the Random House Archive and Library.

Lorenz, Konrad
Selection from *King Solomon's Ring* by Konrad Lorenz, translation copyright © Majorie Kerr Wilson and Methuen Ltd 1952.

McClain, Buzz
'Don't Call Me Mr Mom! Or, what not to say to a Stay-at-home Dad', by Buzz McClain, *slowlane.com* web page. Copyright © 2000 the author.

McCourt, Frank
Extract from *Angela's Ashes* by Frank McCourt, Scribner, 1996. Copyright © Frank McCourt 1996. Reprinted by permission of HarperCollins Publishers.

Marx, Groucho
Extract from *The Groucho Letters* by Groucho Marx, Simon and Schuster, 1967. Copyright © Groucho Marx 1967.

Mead, Margaret
Extract from *Male and Female* by Margaret Mead, copyright © Margaret Mead 1949. Reprinted by permission of The Orion Publishing Group (Victor Gollancz).

Meinke, Peter
'This is a poem to my son Peter' from *Liquid Paper* by Peter Meinke, University of Pittsburg Press, copyright © Peter Meinke 1991. Reprinted by permission of the publisher.

Miller, Henry
Extract from *My Life and Times* by Henry Miller, Playboy Press, 1971. Copyright © Henry Miller and Gemini Smith Inc 1971.

Mitchell, Adrian
'Beattie is Three' by Adrian Mitchell, copyright © Adrian Mitchell. First published in *Heart on the Left: Poems 1953–84* by Bloodaxe Books Limited. Reprinted by permission of PFD on behalf of Adrian Mitchell.

Mitchison, Naomi
Extract from *Small Talk: Memories of an Edwardian Childhood* by Naomi Mitchison, copyright © Naomi Mitchison 1973. Reprinted by permission of The Random House Group Ltd.

Morrison, Blake
Extracts from *And When Did You Last See Your Father?* by Blake Morrison, copyright © Blake Morrison 1985. Reprinted by permission of Penguin Books (Granta).

Mortimer, John
Extract from *Clinging to the Wreckage* by John Mortimer, copyright © John Mortimer 1982. Reproduced by permission of The Orion Publishing Group (Weidenfeld & Nicolson).

Murray, Les
'Fatherhood, from the German' from *Collected Poems* by Les Murray, copyright © the author 1991. Reprinted by permission of Carcanet Press Ltd.

Nabokov, Vladimir
Extract from *Speak, Memory: An Autobiography Revisited* by Vladimir Nabokov, G. P. Putnam's Sons, 1966. Copyright © Vladimir Nabokov 1964.

Narayan, R. K.
Extract from 'Forty-Five a Month', from *Malgudi Days* by R. K. Narayan, copyright © the author 1972, 1982. Reprinted by permission of Viking Penguin, a division of the Penguin Group (USA) Inc.

Nash, Ogden
Extract from *Candy is Dandy*, Methuen, 1985. Copyright © 1985 The estate of Ogden Nash.

Newson, John and Elizabeth
Extract from *Patterns of Infant Care in an Urban Community* by John and Elizabeth Newson, copyright © J. and E. Newson 1965. Reprinted by permission of ITPS on behalf of Routledge.

Nin, Anaïs
Extract from *The Journals of Anaïs Nin*, edited by Gunther Stuhlmann, Harcourt, Swallow Press, 1966. Copyright © Anaïs Nin 1966.

O'Hara, Frank
'To My Dead Father' by Frank O'Hara, copyright © Maureen Granville-Smith 1971. Reprinted by permission of Alfred A. Knopf, a division of Random House, Inc.

O'Neill, Hugh
Extract from *A Man Called Daddy* by Hugh O'Neill, copyright © Hugh O'Neill 1996. Reprinted by permission of the Rutledge Hill Press.

Parsons, Tony
Extracts from *Man and Boy* by Tony Parsons, Sourcebooks, Inc. Copyright © Tony Parsons 1999.

Plath, Sylvia
'Daddy' from *Collected Poems* by Sylvia Plath, Harper & Row, 1981, Copyright © the estate of Ted Hughes 1960.

Plutarch
Extract from *Vitae Parallae*, translated by Bernadotte Perrin 1914–26.

Po Chu-i
'Rising late and playing with A-ts'ui' from *170 Chinese Poems*, translated by Arthur Waley. Reprinted by permission of Constable and Robinson.

Pound, Ezra
Extract from *Sophocles: Women of Trachis*, translated by Ezra Pound, New Directions, 1957. Copyright © 1954.

Raine, Craig
Extract from *Rich* by Craig Raine, Faber & Faber, 1984. Copyright © Craig Raine 1984. Reprinted by permission of Faber & Faber and David Godwin Associates.

Redgrove, Peter
'Early Morning Feed' by Peter Redgrove, from *Poems 1954–1987*, copyright © Peter Redgrove 1959. Reprinted by permission of David Higham Associates.

Roethke, Theodore
'My Papa's Waltz' from *Selected Poems* by Theodore Roethke, copyright © The Estate of Theodore Roethke 1969. Reprinted by permission of Faber & Faber.

Roosevelt, Theodore
Extract from *Voices Offstage* by Marcus Connelly, Holt, Rinehart & Winston, 1968. Copyright © Marcus Connelly 1968.

Roth, Philip
Extract from *Patrimony* by Philip Roth, Simon & Schuster, 1991. Copyright © Philip Roth 1991.

Rousseau, Jean-Jacques
Selections from *Emile* by Jean-Jacques Rousseau, translation copyright © Basic Books 1979. Reprinted by permission of Basic Books.
  Extract from *The Confessions*, translation copyright © Christopher Kelly 1995.

Russell, Bertrand
Extract from *Marriage and Morals* by Bertrand Russell, copyright © Bertrand Russell 1929. Reprinted by permission of ITPS on behalf of Routledge.

Sandburg, Carl
Extract from *Always the Young Strangers* by Carl Sandburg, Harcourt & Company, 1952. Copyright © Carl Sandburg 1952. Reprinted by permission of Harcourt Inc.

Saroyan, Aram
Quoted in Jon Winokur, *Fathers*, Dutton Books 1993.

Saroyan, William
Extract from *Here Comes, There Goes, You Know Who* by William Saroyan, Simon & Schuster, 1961. Copyright © William Saroyan 1961. Reprinted by permission of Pocket Books, a division of Simon & Schuster.

Sartre, Jean-Paul
Extract from *The Words* by Jean-Paul Sartre, translation copyright © George Braziller Inc 1964.

Scannell, Vernon
'Growing Pain' and 'Nettles' from *Collected Poems 1950–1993* by Vernon Scannell, copyright © Vernon Scannell 1993. Reprinted by permission of Robson.
 'Poem for Jane' from *Selected Poems*, copyright © Vernon Scannell 1971. Reprinted by kind permission of Allison & Busby, London.
 Extract from *The Tiger and the Rose*, copyright © Vernon Scannell 1971. Reprinted by permission of Penguin UK.

Schulberg, Budd
Extract from 'A Short Digest of a Long Novel' by Budd Schulberg, first published in *Some Faces in the Crowd* by Budd Schulberg, Random House, 1953. Copyright © the author 1953. Reprinted by permission of Miriam Altshuler Literary Agency.

The Simpsons
Extract from script of *The Simpsons*, copyright © 20th Century-Fox Television 1991.

Smith, Stevie
'Papa Love Baby' by Stevie Smith, from *Collected Poems of Stevie Smith*, copyright © Stevie Smith 1975. Reprinted by permission of James & James on behalf of the estate of James MacGibbon.

Spencer, Charles
Extract from 'Trying Times' by Charles Spencer, copyright © Charles Spencer 1997. Reprinted from *Fatherhood*, Gollancz, by permission of the author.

Spender, Stephen
'To My Daughter' from *Selected Poems* by Stephen Spender, copyright © the estate of Stephen Spender. Reprinted by permission of Faber & Faber.

Steinbeck, John
Extract from *Steinbeck: A Life in Letters*, edited by Elaine A. Steinbeck and Robert Wallsten, Viking Penguuin, 1975. Copyright © John Steinbeck 1952, copyright © E. A. Steinbeck and Robert Wallsten 1975.

Strauss, Barry
Extract from *Fathers and Sons in Athens* by Barry Strauss, copyright © Barry Strauss 1997. Reprinted by permission of ITPS Ltd on behalf of Routledge.

Su Tung-P'o
'On the Birth of His Son' from *170 Chinese Poems*, translated by Arthur Waley 1919. Reprinted by permission of Constable & Robinson.

Thomas, Dylan
'Do Not Go Gentle into that Good Night' by Dylan Thomas, copyright © Dylan Thomas 1971. Reprinted by permission of David Higham Associates.

The Times
Extracts from *The Times*, copyright © Times Newspapers Limited 1999, 2000. Reprinted by permission of News International Syndication.

Trumbo, Dalton
Extract from *Additional Dialogue: Letters of Dalton Trumbo, 1942–1962*, Evans, 1976. Copyright © Dalton Trumbo 1976.

Turner, Janine
Extract from *Behind Closed Doors* by Janine Turner, copyright © Janine Turner 1988.

Waugh, Auberon
Extracts from *Will This Do?* by Auberon Waugh, copyright ©
Auberon Waugh 1991. Reprinted by permission of Peters, Fraser
& Dunlop.

Wells, H. G.
Extract from *Ann Veronica* by H. G. Wells, copyright © H. G.
Wells 1909.

Williams, Hugo
Extract from 'What Shall We Do Now That We Have Done
Everything?' by Hugo Williams, copyright © Hugo Williams
1992. First published in *Fatherhood*, edited by Sean French,
Virago 1992. Reprinted by permission of the author.

Williams, William Carlos
Extracts from *The Selected Letters of William Carlos Williams*,
edited by John Thirlwell, McDowell Obolensky. Copyright ©
William Carlos Williams 1957.

Yeats, W. B.
'A Prayer for My Daughter' from *Collected Poems*, copyright ©
Macmillan Publishing Company 1924. Renewed 1952 B. G. Yeats.
Reprinted by permission of A. P. Watt Ltd.